THE CALIFORNIA AND HAWAIIAN SUGAR REFINING CORPORATION

View of the Refinery of the California and Hawaiian Sugar Refining Corporation, Showing a Portion of the Town of Crockett

STANFORD BUSINESS SERIES
No. II

THE CALIFORNIA AND HAWAIIAN SUGAR REFINING CORPORATION
of San Francisco, California

A Study of the Origin, Business Policies, and Management of a Co-operative Refining and Distributing Organization

By

BORIS EMMET, Ph.D.

AMS PRESS, INC.
NEW YORK

Reprinted from the edition of 1928, Stanford
First AMS EDITION published 1970
Manufactured in the United States of America

International Standard Book Number: 0-404-02353-3

Library of Congress Catalog Card Number: 76-126654

AMS PRESS, INC.
NEW YORK, N.Y. 10003

FOREWORD

Educators are sometimes spoken of as standing on the sidelines of life instead of being a part of it. The charge is somewhat overdrawn; nevertheless, detachment of teachers from the activities about which they are teaching is a danger against which education has to guard itself. This applies especially to professional education, and most of all, perhaps, to the pioneer task of educating young people for leadership in business.

The Graduate School of Business at Stanford has from the start regarded its contacts with business as a matter of prime importance. The persons charged with developing and enforcing the policies of the School have believed it to be necessary for members of the faculty to draw material for teaching from situations with which business concerns have actually dealt in the past or are having to deal now. It is considered essential for teachers to so command the actual facts of such situations that they can speak with authority concerning the degree of significance of different facts in connection with the business principles they are trying to teach.

The managers of the School have also considered it essential for students from the very beginning of their course to know business men and to hear from the lips of business men about the difficulties they have had to overcome and how they actually went about the task. To promote this object, visits have been arranged to the plants of numerous concerns, whose executives have agreed in advance to spend as much time as necessary going over their problems with students, according to a plan worked out by the executives and the teacher in charge of the visits. It has been felt that this touch of reality at the start has furnished the best available antidote to the students' obvious lack of experience and to the tendency toward easy generalization on the basis of insufficient facts—the tendency to theorize—with which even the best students often come out of their undergraduate course. In connection with these visits, students are encouraged to ask questions and to make suggestions, and everything possible is done to remove any notion of a mere sight-seeing tour.

The officers of the California and Hawaiian Sugar Refining Corporation have from the start co-operated fully in this plan of plant visits and have been generous indeed in placing their time and thought at the disposal of the School. Moreover, this company has been conspicuous for having worked out far-reaching management policies. Its activities have been concerned with the production of raw materials, transportation of materials and product, manufacture, distribution, finance, and control in such a way as to make it an exceptionally good medium for emphasizing the central management point of view in teaching. The Graduate School of Business has tried in all its teaching to keep this central point of view in the front of the picture, as against that of divisional or functional management. All these reasons, in addition to its accessibility, have resulted in the California and Hawaiian Sugar Refining Corporation being one of the first concerns with which our entering students have come in contact.

The natural maturing of these contacts and the fact of Dr. Emmet's wide experience as a business investigator, as well as business man and teacher, led to the suggestion that he undertake a comprehensive study of this company. The immediate response from officers of the Corporation, and the prompt authorization by its board of directors to go ahead, made it possible to get the study under way in the fall of 1927. During the intervening months both Dr. Emmet and representatives of the Corporation have spent a vast amount of time in going over company records and trying to arrive at the basic factors in the

FOREWORD

policies the company has followed. Great effort has also been made to set forth clearly the essential facts and the nature of the chief problems which the company has to solve. The principles of management are the same in the sugar industry as they are in any other business, but, as noted, there are certain factors in this business that make it peculiarly suitable and timely for a study of the sort here undertaken. We hear a great deal about co-operation. The word usually suggests joint action either on the part of agricultural producers, or on the part of consumers. In both cases its prime object is to eliminate or reduce middlemen's profits in advancing goods from producer to consumer. There is, however, a form of cooperation, whether technically organized as a co-operative or as a corporation for profit, in which the whole process of production from raising the raw material to delivery of the ultimate product is brought within the scope of a well-articulated policy of production and distribution.

This number of the Stanford Business Series has to do with activities essentially of the sort just described. The data with which it deals cover nearly the whole sweep of the production and distribution process. Space has not permitted the author to go into all phases of relationships with planters in Hawaii nor to develop at length all of the influences that affect distribution of the product. But enough has been said to bring out these relationships and to show how important they are.

Still another reason makes the California and Hawaiian Sugar Refining Corporation an appropriate subject for an initial study of this kind, and that concerns the international and social phases of its activity. Here again neither space nor the immediate purposes of the study permit going into the social, racial, educational, and industrial problems of the planters in Hawaii, nor into the ramifications of the ocean transportation involved in bringing raw cane sugar from the Islands to California and in shipping refined sugar East. However, no competent study of this company can be made without emphasizing, tacitly at least, the far-flung international and social forces that come within the purview of business policy. This is especially true of a business that has its starting-point in the Islands of the Pacific. This wide-angle view of business is another of the lessons that the Graduate School of Business is trying to drive home.

Business policy has its roots in economic history. The California and Hawaiian Sugar Refining Corporation is important historically as well as for its present activity. Its development constitutes a significant factor in the industrial growth in the North Bay section of the San Francisco metropolitan area. It is the hope of those who are responsible for launching the Graduate School of Business and for developing its policy that the School may become a center of scholarly research especially in connection with the history of business on the Pacific Coast. This study has been made with the thought that it will make a fitting start toward the realization of such a purpose. It is regarded by the authorities of the School as a forerunner of other similar studies, in which, alongside of present policies and problems of outstanding concerns, the historical background out of which these concerns have sprung will be set forth.

At the conference held in connection with the opening of the Graduate School of Business, considerable attention was devoted to the subject of research. It has not seemed wise nor timely to establish at Stanford a formally organized bureau of business research like those which have rendered such good service in numerous other universities. It is our purpose, however, to have the quest for knowledge about business permeate all the activities of the School and the aims of each and every member of the faculty.

FOREWORD

The task of securing material from business for use in the teaching of business is extremely complex, and calls for the exercise of discriminating judgment and a scholarly outlook in selecting and interpreting facts and in setting them forth. So great is this need that it seems wise, for the present, to entrust the task only to the members of the faculty or to other mature and trained men who are skilled both as investigators and as practical men.

This study is in pursuance of the policy of stimulating individual and co-operative faculty research. The contacts out of which it developed illustrate the kind of team play between education and practical business upon which the newly assumed task of university education for business leadership must largely depend for its success. I shall not deprive the author of the pleasant task of expressing his gratitude to the officers of the California and Hawaiian Sugar Refining Corporation who have given so freely of time and thought. In behalf of the Graduate School of Business, however, and of Stanford University, it is appropriate for me to say that we all join in this feeling of appreciation. Everyone connected with the School has had great satisfaction in the progress of this undertaking to such a gratifying conclusion.

WILLARD E. HOTCHKISS

STANFORD UNIVERSITY, CALIFORNIA
December 1, 1928

PREFACE

The volume of sales of this company increased almost eight and one-half times since 1906, the first year of operation. During 1927 the company did a volume of business of about eighty millions.

The business and management problems involved in an institution of the character and magnitude of the California and Hawaiian Sugar Refining Corporation, engaged in an industry subject to seasonal fluctuations both in the supply of raw material and in the demand for the refined product, are such that ultimate success is possible only through the application of business foresight, unremitting attention to detail, the utilization of every known scientific and technical help, and continuous research in the management and chemical phases of sugar refining.

The California and Hawaiian Sugar Refining Corporation has fostered experimentation in co-operative business, modern management methods, and in the advanced technology of sugar refining. It has been liberal, in plans and expenditures, in the promotion of a better understanding between employer and employee, in an effort to stabilize production, improve quality and service, and reduce costs. The organization enjoys public favor because of its open and above-board methods of doing business, and because of its general business integrity.

To the student of business organization, the management policies of this company are of especial significance, because of the success attained in its business, through the smooth co-ordination of all activities throughout the organization. Much of this success is due, no doubt, to effective team work among the staff. There is ample indication, however, that the reins in the hands of its general officers connect with every phase of its refining and distribution activities.

At the start of this study, conferences were held with all of the major executives of the Corporation for the purpose of getting a comprehensive idea of their aims and business problems. Inquiries were also made as to the means by which the management proposed to solve the various complexities of its refining and distribution. An attempt was also made to verify the extent to which the policies thus outlined were actually being carried out, from the following points of view: (1) the business organization, (2) its actual functioning, and (3) the effectiveness of co-ordination of separate activities into one whole.

Careful study was made of progress achieved in the quality of product, technology of refining, production costs, control of expense, and methods utilized in accounting and finance.

Without exception, access was had to all refinery and general business files, accounting records, and annual and special reports. Throughout this survey all of the principal executives of the Corporation have assumed an attitude of full and frank discussion of their problems. Their idea, fully as much as that of the Graduate School of Business, was to make the study analytical.

The relative wisdom of any business policy is susceptible of verification, mathematically or otherwise. The effect of a definite industrial relations policy is verifiable through an analysis of the extent of labor stabilization and by improvements shown in production and service. The wisdom of a certain distribution policy may be seen in the volume of business and in sales costs. The worthwhileness of regularization of manufacturing operations should be reflected in reduced unit costs, greater operating smoothness, improved quality of product, and in increased annual earnings of workmen. The desirability of budgeting, too, may be seen, by results achieved in increasing the effectiveness of control over expenditures.

PREFACE

The merits of this report, if any, are due in a large measure to the whole-hearted co-operation and advice of Mr. George M. Rolph, President, and Messrs. A. M. Duperu, Louis R. Campiglia, and William F. Sampson, Vice-Presidents, of the Corporation. Mr. Fred W. Vieth, Assistant to the Treasurer, has contributed much in the preparation of the study. Thanks are due to Dean Willard E. Hotchkiss for encouragement and advice, and to Dr. William Leonard Crum, for assistance in determining the proper statistical methods for the computation of the index of seasonality in the demand for sugar.

The responsibility for all shortcomings, however, rests solely upon the author.

TABLE OF CONTENTS

	PAGE
LIST OF FIGURES	xvii
LIST OF TABLES	xix
I. INTRODUCTION	1
1. Note on History of the Corporation	1
2. The Co-operative Agreement	3
3. Capital Structure	8
4. General Character of Organization	10
II. THE REFINING DIVISION	15
1. General Organization of Refinery	15
2. Refinery Budgets	17
3. Description of Refining Processes	29
4. Technical or Chemical-Control Department	41
5. Operating Department	48
6. Plant Sanitation and Cleanliness	52
7. Inspection Department	52
8. Industrial Relations Department	55
9. Engineering and Maintenance Department	99
10. The Warehouse	120
11. Refinery Office	127
12. Stores Accounting	133
13. Physical Inventories	136
III. THE SALES DIVISION	139
1. Central Sales Organization	139
2. Varieties of Product	140
3. Volume of Sales	140
4. Sales Terms: Coast and East	142
5. Geographical Distribution of Brokers' Offices	145
6. Customer Classification	146
7. Sales by Grades of Product	148
8. Increases in "Specialty" Sales	150
9. Sales Forecasts and Budgets	150
10. Marketing of Molasses	152
11. Advertising	153
12. Seasonality of Demand for Sugar	155
IV. THE FINANCE AND ACCOUNTING DIVISION	163
1. Organization of Division	163
2. Financial Operations and Accounting Ratios	165
3. Budgeting	170
4. General Accounting	172

		PAGE
5.	Order Department	173
6.	Credit Department	174
7.	Billing	175
8.	Accounts Receivable	176
9.	Accounts Payable	177
10.	Cashier	178
11.	Consignment	180
12.	Tabulating Department	181
13.	Central Stenographic Service	182
14.	Mail and File Section	182
15.	Telephone and Telegraph Service	183
16.	Purchasing Department	183
17.	Stores Department	186
18.	Traffic Department	189
19.	Insurance and Tax Department	190
20.	Auditing Department	195
21.	Commercial and Statistical Research	197
22.	Salary Standardization	200
23.	Classification of Accounts	204

V. THE LEGAL DEPARTMENT 205

VI. PROGRESS AND RESULTS 207
    1. Progress in Extraction 207
    2. Interpretation of Results 210
    3. Regularization of Production, 1923–1927 . . . 211
    4. Effect of Rate of Melt upon Unit Cost of Refining . 216
    5. Labor Stabilization 220
    6. Productivity of Refinery Labor 231
    7. Productivity of Capital 232
    8. Productivity of Refinery Machinery and Equipment 233
    9. Instances of Improvement in Material and Equipment 235
   10. Inventions by Employees 240
   11. Progress in Cost Reduction 242

APPENDIX 257
    Classification of Accounts 257

INDEX 285

LIST OF FIGURES

FIGURE		PAGE
1.	Chart of Co-operative Agreement	9
2.	Chart of General Organization	11
3.	Chart of Refining Division	16
4.	Chart of Operating Department	50
5.	Chart of Industrial Relations Department	58
6.	Diagram of Warehouse Conveyor System	124
7.	Map Showing Geographical Distribution of Brokers' Offices	144
8.	Graph Showing Seasonality of Demand for Sugar	162
9.	Chart of Finance and Accounting Division	164
10.	Graph Showing Relative Regularity of Refining Operations, 1923–27	214
11.	Graph Showing Comparison of Seasonal Trend of Production in 1924 and 1927 with Average Seasonal Demand for Sugar	216
12.	Graph Showing Effect of Rate of Melt upon Union Cost of Refining	218
13.	Graph Showing Seasonality of Labor Turnover, 1923–27	230

xvii

LIST OF TABLES

TABLE		PAGE
1.	Refinery Calendar for 1928	17
2.	Comparison of Budgeted with Actual Production, 1927	20
3.	Comparison of Budget with Actual Money Expenditures, 1927 (by Objects of Expenditure)	23
4.	Comparison of Budget with Actual Money Expenditures, 1927 (by Functions)	24
5.	Comparison of Budget with Actual Unit Costs, 1927 (by Objects of Expenditure)	25
6.	Comparison of Budget with Actual Unit Costs, 1927 (by Functions)	26
7.	Labor Budget for First Quarter of 1928	27
8.	Methods of Wage Payment	67
9.	Age Distribution of Employees	87
10.	Length of Service of Employees	88
11.	Cost of Industrial Relations Activities	89
12.	Membership of Employees' Mutual Benefit Association	93
13.	Statement of Revenues and Expenses of E.M.B.A.	95
14.	Group Insurance in Force	98
15.	Distribution of Cost of Group Insurance	99
16.	Relative Volume of Sales, 1914–1927	140
17.	Average Tonnage per Customer Invoice	141
18.	Sales on Consignment, 1922–1927	143
19.	Comparison of Direct Selling Expense, Coast and East, 1927	145
20.	Sales by Types of Customer—Total Territory	146
21.	Sales by Types of Customer, in Percentages	147
22.	Sales by Grades of Product—Total Territory, in Percentages	148
23.	Sales by Grades of Product—All Territories, 1927	149
24.	Sales by Grades of Product—All Territories	149
25.	Percentage of Quota Actually Delivered in Each Territory	152
26.	Link-Relatives for Monthly Tonnages of Sales, 1922–1927	156
27.	Multiple Frequency Distribution of Link-Relatives	156
28.	Computation of Adjusted Index Showing Seasonality of Sales for Combined Years of 1922–1927	161
29.	Accounting Ratios, 1922–1927	167
30.	Annual Extraction Results—1915 to 1927	208
31.	Annual Extraction Results—1915 to 1927	209
32.	Regularity of Refinery Operations	213

xx THE C & H SUGAR REFINING CORPORATION

TABLE	PAGE
33. Comparison of Relative Increase in Melt, Number of Men Required, and Wage Cost	217
34. Gross Total of Refinery Labor Turnover, 1923–1927	222
35. Percentage Gross Labor Turnover, by Departments	223
36. Percentage of Net Labor Turnover by Departments	224
37. Causes of Separations	225
38. Reasons for Voluntary Separations or "Quits"	227
39. Causes of Discharges and "Lay-offs for Cause"	227
40. Seasonality of Labor Turnover	229
41. Reduction in Cost of Maintaining Working Personnel of Refinery, 1923–1927	231
42. Average Daily Labor Productivity, 1925–1927	232
43. Changes in Capital Productivity, 1923–1927	232
44. Changes in Productivity of Machinery and Equipment, 1922–1927	234
45. Distribution of Total Business Cost, 1927	243
46. Percentage Distribution of Total Wholesale Price to Major Items of Expense, 1923–1927	243
47. Percentage Changes in Relative Cost of Principal Items of Expense, 1923–1927	245
48. Annual Index of Comparative Unit Costs	245
49. Distribution of Total Refinery Unit Cost	247
50. Comparison of Unit Costs of Major Refining Functions, 1925–1927	248
51. Comparison of Percentage Unit Costs of Major Refining Functions, 1925–1927	249
52. Comparison of Total Expenditures, Cost per Unit (100 lbs.), and Volume of Sales in Percentage of 1922	250
53. Percentage Increased Productivity per Office Employee	253
54. Classified Items of Expense, 1922, 1927	255

THE CALIFORNIA AND HAWAIIAN SUGAR REFINING CORPORATION

I. INTRODUCTION

1. NOTE ON HISTORY OF THE CORPORATION

From a commercial point of view, the history of sugar in the Hawaiian Islands commences with the reciprocity treaty of 1877 between Hawaii and the United States, under the terms of which the United States granted Hawaii the free entry of its sugars into this country in exchange for a naval coaling station at Pearl Harbor. Prior to that time Hawaii could not economically produce sugar to compete with sugar from Cuba and other foreign countries. It was not until August 1, 1898, however, with the annexation of Hawaii by the United States, that the Hawaiian sugar producers felt a sense of security and permanency sufficient to warrant the investment of large sums of money in sugar plantations, irrigation projects, and water works. Thereafter the Hawaiian sugar industry began to expand. The produce was shipped to the mainland where it was purchased in the open market by Atlantic seaboard and Gulf refiners.

Owing to the cost and uncertainty of transportation around Cape Horn, the long time consumed in transit, and other adverse conditions in the sugar trade, it became apparent to the producers of Hawaii that their industry could be made to thrive and expand far more rapidly by the establishment of a central refining and distributing agency on the mainland. In 1904 the Sugar Factors, Limited, was organized for this purpose, with a capital stock of $5,000,000.

In the early days what is now the town of Crockett was called Wheatport. Large quantities of wheat were shipped there by rail from the San Joaquin and Sacramento valleys. The wheat was ground into flour at the Starr flour mill, one of the first flour mills to be built in the state of California. The Starr mill occupied the site of the present sugar refinery. The close proximity of the location to rail and water facilities made it ideal in those days as a receiving point for wheat and a shipping point for flour. The same facilities make Crockett an advantageous location for the sugar refinery today.

The town of Wheatport was a part of one of the original Spanish land grants—the Rancho Cañada del Hombre. In later years there was long and bitter litigation in the courts over conflicting rights and boundaries within the Rancho. Joseph B. Crockett, an early pioneer and lawyer, received a portion of the Rancho as his fee for legal services. Later he became a Justice of the Supreme Court of California, and in his honor the name of the town of Wheatport was changed to Crockett. It has not been incorporated.

With the adaptation of the rich valley lands to the cultivation of products more profitable than wheat, and the opening of other avenues of commerce and transportation, the importance of the Starr flour mill gradually declined. This mill was purchased and converted into a beet and cane sugar refinery (the California Beet Sugar and Refinery Company) in 1898. The attempt to operate a combination beet and cane refinery was short-lived, however, because of the unsuitability of adjacent lands to the raising of sugar beets. The California Beet Sugar Refinery was purchased by the Sugar Factors Company in 1905, and the plant was overhauled and remodelled. Its operation as the California and Hawaiian Sugar Refining Corporation commenced on March 10, 1906, strictly as a cane sugar refinery, under the management of Mr. George M. Rolph, who is president of this company today.

During the first year of its operation by the present

company, the Crockett refinery melted 67,000 tons of Hawaiian raw sugars. Today the plant is one of the largest and most modern sugar refinery units in the United States, with an actual melting capacity of 2,500 tons of cane sugar per day, or about 700,000 tons per year. The refinery is owned and controlled by a group of thirty-three Hawaiian sugar plantations, whose output represents about 80 per cent of all the raw cane sugar produced in Hawaii. The value of these plantations—land, machinery, and equipment—is said to be over one hundred million dollars.

Shipment of raw cane sugar from the islands.—The steamers which transport the raw sugar to Crockett are specially constructed for sugar service, with cargo capacities up to 12,000 tons. The monthly production of raw sugar varies. Production begins slowly in December and January, reaches its peak in April, May, and June, and starts tapering off as the harvesting nears completion in September. A large fleet of steamers is therefore required to handle shipments. Tonnage must be provided for the peak-load periods, because of lack of storage space in the Islands, and because the greatest consumption on the mainland takes place at those times. The raw sugar is brought to California by the Matson Navigation Company, which maintains a fleet of modern sugar-carrying vessels capable of handling up to 90,000 tons per month. These vessels operate on regular schedules between San Francisco Bay and Hawaiian ports, where they load the sugar which has been transported by rail from the various plantations to the coast.

2. THE CO-OPERATIVE AGREEMENT

Co-operation or pooling of production begins with the shipment of raw sugar to the mainland. Up to this point each of the thirty-three plantations is an independent producing or growing unit, with its own methods of irrigation, agriculture, grinding, machinery and equipment, storage facilities, and management. The advantages achieved through the existence of one large central refining and distributing organization, as against thirty-three separate and distinct small units, are readily apparent and need but little comment. The first great advantage lies in the ability of the combined producers to secure a modern up-to-date fleet of vessels for transporting their product to the mainland with proper speed and under proper air and moisture conditions. The Matson Line which does all the transporting for this group maintains such a fleet. No such transportation could be had without the assurance to the Matson Line of a business of several hundred thousand tons of cargo per annum.

The problem of storing raw sugar is greatly simplified for the planters through the existence of ample raw-sugar storage space at Crockett.

Under the old system of refining and distribution, the potential number of customers for the raw sugar of the plantation group was limited to not over five refineries on the Atlantic Coast, with perhaps an additional one on the West Coast. Such a limitation of outlets was naturally disadvantageous to the planters. They were practically at the mercy of a few refiners. This fact reduced greatly the planters' bargaining power in the disposition of their product. Under the present co-operative system of refining and sale, the number of outlets for the planters is equivalent to the very large number of customers of the California and Hawaiian Sugar Refining Corporation.

Like most other agricultural industries, the growing of cane is seasonal. The average harvesting season is about seven months. Were each plantation to maintain a refinery of its own, the investment in such a plant would be idle five months each year. The co-operation achieved through the maintenance of the refinery at Crockett has had a definite tendency to effect economies in overhead expense by lengthening the refining period. As shown elsewhere in this study, production at Crockett has been regularized to a point where the refinery operates at maximum capacity, twenty-four hours a day, for about eleven months per year. The result of this regularization of operations and of production at capacity has been greatly to reduce refining costs. This great saving has benefited each member of the plantation group, in accordance with the amount of raw sugar delivered.

The cost of distribution, too, would almost certainly be greatly increased if each plantation was to maintain a selling and distribution organization of its own, instead of the one centralized distribution mechanism now in operation. As a matter of fact, many of the plantations are not sufficiently large to make individual refining and distribution possible. The method of distribution in vogue in the sugar industry—namely, distribution through brokers and wholesalers—makes it difficult for even a large and well-managed centralized sales organization to exercise proper control over distribution. A small organization could not possibly cope efficiently with such a decentralized and complicated form of distribution.

The question is often asked why the planters of this group could not maintain one central refinery in the islands. As a matter of fact, one plantation (outside of this group) with a capacity of 30,000 tons per annum does refine its raw cane in the Islands. This plantation, however, disposes of the greater part of its refined product within the Islands. A central Island refinery for the co-operative group would double its transportation costs. The thirty-three plantations are located on five different islands, and the cost of transporting the raw sugar to a central point on one of the islands would be about equivalent to the cost of loading and transporting it to the mainland of the United States. There would then be the additional cost of transporting the refined product to the mainland. Today there is only one charge—that of transporting the raw sugar to Crockett. One naturally wonders why this co-operative scheme does not extend all the way to the growing, grinding, and milling of the cane. The only possible answer to this is custom and tradition. Some of the plantations in this group have been in existence, as independent growing units, from seventy-five to one hundred years. With increasing pressure of competition, the advantages of this sort of co-operation are bound to be more keenly appreciated by each of the plantations. There will then be a definite tendency for co-operation in the growing and grinding of the cane, akin to the pooling now in force in the refining and distribution end. The advantages to be had by co-operative effort in the growing and milling of the cane appear to be as great as the advantages already achieved through co-operation in refining and distribution. The introduction of uniform methods of fertilization, irrigation, milling, and engineering would, there is little doubt, bring inestimable benefits to the group. The standardization of supplies and equipment and the centralization of the buying of such supplies and materials would save, it is believed, many millions of dollars. One instance will illustrate this point. At the present time each plantation determines its own specification, make, and size of bags for the shipment of raw sugar. The standardization of the size of the bag to 100 lbs. would alone result, it is reliably estimated, in an annual saving of over $200,000. That the advantages of this sort of co-operation are becoming more obvious may be seen from the fact that the plantations at the present time maintain jointly a central experimental station for the study of the various agricultural and chemical problems involved in the raising and milling of cane sugar.

INTRODUCTION

The California and Hawaiian Sugar Refining Corporation is but one link in the chain of a co-operative organization—the growing, milling, refining, and distribution of sugar. As already stated, the refinery at Crockett is owned by thirty-three separate corporate entities or plantations. These are organized into six distinct groups, each represented on the mainland by a "sugar agency." The legal title to the refinery at Crockett is vested in six trustees elected by the six agencies.

To facilitate the movement of the raw sugars an intermediate corporation, the Sugar Factors, Ltd., was organized. Its principal function is that of arranging for deliveries of raw sugars from the plantations to the refinery at Crockett, on a predetermined schedule agreed upon annually.

The California and Hawaiian Sugar Refining Corporation refines and sells the sugar for account of the producers. To give the latter sufficient working capital through the growing and grinding campaign or season, the contract provides for a payment on account for each raw sugar cargo delivered as follows:

A. An initial payment of 75 per cent of the value of the cargo, plus or minus polarization allowances. For arriving at this initial payment the average New York market price of 96 per cent polarization sugar, full duty paid, for ten consecutive market days, of which the date of arrival at San Francisco is the fifth, is taken.

B. A final payment to the plantation in proportion to the weight of sugar shipped during the contract year ending November 30. This final payment is determined in the following manner: A total is made of

1. The gross proceeds of all sales made prior to the end of the year, plus
2. the estimated value of all sugars and molasses remaining unsold as of November 30, plus
3. all other income from every source.

From the total of the three above-mentioned items, the following are then deducted:

1. The initial payment above referred to.
2. The purchase price of all other sugars, raw, refined, or beet, purchased from anyone other than the thirty-three plantations represented.
3. The amount of any overestimate made as of the previous November, of the value of unsold sugars.
4. All manufacturing, marketing, operating, and other expenses incurred by the refinery.
5. A fixed percentage of the capital worth of the Corporation as per the "Withholding Provision" of the contract, to provide the Corporation with funds to cover: (a) Plant improvements, betterments, and additions; (b) Sinking-fund requirements for bond redemption; (c) Dividends on common stock, when, and if, declared.

The plantation's share of the remainder, as determined above, constitutes the final payment, to be made not later than the following December 15.

The company is privileged, when financial position warrants, to make partial payments throughout the year to plantations, in proportion to the sugar shipped by each to date. These partial payments then become a further deduction in arriving at the final payment.

The following chart (Fig. 1) shows graphically the co-operative nature and organization of this business.

3. CAPITAL STRUCTURE

On November 30, 1927, the capital structure of the Corporation consisted of an authorized common stock issue of 150,000 shares (par value $100) of which only 100,015 shares, valued at $10,001,500, were actually issued. In addition there was an outstanding issue of $7,000,000 of 7 per cent gold bonds, redeemable at the rate of $700,000 per year. The bonds are secured by a first mortgage on the real estate, plant, and equipment owned by the company.

The capital assets of the Corporation, as of November 30, 1927, were: current and working assets, $12,921,725;

INTRODUCTION

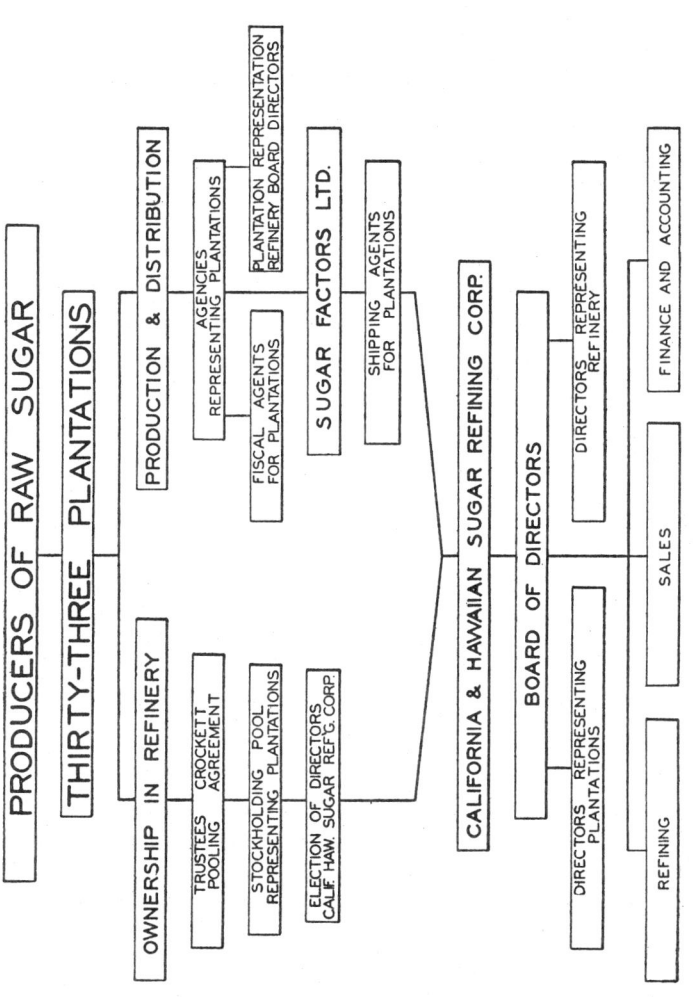

Fig. 1.—Chart of co-operative agreement

fixed assets less bonds, $5,276,031; other assets, $2,475,414. From the total thus obtained—$20,673,170—there should be deducted a contingent liability to the sugar planters of $3,057,668. The total proprietary capital of the company was therefore $17,615,502. The amount of borrowed capital was $11,384,174. The fixed part of this borrowed capital was represented by a bond issue of $7,000,000. Current borrowings consisted of: accounts payable, $927,995; reserve for fixed charges, $398,511; and the contingent liability to the planters of $3,057,668.

4. GENERAL CHARACTER OF ORGANIZATION

The chart given below (Fig. 2) shows the present Corporation ownership, administrative control, and executive management of the Corporation. The stockholders or owners are identical with the groups of planters who produce the raw cane sugar in Hawaii.

The actual administration is carried on through a Board of Directors of fifteen members, headed by a Chairman of the Board. Of the fifteen members, eleven represent the plantations and four the actual management of the refinery. The refinery representatives are its President and the three Vice-Presidents.

With the exception of fifteen shares held by some of the directors all the outstanding stock of the Corporation (100,000 shares of common stock, par value $100) is owned and held by the plantations.

The Board of Directors represents the policy-forming mechanism. One might call this board the directive agency of the business, as distinct from its executive management. The management is in the hands of an executive committee of nine, consisting of the Chairman of the Board of Directors, the President of the Corporation and the three Vice-Presidents (in charge, respectively, of Refinery, Sales, and Finance and Accounting), and four Directors representing the plantations.

INTRODUCTION 11

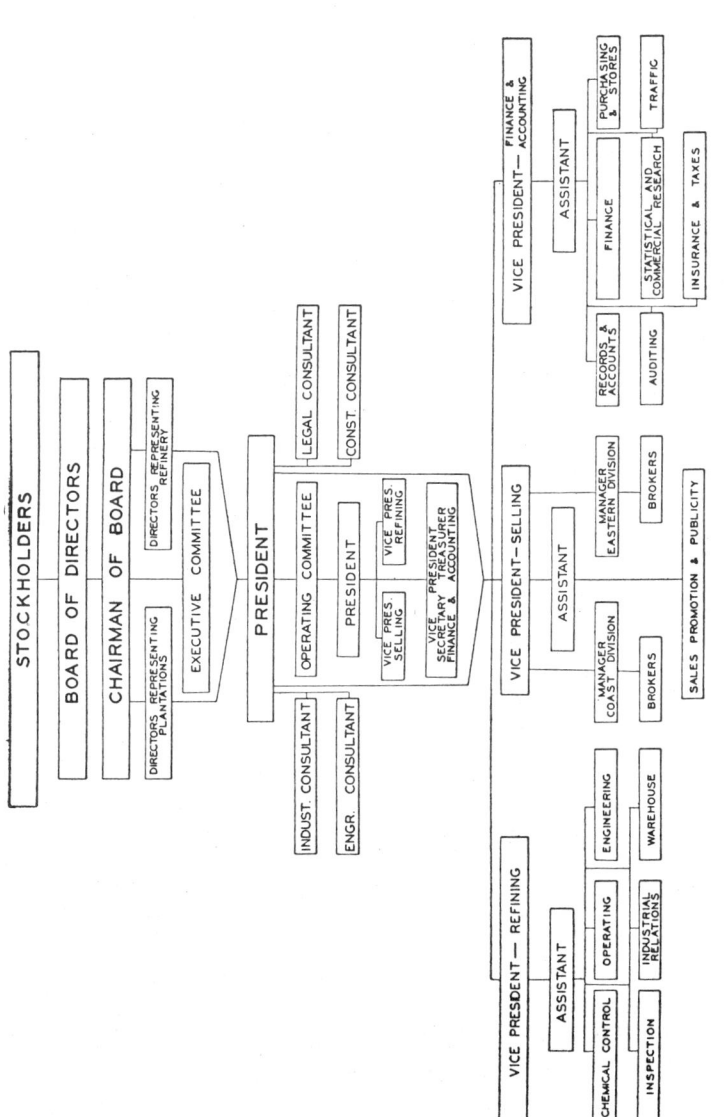

Fig. 2.—Chart of general organization

In addition to his regular staff, the President has a consulting staff of four for special problems—an industrial consultant, a legal consultant, a construction consultant, and a consulting engineer. Originally the three major associates of the President, in charge, respectively, of Refinery, Sales, and Finance and Accounting, were not members of the directorate. This lack of close relation between the men who formulated policies and those who were called upon to execute them was found unsatisfactory. In 1920, these three major assistants to the President were organized into an advisory staff committee, and on February 11, 1925, they were elected Vice-Presidents and placed on the Board of Directors of the Corporation.

Each of the three Vice-Presidents has an assistant as an understudy; there is, therefore, an Assistant to the Vice-President in charge of Sales, an Assistant to the Vice-President in charge of Finance and Accounting, and an Assistant to the Vice-President in charge of the Refinery. The last-named assistant is also technical superintendent of the refinery.

The activities of the three main divisions of the organization are co-ordinated, first by frequent conferences between the three Vice-Presidents, and finally through review by the President himself. There is an official weekly staff meeting in San Francisco, presided over by the President and attended by the three Vice-Presidents.

The proper functioning of the Corporation involves, to a great extent, a co-ordination of the functions of one division with those of the rest. For instance, the Sales Division plans and formulates the selling budget of the refinery, determining the amounts of the various grades, varieties, and packages to be sold. The execution of the production budget, however, involves (1) receipt of raw sugars from the Islands—a function the supervision of which is in the hands of the refinery; and (2) the furnishing of materials, supplies, and containers, and a familiarity with the existing condition of stocks in the hands of brokers and in transit—functions of the Finance and Accounting Division. The production budget, although nominally originating in the Sales Division, is really the result of co-operative thought on the part of the other two divisions. Again, the formulation of expense and improvement budgets, though supervised by Finance-Accounting, in reality originates in the Refinery. Auditing, cost-keeping, and budget-keeping are functions of Finance-Accounting, although the major part of all actual expenditures is incurred by the Refinery and by the Sales Division.

Day-to-day co-ordination of the Refinery with Finance-Accounting is achieved through an official of the latter division (the assistant to the treasurer), who is located at the refinery, but is independent of, although working closely with, the plant manager.

A close study of the operations of the Corporation makes one feel that its organization is effective both in the formulation of general policies and in their execution. The reason for this effectiveness lies in the harmony and understanding existing between the five men running the business—the Chairman of the Board of Directors, the President, and the three Vice-Presidents. Each Vice-President is interested in the business as a whole, aside from his own particular sphere of activity. The Vice-President in charge of Finance and Accounting is versed in the general problems of the refinery, as well as in the problems involved in distribution and sales. The Sales executive takes an interest in the operations of the refinery and in problems of finance and accounting. The Vice-President in charge of Refining takes a vital interest in the work of his colleagues. Discussions of each other's problems are welcomed and not considered meddlesome.

One can hardly fail to notice that credit for this sort of co-operation—most desirable and necessary in any business institution—is due to the personality of the President who is the chief co-ordinator. The character and ability of the men he has selected as his major associates make co-ordination possible.

The difficulty with the Chart of General Organization (Fig. 2) presented in this report is the fact that it is impossible to bring out graphically co-ordinative effectiveness. In its actual operation this company is far from being an organization divided into watertight compartments with the idea that "this department is yours and this is mine."

The management stresses the development of understudies for each of the major executives. One of the Vice-Presidents is the official understudy of the President, ready and capable to take up the reins of office when called upon. The relationship between the understudies is similar to the relationship between their superiors. Each one functions within his own field and co-operates with the others. This policy of the development of understudies is found throughout the entire organization—among operating executives and department heads as well as at the top of the business structure.

II. THE REFINING DIVISION

1. GENERAL ORGANIZATION OF REFINERY

The refinery is managed by the Vice-President in charge of Refining, referred to as the plant manager. The organization of the refinery is shown on the chart presented herewith (Fig. 3, p. 16). The assistant to the plant manager is also the technical superintendent, in charge of one of the main departments, namely, that of chemical control. The other two major refining departments are concerned with operation and inspection. The fourth department is that of warehousing and deals with the receiving and delivery of raw sugar to the refinery and with the storing and shipping of the refined product. In addition to the four mentioned departments, there are departments of engineering and maintenance and of industrial relations. The last two departments are, by their very nature, service departments. Their effectiveness depends wholly upon the rendering of proper and timely service to the departments actually operating the plant.

In July 1922 after many weeks of study, the operation of the refinery was put on a continuous 12-day basis, instead of operating the refinery six consecutive days and then shutting it down on Saturday and Sunday. A shift arrangement of the working force keeps the maximum weekly hours of labor at forty-eight. The result to the men, in number of days off, was the same. The change, however, resulted in economy and increased efficiency. Much time and energy had been lost in stopping operations at the close of each week. The quality of the sugar had often suffered by reason of frequent stops and starts. Such stopping and starting is as undesirable today as before, but the number of shut-downs has been cut in half. The plan is also popular with the employees, as it gives them longer week-ends.

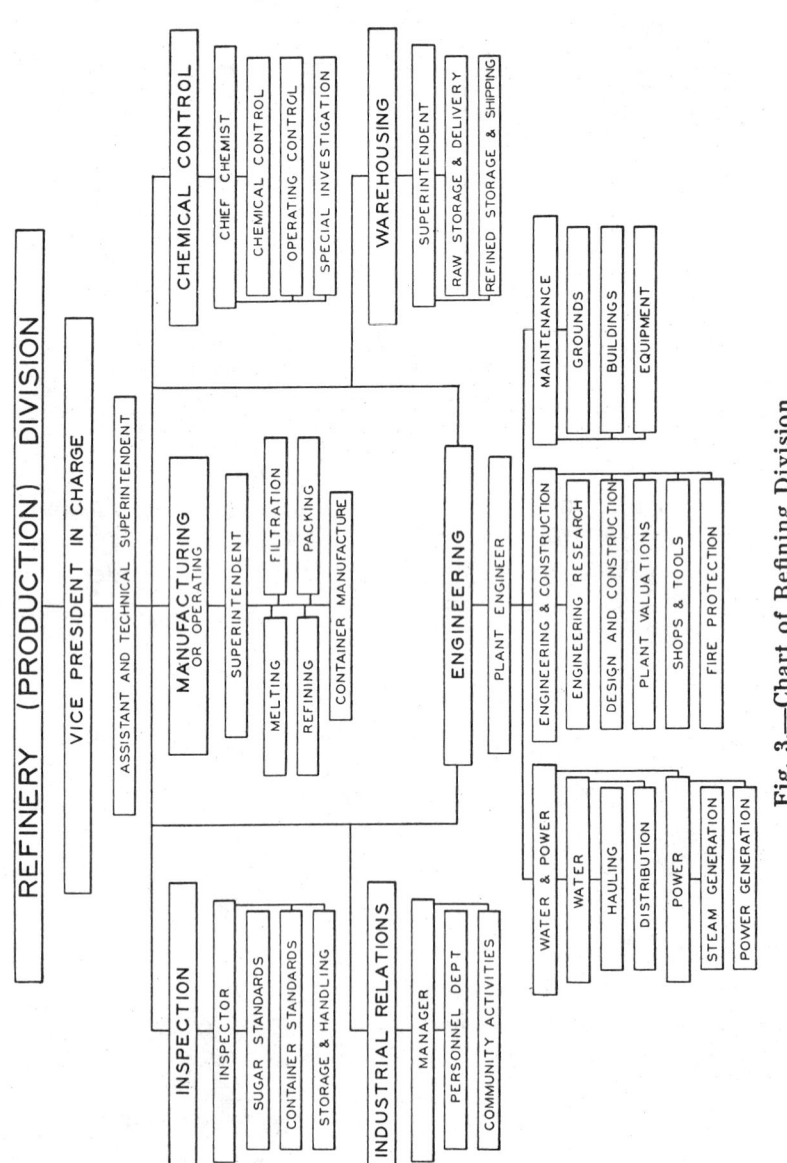

Fig. 3.—Chart of Refining Division

Operating schedule for 1928.—The following table (Table 1), known as the Refinery Calendar, shows operating and shut-down days for 1928, also days designated for stock taking:

TABLE 1
REFINERY CALENDAR FOR 1928

No.	Start	\multicolumn{11}{c	}{OPERATING PERIOD}	OPR. DAYS	SHIFT CHANGE	STOCK DAY
		M	T	W	T	F	S	S	M	T	W	T	F	S	S			
--	Jan.	-	-	-	-	-	-	-	-	-	-	-	-	-	1			
1	Jan.	[2]	3	4	5	6	7	8	9	10	11	12	13	[14	15]	11	Jan.15	-
2	Jan.	16	17	18	19	20	21	22	23	24	25	26	27	[28	29]	12	Jan.29	Jan.28
3	Jan.	30	31	1	2	3	4	5	6	7	8	9	10	[11	12]	12	Feb.12	-
4	Feb.	13	14	15	16	17	18	19	20	21	22	23	24	[25	26]	12	Feb.26	Feb.25
5	Feb.	27	28	29	1	2	3	4	5	6	7	8	9	[10	11]	12	Mar.11	-
6	Mar.	12	13	14	15	16	17	18	19	20	21	22	23	[24	25]	12	Mar.25	Mar.24
7	Mar.	26	27	28	29	30	31	1	2	3	4	5	6	[7	8]	12	Apr. 8	-
8	Apr.	9	10	11	12	13	14	15	16	17	18	19	20	[21	22]	12	Apr.22	Apr.21
9	Apr.	23	24	25	26	27	28	29	30	1	2	3	4	[5	6]	12	May 6	-
10	May	7	8	9	10	11	12	13	14	15	16	17	18	[19	20]	12	May 20	May 19
11	May	21	22	23	24	25	26	27	28	29	30	31	1	[2	3]	12	Jun 3	-
12	Jun	4	5	6	7	8	9	10	11	12	13	14	15	[16	17]	12	Jun 17	Jun 16
13	Jun	18	19	20	21	22	23	24	25	26	27	28	29	30	1			
--	Jul	2	[3	4	5]	-	-	-	-	-	-	-	-	-	-	15	Jul 4	-
14	Jul	-	-	-	-	6	7	8	9	10	11	12	13	14	15			
--	Jul	16	17	18	19	20	[21	22]	-	-	-	-	-	-	-	15	Jul 22	Jul 21
15	Jul	23	24	25	26	27	28	29	30	31	1	2	3	[4	5]	12	Aug. 5	-
16	Aug.	6	7	8	9	10	11	12	13	14	15	16	17	[18	19]	12	Aug.19	Aug.18
17	Aug.	20	21	22	23	24	25	26	27	28	29	30	31	[1	2]	12	Sep. 2	-
18	Sep.	[3]	4	5	6	7	8	9	10	11	12	13	14	[15	16]	11	Sep.16	-
19	Sep.	17	18	19	20	21	22	23	24	25	26	27	28	[29	30]	12	Sep.30	Sep.29
20	Oct.	1	2	3	4	5	6	7	8	9	10	11	12	[13	14]	12	Oct.14	-
21	Oct.	15	16	17	18	19	20	21	22	23	24	25	26	[27	28]	12	Oct.28	Oct 27
22	Oct.	29	30	31	1	2	3	4	5	6	7	8	9	[10	11]	12	Nov.11	-
23	Nov.	12	13	14	15	16	17	18	19	20	21	22	23	24	25			
--	Nov.	26	27	28	[29]	-	-	-	-	-	-	-	-	-	-	17		Nov.29
--	Nov.	-	-	-	-	30	1	[2]	3	4	5	6	7	8	[9]	--		
--	Dec.	10	11	12	13	14	15	[16]	17	18	19	20	21	22	[23]	--		
--	Dec.	24	[25]	26	27	28	29	[30]	31	-	-	-	-	-	-	--		

NOTES :- ☐ Dates on which Refinery is scheduled to be shut down.

Calendar arranged so that Easter Sunday falls on a non-operating day.

2. REFINERY BUDGETS

As stated elsewhere, much success has been attained in the regularization of operations to avoid the excessive and fluctuating costs due to the irregularity of melt. Plans were adopted which made possible the operation of the refinery at maximum capacity, for the greatest number of days consistent with raw-sugar deliveries. The success achieved in regularization has made effective budgeting of refinery expenditures really practical.

Budgeting at the refinery involves the following:

1. The quarterly preparation of detailed melt and production schedules.
2. The quarterly preparation of refining-cost budgets, comprising costs of labor, material, and supplies, expense, maintenance, and fixed charges.
3. The quarterly preparation of improvement budgets, covering expenditures to be made for plant and equipment additions and alterations.

Melt and Production Budget.—The refinery begins its operations with new-crop sugar about January 1 of each year. The basis of the melt budget consists of crop estimates received from the growers. These estimates reach the refinery during November, and immediately thereafter tentative plans are drawn for the next year's "campaign" or season and an operating schedule or calendar for the year is drawn up. The calendar for 1928 is shown, as Table 1, on page 17. At the time these estimates of raw crop are made, the growing cane is still in the fields. This first estimate is therefore treated as preliminary to more accurate figures which become available after the start of the grinding season.

From this tentative or preliminary annual forecast there follows the actual development of the first quarter's production budget. From the sales forecast already prepared covering the three-months period, the requirements of grades and packages are determined. The total output of the refinery for the budget period is shown by the melt schedule. The difference between these two (that is, between melt and sales forecasts) shows the expected increase or decrease in the inventory during the three months, so that an estimate may be had of the ending inventory. The proper distribution of this inventory to grades and packages is then prepared. This considers the

THE REFINING DIVISION

requirements of the refinery inventory to meet demands for direct shipments to the Coast and River territories and boat shipments to the Southern territory.

Some factors prevent a perfect distribution of the planned inventory. Certain grades deteriorate rapidly in storage, and these must be kept at a minimum; other grades are highly seasonal and at certain times in the year need not be kept in stock. Frequently the possibility of discontinuing a certain grade makes it advisable to reduce the inventory on this one grade.

When the plan for the probable inventory has been completed, these quantities are added to the estimated quantities of sales. This tells how much of each package must be made available within the three-month period. By deducting the inventory of each package on hand at the first of the period, the quantity which must be produced is derived. The following sample tabulation shows more clearly how the production schedule is prepared; the figures are in tons.

Grade	Estimated Sales	Inventory— End of Period	Needed	Inventory— Start of Period	Quantity to Produce
Totals	200,840	61,413	262,253	67,818	194,435
Granulated ...	173,426	46,961	220,387	57,613	162,774
Confectioners'	9,732	5,446	15,178	4,694	10,484
Pressed	1,743	983	2,726	715	2,011
Softs	9,559	5,040	14,599	3,389	11,210
Powdered	6,380	2,983	9,363	1,407	7,956

All of the foregoing may meet with some modification, contingent upon the refinery's ability to carry out the schedule. Refining and packing capacities must be considered with particular reference to more or less uniform rates of melt. Furthermore, it is not economical to have idle equipment, or to work second or third shifts for varying periods.

20 THE C & H SUGAR REFINING CORPORATION

On the first of each month performance is checked with forecasts. Revisions in sales estimates are balanced against production, and revisions are made in the production budget if required. The production budget is used by the refinery superintendent as the basis for estimating his production ratios, such as the percentage of soft sugar and specialty sugars to be produced. Schedules are then prepared covering the refining equipment and the personnel required.

The purchasing department then proceeds to purchase and arrange for delivery of materials; the warehouse department plans storage and handling; the engineering department plans and prepares its budgets covering operating units under its supervision. The preparation of the refining-cost budget then follows.

The degree of closeness with which production budgets are formulated at the present time is shown by Table 2,

TABLE 2

COMPARISON OF BUDGETED WITH ACTUAL PRODUCTION, IN PERCENTAGES, 1927

Product	Budget	Actual Production in Percentage of Budget	Percentage of Total Actual Production
Fine Standard	100.00	101.22	55.19
Berry	100.00	100.63	30.64
Coarse	} 100.00	104.74	5.50
Confectioners' "A"			
Confectioners' "AA" and Special			
Cube and Cubelets	100.00	121.98	.76
Extra "C"	100.00	111.37	.34
Golden "C"	100.00	105.03	2.72
Yellow "D"	100.00	109.11	.68
Powdered	100.00	99.14	3.80
Dessert	100.00	132.82	.07
Brown (1-lb. pkgs.)	100.00	96.47	.30
Totals	100.00	101.46	100.00

which presents a comparison of budgeted with actual production for 1927. The last column of the table furnishes an idea as to the relative importance of a specific over- or under-estimate by giving the percentage of total actual production of each budgeted item. Total production for 1927 was slightly less than one and one-half per cent greater than the production budget. The largest proportion of production over the budget, 32.82 per cent and 21.98 per cent, took place, respectively, in "Dessert" and "Cube and Cubelets." These items of specialty sugars are, however, relatively unimportant as may be seen from the last column of the table, they having been responsible for less than one per cent of the total production of the refinery for the year.

Refining Cost Budget.—Operating expense budgets are prepared quarterly and cover expenditures for salaries and wages, materials, supplies, and expense, fixed, and other charges. The budget for salaries and wages in all departments, except manufacturing, is based on the number of employees to be carried in each department, at established rates of pay.

In the operating department each station has a standard number of employees per shift for a given daily rate of melt. The production budget determines the number of shifts required on each station. There is also a standard rate of pay for each station. Therefore the estimated cost is calculated by multiplying the number of operating days by the daily cost of each station, and adding to this the cost of labor used on non-operating days. Each department prepares its own labor estimates.

The major items of material, except container material, are calculated on a rate per hundred ton of melt. This rate is arrived at from past performance covering a two-year period. Container costs are arrived at by taking the estimated number of containers for the quarter and multiplying by the current cost of materials used in making the finished containers. To this is added the standard labor cost for container manufacture.

Supplies and expense items are based on an estimated rate per 100 tons of melt. The budget for maintenance and repairs is prepared by the engineering department and covers the estimated amount to be expended, by stations. The total actual charges are made to a reserve account and pro-rated to each department on a theoretical rate based on estimated melts. Theoretical rates are used because the budget, as prepared by the engineering department, covers a full year, while the expense budgets are prepared quarterly. It is difficult to determine in what months heavy expenditures for maintenance and repairs will be made. If the charges were made direct to operating accounts the result would cause the monthly rates per hundred pounds of net output to fluctuate considerably.

Taxes, insurance and depreciation are charged to the various departments on a pre-determined rate per hundred pounds of net output. Other charges, covering bone coal renewals, contingencies, and lay-by expense, are also calculated on a predetermined rate per hundred pounds of net output. Lay-by expenses are those incurred during the period in which the plant is idle because of extraordinary repairs and for general cleaning.

All of the budgets are turned in to the accounting department, where a consolidated statement is made showing the estimated cost by departments and by objects of expenditure and functions. During each budget period, daily comparisons by stations are made. At the end of each quarter a statement covering all departments is made showing a comparison of budget with actual expense, both by objects of expenditure and by functions. This comparison is made by the accounting department, and where the actual controllable items vary to any extent from the estimated amounts, explanations are requested.

The figures thus obtained, with explanations, are incorporated in the comparative statement rendered by the accounting department. The first budget year was 1926. The estimated budgets for manufacturing, the largest item of expense, were shown during 1926 to have been about 8 per cent greater than actual expenditures for the year. On the whole, the average unit cost of production was 5.73 per cent less than the budget figures. Expenditures on salaries and wages during the same year exceeded estimates by less than one per cent.

The improvement in budget technique, enabling closer forecasting and more effective execution, is shown by the results of budget operation for 1927. These results are shown in Tables 3, 4, 5, and 6. The basis of comparison

TABLE 3

COMPARISON OF BUDGET WITH ACTUAL MONEY EXPENDITURES, IN PERCENTAGES, 1927

By objects of expenditure

Objects of Expenditure	Budget	Actual Expenditure in Percentage of Budget	Percentage Distribution of Total Actual Expenditure
Salaries and wages	100.00	99.77	25.15
Materials	100.00	100.06	55.99
Supplies	100.00	110.58	1.16
Expense	100.00	140.48	3.38
Maintenance and repairs	100.00	103.50	9.00
Fixed charges	100.00	98.67	12.57
Other charges	100.00	96.00	5.68
Total	100.00	100.85	112.93
Department credit	100.00	101.40	-12.93
Net Total	100.00	100.78	100.00

24 THE C & H SUGAR REFINING CORPORATION

is the budget, actual expenditures being expressed in terms of a percentage of those estimated. Budgets and expenditures are shown in dollars and in unit costs per hundred pounds, both by objects of expenditure and by function.

TABLE 4

COMPARISON OF BUDGET WITH ACTUAL MONEY EXPENDITURES, IN PERCENTAGES, 1927

By functions

Functions	Budget	Actual Expenditure in Percentage of Budget	Percentage Distribution of Total Actual Expenditure
Manufacturing	100.00	100.33	69.87
Technical control	100.00	88.25	1.65
Water and power	100.00	94.99	13.62
Engineering and mechanics	100.00	104.59	3.72
Purchasing and stores	100.00	93.78	1.26
Transportation	100.00	102.02	.24
Industrial relations	100.00	112.60	2.38
Accounting and statistical	100.00	89.16	.66
General plant expense	100.00	111.51	6.33
Administrative expense	100.00	121.24	2.48
Sub-total	100.00	100.64	102.21
Department credit	100.00	99.50	−11.38
Total	100.00	100.78	90.83
Warehouse	100.00	103.12	9.17
Net Total	100.00	100.99	100.00

Table 3 shows for net total an over-expenditure of about ¾ of one per cent for the year. Table 4 shows an excess of expenditure, over total budget, of slightly less than one per cent; Table 5, an over-expenditure of about one-sixth of one per cent; and Table 6, an excess of expenditure, over budget, of about ⅜ of one per cent.

Aside from improvement in budgetary technique, the close approximation of budgets to actual expenditures was due to a greater regularization of operations. Such stabilization of operations made possible closer forecasting and a closer day-to-day check on actual expenditures. The Division of Finance and Accounting, in charge of

TABLE 5

COMPARISON OF BUDGET WITH ACTUAL UNIT COSTS (PER 100 LBS.), IN PERCENTAGES, 1927

By objects of expenditure

Objects of Expenditure	Budget	Actual Expenditure in Percentage of Budget	Percentage Distribution of Total Actual Unit Cost
Salaries and wages	100.00	99.14	25.15
Materials	100.00	99.43	55.99
Supplies	100.00	109.82	1.16
Expense	100.00	139.66	3.38
Maintenance and repairs	100.00	102.86	9.00
Fixed charges	100.00	98.05	12.57
Other charges	100.00	95.41	5.68
Total	100.00	100.22	112.93
Department credit	100.00	100.76	−12.93
Net Total	100.00	100.16	100.00

budget enforcement, is in daily touch with almost every official making expenditures. These men know from day to day just how they stand with reference to actual expenditures of the budgeted items. This fact, perhaps, as much as any other, made for greater effectiveness in budget formulation and budget execution during 1927.

Labor Cost budget.—A good illustration of the care with which budgets are compiled is furnished by the labor budget, compiled quarterly. This budget estimates in great detail, by station and sub-station, the number of workmen, classified by sex and method of pay (monthly, hourly, premium and piece work), which will be required for daily melts of 1,800, 2,000, 2,200 and 2,400 tons.

TABLE 6

COMPARISON OF BUDGET WITH ACTUAL UNIT COSTS (PER 100 LBS.), IN PERCENTAGES, 1927

By functions

Functions	Budget	Actual Expenditure in Percentage of Budget	Percentage Distribution of Total Actual Unit Cost
Manufacturing	100.00	99.70	69.87
Technical control	100.00	87.60	1.65
Water and power	100.00	94.40	13.62
Engineering and mechanics	100.00	103.94	3.72
Purchasing and stores	100.00	93.20	1.26
Transportation	100.00	101.61	.24
Industrial relations	100.00	111.95	2.38
Accounting and statistical	100.00	88.66	.66
General plant expense	100.00	110.82	6.33
Administrative expense	100.00	120.44	2.48
Sub-total	100.00	100.01	102.21
Department credit	100.00	98.87	11.38
Total	100.00	100.16	90.83
Warehouse	100.00	102.48	9.17
Net Total	100.00	100.36	100.00

Space does not permit a detailed reproduction of all of the various steps involved in the preparation of the labor budget, interesting and instructive though it might be. The detailed labor budget finally takes the form of summary figures of labor requirements, for each melt, as follows (Table 7):

TABLE 7
LABOR BUDGET FOR FIRST QUARTER OF 1928

	Monthly Employees							
	Men				Women			
	1,800 Tons	2,000 Tons	2,200 Tons	2,400 Tons	1,800 Tons	2,000 Tons	2,200 Tons	2,400 Tons
Melting raws	7	7	7	7	..	..	..	..
Filtration	24	24	24	24	..	..	..	..
Refining	29	29	29	29	..	..	..	..
Packing	4	4	4	4	..	..	..	..
Containers	2	2	2	2	..	..	..	..
Sugar inspection	4	4	4	4	..	..	..	..
Supervision	5	5	5	5	2	2	2	2
Reprocessing	..	..	..	..	..	..	..	..
Sanitation	1	1	1	1	..	..	..	..
Bag laundry	..	..	..	..	..	..	..	..
Powdered sugar	2	2	2	2	..	..	..	..
	78	78	78	78	2	2	2	2

	Daily Employees							
Melting raws	36	41	43	45	..	..	..	..
Filtration	128	128	128	128	2	2	2	2
Refining	109	115	121	121	..	..	..	..
Packing	104	109	112	115	21	21	21	21
Containers	21	22	23	23	53	61	63	66
Sugar inspection	...	...	...	...	1	1	1	1
Supervision	...	...	...	...	..	..	..	..
Reprocessing	2	2	2	2	..	..	..	..
Sanitation	26	26	26	26	..	..	..	..
Bag laundry	24	27	33	33	..	..	..	..
Powdered sugar	28	28	28	28	9	9	9	9
	478	498	516	521	86	94	96	99

	1,800 Tons	2,000 Tons	2,200 Tons	2,400 Tons
Totals, Monthly Men	78	78	78	78
Totals, Monthly Women	2	2	2	2
Totals, Daily Men	478	498	516	521
Totals, Daily Women	86	94	96	99
Grand Total, Employees	644	672	692	700

Improvement budgets.—The improvement budget represents allotments of money for the installation of new buildings, machinery, and equipment, as well as for renewals or alterations of the present equipment. There is a persistent attempt on the part of the company to introduce new machinery and improved methods of production. The first definitely formulated and specifically executed improvement budget was prepared for 1927, and involved an expenditure of $428,000. The improvement budget for 1928 calls for an expenditure of $475,000.

The formulation of the improvement budget for 1927 was an integral part of the budgeting policies instituted in 1925. That large sums were expended for plant improvement and betterment prior to 1927 may readily be inferred from the fact that the cost value of the refinery, machinery, and equipment has been progressively on the increase since 1921.

The improvement budget originates with the various officials of the refinery in charge of operating, chemical control, and engineering. The actual compilation of the tentative budget is made by the chief engineer. A number of conferences are then held by the plant manager, at which all parties interested are present. The real object of these conferences is to establish (1) the necessity of the specific improvement from the point of view of operation, (2) its necessity from the point of view of better quality, and (3) the approximate cost and the possible return on this investment.

In a large plant such as this, with a progressive type of organization, the aggregate of total contemplated improvements is usually larger than that which could be accomplished within a given period. These conferences therefore establish, by discussion, a priority for certain installations. The plant manager vetoes some projects, approves of others for immediate execution, and refers the rest "for further study, investigation, and more detailed reports."

After the tentative improvement budget has been passed by the plant manager, it goes for final approval to the operating committee of the company. This committee, as already stated, consists of the President and the three Vice-Presidents.

The very nature of expenditures involved in the improvement budget makes it most difficult to estimate costs closely. Most of the work contemplated by this budget—special new construction, improvements, and renewals—is to be done for the first time. The improvement budget is therefore the hardest of all budgets to formulate with close approximation. Another of the difficulties involved in the planning and execution of a budget such as this is due to the fact that the improvements contemplated are seldom completed on definite fiscal dates. There are always projects only partly completed, and jobs started during one fiscal period but completed during another.

3. DESCRIPTION OF REFINING PROCESSES

A brief description of the processes used at Crockett in the refining of sugar is essential to an understanding of the operations of the refinery and the results achieved. W. A. Allen, assistant editor of *Chemical and Metallurgical Engineering,* after a careful investigation of manufacturing processes at Crockett, published[1] in 1925, an article describing the methods of manufacture followed. With the permission of Mr. Allen this article, with some revisions which bring the description of processes up to date, is reproduced herewith.

[1] Volume XXXII, No. 9, March, 1925.

A Description of the Plant, Processes, and Technical Achievements of the California and Hawaiian Sugar Refining Corporation

The preliminary operations at or near the plantation serve to produce raw sugar containing about 96 to 97.5 per cent of sucrose. The cane is crushed between rolls and the resultant juice purified by treatment with lime and heat and by settling the solid impurities. Evaporators are used to concentrate the clear liquor to a thick syrup and crystallization is brought about subsequently in vacuum pans. The product, a mixture of comparatively coarse crystals and molasses, is centrifuged, and the resulting raw sugar is packed in jute bags. These are shipped in special freighters of the Matson Navigation Company to the refinery at Crockett. Much of the molasses produced at the plantations is shipped to the United States, to be used for the manufacture of industrial alcohol, stock feed, or vinegar.

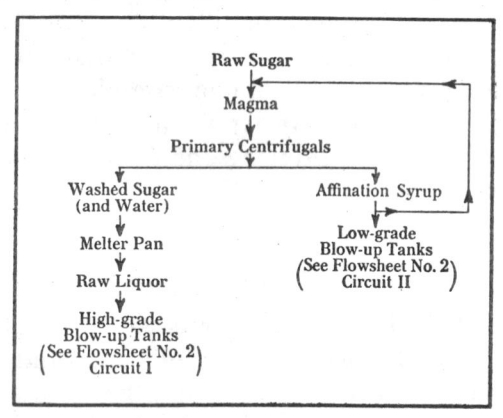

```
                    Raw Sugar
                       ↓
                     Magma
                       ↓
               Primary Centrifugals
              ↓                    ↓
      Washed Sugar           Affination Syrup
      (and Water)                   ↓
            ↓                  Low-grade
       Melter Pan            Blow-up Tanks
            ↓               (See Flowsheet No. 2)
       Raw Liquor           (     Circuit II    )
            ↓
       High-grade
     Blow-up Tanks
   (See Flowsheet No. 2)
   (     Circuit I     )
```

FLOWSHEET No. 1.—The preparation of sugar liquor

The Crockett refinery operates for twelve days continuously, then shuts down for two days. This arrangement, welcomed by employees and employers alike, permits the reservation of one day in seven to all workers, and enables the mechanical department to keep the equipment in first-class condition.

Constant improvement and development is in evidence to minimize handling costs by the maximum possible use of mechanical equipment. (Conveying equipment installed at the wharf

THE REFINING DIVISION

in 1924 has obviated the employment of 35 truckers.) On arrival of the raw sugar at Crockett, its grade is determined by tests made on samples taken from each sixth bag unloaded, a tryer scoop being used, which is driven through the unopened bag. The sampling is done by an independent concern, checks being delivered to the refining company and to the plantation. Agreement is usual; in the event of dispute, the sucrose content of an umpire sample is accepted as correct.

Formerly, the bags of incoming sugar were loaded, in lots of five, by hand onto a truck for weighing. Recently a new system was installed, whereby weighing is accurately and inexpensively performed, the tryer sample being obtained, as mentioned above, from each sixth bag. Accuracy is essential in the recording of the weight of a material of such a comparatively high value, especially in view of the immense tonnage being handled. Automatic weighing on a moving belt conveyor, as practiced in the metallurgical industries, is hopelessly inaccurate for the refiner of sugar. The average error may amount to 1.5 per cent. The weighing of sugar by hand is inevitable in a refinery taking the output of several plantations, personal supervision being necessary to group the output from each. The plan successfully adopted at Crockett involves the weighing by rapid hand adjustment of a short length of conveyor, on which six to eight sacks of sugar are placed. The deflecting of the bags with hook to the appropriate moving platform is done so quickly, the adjustment of the scale is so rapid, and the result is so accurate that the ideal of cheapness and efficiency appears to have been attained. With the large quantities of raw product being handled at Crockett daily, it is evident that moisture content must be estimated before appreciable evaporation has occurred in the sample. To minimize error in this connection, steps are to be taken to provide a room where humidity and temperature are kept constant during the handling and the quartering of the samples.

Storage for 115,000 tons of raw and refined sugar is available to form an adequate reserve in abnormal periods of supply and demand. The raw sugar delivery system is planned so that the cargo as discharged from the ship can be sent direct to processing and thus avoid the cost of unnecessary storage and handling. An interesting feature in the delivery system is the electric control of the conveyors and the means of intercommunication between the supply and receiving departments. The total time taken to wash, melt, refine, crystallize, dry, and pack the finished product is about twelve hours; and in one part of the plant may be seen a 36-in. belt conveyor, on the top of which raw sugar enters the refinery, and on the bottom of which the bags of refined product leave the plant.

In a normal day's operation, the jute bags from the plantations, after the contents have been dumped by hand through a grizzly into the primary bin, contain about six tons of sugar. The laundering of these bags and the recovery of the adhering sugar is therefore an important step in the process. The "sweet water" resulting joins the other liquors of similar density, the sugar being ultimately recovered as a refined product. To facilitate accounting, the bags are marked at the plantations with washable ink, to designate origin; the same bags, repaired if necessary, lined with an inner cotton bag and printed in color according to the type of final product contained, are used for the refined sugar. After laundering, the bags are dried during passage on a hanging conveyor over the boilers.

The raw sugar, containing 96 to 97.5 per cent of sucrose, is discharged from the bottom of the storage bin by drag conveyor, and then goes to two mixers, termed minglers, similar in construction and operation to the machines used in the pottery industry for the pugging of clay. In these it is incorporated with sufficient crude syrup to insure fluidity of the mass and easy control of load into the centrifugals, where primary washing is effected. Twenty-two Watson-Laidlaw, self-discharging type machines are used, each being motor driven at a maximum speed of 870 r.p.m. A normal load of each is about 1,226 lb. of magma, as the mixture is called. The wash averages about 25 lb. per charge, the amount being controlled by an electrically operated device. An automatic electrically operated baffle deflects the wash liquor into a separate channel from that taken by the syrup thrown off in the initial stages of centrifuging.

Washed sugar from the primary centrifugals, averaging over 99 per cent sucrose, is then ready for melting and refining. Attention may well be directed to the exceedingly small amount of impurities remaining, for the removal of which the most elaborate processing is necessary. However, this processing is not alone for the purification of the sugar; it makes possible the ultimate production of a saleable product in a wide variety of forms and character, each of which has its application in the economics of sugar as a food, in preserves, or for decorative or for flavoring purposes.

THE REFINING DIVISION

FILTRATION AND DECOLORIZING OF SUGAR SYRUP

It is pertinent to note that the filtration and decolorizing of the raw-sugar liquor is an important phase of processing, to produce a clear and clean crystal or a snow-white powder. The work is done in two stages. Filtration, aided by an inert granular material, kieselguhr (this designation for diatomite, customary in the sugar industry, will be retained throughout this article), is followed by decolorizing with bone char. Pressure varies according to the resistance encountered. Gravity, from a height, is adopted in the initial stages of filtration and in the final stage of decolorizing. Pump pressure is used in the filter press after a layer of filter aid has been deposited on the leaves; and atmospheric pressure, induced by vacuum on the filtrate side of the medium in the continuous filters, assists percolation of wash water, and cleanses the filter aid of associated sugar.

Particular interest is attached to the use of kieselguhr to assist filtration, because it was at Crockett that the pioneer work was done with the Californian product in connection with the purification of sugar juices in refineries. The washed sugar from the primary centrifugals, 710 lbs. per charge, falls into a dissolving tank, known as a melter, where sufficient hot water is added to produce a dense liquor with a moisture content of about 37 per cent. This is pumped to the top of the building and distributed to three cylindrical tanks, each 10 ft. by 10 ft. 6 in., equipped with steam coils to heat the liquor to 80° C. This reduces viscosity and insures efficient filtration. The capacity of the "blow-ups," as they are called, is 3,800 gallons apiece, 3,500 gallons being the normal load. The charge in each contains about twelve tons of sugar liquor. Kieselguhr is added in separate and distinct quantities: (1) to form a pulp by which a preliminary "smear" is obtained in the presses, and (2) to assist the filtration of the bulk of the liquor. In the former instance about 750 lb. of kieselguhr is added per tank; in the latter, about 75 lb. per tank. Compressed air is used to keep the mass in agitation and to prevent the settlement of solids, hence the designation "blow-up."

The heavier pulp, when properly mixed, is delivered by gravity to part of a battery of thirty-eight No. 12 refinery-type Sweetland filter presses, each with 72 leaves and a filtering area of 1,044 sq. ft. This press is of the suspended-leaf, inclosed type. It consists essentially of a cylinder, divided along its horizontal axis into two parts, the lower of which is hinged to the upper, to permit the removal of cake or the cleansing of the filter leaves, the latter conforming to the shape of the cross-section of the cylinder. The two halves of the cylinder are provided with a packing joint, to withstand internal pressure when the press is closed; and each filter leaf is connected to a manifold through a sight glass, thus permitting the immediate detection of contamination in consequence of the rupture of the filter medium.

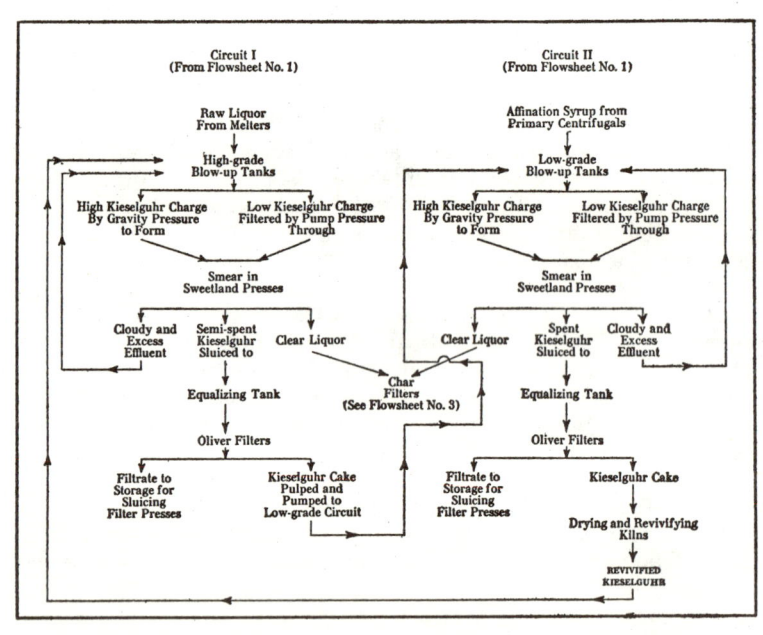

```
                    Circuit I                              Circuit II
               (From Flowsheet No. 1)                 (From Flowsheet No. 1)

                  Raw Liquor                          Affination Syrup from
                  From Melters                         Primary Centrifugals
                       ↓                                      ↓
                  High-grade                              Low-grade
                  Blow-up Tanks                          Blow-up Tanks
                  ↓         ↓                            ↓         ↓
   High Kieselguhr Charge   Low Kieselguhr Charge   High Kieselguhr Charge   Low Kieselguhr Charge
   By Gravity Pressure      Filtered by Pump Pressure  By Gravity Pressure    Filtered by Pump Pressure
   to Form                  Through                    to Form                Through
                  ↓         ↓                            ↓         ↓
                   Smear in                               Smear in
                 Sweetland Presses                      Sweetland Presses
              ↓            ↓                           ↓            ↓
          Cloudy and   Semi-spent                    Spent      Cloudy and
           Excess      Kieselguhr  Clear Liquor    Kieselguhr     Excess
           Effluent    Sluiced to          ↘     Clear Liquor  Sluiced to    Effluent
                           ↓                Char                 ↓
                    Equalizing Tank        Filters         Equalizing Tank
                           ↓        (See Flowsheet No. 3)        ↓
                     Oliver Filters                         Oliver Filters
                     ↓       ↓                              ↓       ↓
                 Filtrate to  Kieselguhr Cake         Filtrate to   Kieselguhr Cake
                 Storage for  Pulped and              Storage for         ↓
                 Sluicing     Pumped to               Sluicing     Drying and Revivifying
                 Filter Presses Low-grade Circuit     Filter Presses       Kilns
                                                                          ↓
                                                                      REVIVIFIED
                                                                      KIESELGUHR
```

FLOWSHEET NO. 2.—Filtration of sugar liquors with kieselguhr and revivification of kieselguhr.

The high-kieselguhr liquor is delivered by gravity to the interior of the press, the filtration cocks and manifold being open; and in five to ten minutes a deposit of filter aid is formed on the leaves. The filtration of this high-kieselguhr liquor is continued until the filtrate is clear, and the cloudy effluent being returned from the press goes back to the blow-up tanks. The feed is then diverted and replaced with liquor with the smaller load of kieselguhr. Pressure is obtained with a centrifugal pump to a maximum of about 60 lb. per square inch. The cycle of operation in each press occupies about 2 hr. 30 min., after which the cylinder is drained of surplus liquor, which is pumped back to the blow-up tanks.

Two separate systems of liquor are maintained, to insure against the contamination of the high-purity liquors by the low-purity syrups. Each system has its special apparatus. The clear liquor from the high-purity Sweetlands is ready for decolorizing with bone char. The cakes in the presses are then sluiced off with hot, low-density sweet water, without opening the apparatus, by means of a series of arcing nozzles, the resultant kieselguhr pulp going to an equalizing tank, thence to one of four 12-ft. Oliver vacuum filters. The cake from this, after "sweetening off," is pumped back to the low-purity blow-ups, where it is used once again as a filter aid, passing to the low-purity Sweetlands, thence to the low-purity Oliver filters. The kieselguhr is therefore used twice before passing to the revivification plant. The cake formed on the drum of the Oliver filter is sprayed with water, the filtrate going to the clear sluice tank, which supplies the sluicing water for the discharge of the cake in the Sweetland presses.

The Sweetland presses have bronze-wire leaves, covered with monel-metal screens for both the high- and low-purity liquors; they are opened every eight hours for inspection and, if necessary, for the thorough cleasing of the leaves by hose. The Oliver filters are equipped with monel-metal screens, 80–74 meshes to the inch. Phosphor bronze and nickel have been tried but monel metal has been found superior. Brass or bronze has replaced iron generally in the fittings of the Oliver filters. The kieselguhr is abrasive. Pumps employed to convey it, as a constituent of a filter pulp, are provided with high-pressure gland water service, to minimize scoring of the shaft and to protect the packing. An unusually gritty kieselguhr is a poor filter aid; and it is therefore evident that strict standardization of product is essential to success and uninterrupted efficiency in the application of this material to the problems of clarifying sugar juices.

Bone-char decolorizing at the Crockett plant takes place in 108 char filters, each 10 ft. diameter and 25 ft. high. In all of these the filter cloth, of heavy cotton twill, rests on an iron plate perforated with small holes, placed about 4 in. above the bottom of the filter. The blanket is about 2 ft. larger in diameter than the tank at the point of support. The excess is available for edge packing, for which metal weights are used, held in place with wooden wedges. Fifty tons of char (minus 8 plus 24 mesh, specification, weighing about 45 lb. per cubic foot when new) is fed in to each tank with the sugar liquor, the exit valve being closed meanwhile. When the tank is full of liquor and char, the filling port is sealed, and a steady stream of liquor is delivered direct by pipe from the storage tanks on the floor above. The effluent pipe from each char filter is carried upward, so that the char is always submerged, irrespective of rate or amount of flow.

The rate of flow varies from 1,000 to 3,500 gal. per hour, depending on the product, the liquor remaining in contact with the char for from 2½ to 8 hours. After 12 to 60 hours of service, depending on the product filtered, the char becomes impaired, indicated by a failure to decolorize satisfactorily. The filter is then drained, the syrup being returned to the filter circuit. The char is "sweetened off" with hot water, to recover the greater portion of sugar, washed with hot water, then discharged through manholes near the bottom. The blanket is washed between each cycle, and removed for repair, if necessary. The problem of insuring an intimate mixture of char and syrup in the first instance was one that involved considerable research. As mentioned before, both are now added simultaneously, thorough wetting being effected by an ingenious arrangement of staggered funnels, placed in the neck of the filter. In view of the importance of close control of the color of the various liquors, the correct handling of these to and from the char filters involves considerable personal attention. The liquor distribution room, where samples are continuously being taken of all inflows and effluents, is the "signal tower" as well as the "operating platform" of this part of the plant. Here the liquor from each filter is tested, returned for additional decolorizing, or sent to the vacuum pans for crystallization.

Carefully controlled heating is the essential step in the treatment of spent kieselguhr or bone char, whereby each is made available for further use as a filter aid and as a decolorizing absorbent, respectively. It is worthy of note that the practicability of the revivification of kieselguhr was first demonstrated as a result of pioneer research by the California and Hawaiian technical staff. After double usage, the cake from the Oliver filters that handle the sluicings from the low-purity Sweetlands is passed through two revolving kilns. The first of these acts as a drier, and the material is deprived of sufficient water to permit disintegration by a pair of rolls, placed between the two kilns. In the second kiln the temperature is raised by oil fire to about 1,200° F., whereby the activity of the kieselguhr is restored. The dust is

THE REFINING DIVISION

collected by water spray, and the pulp is dewatered on an Oliver filter before being returned to the blow-up tanks.

The bone-char retorts are of the standard type, 80 forming a kiln, of which 45 are in use. The nominal output is 50 cu. ft. of char per kiln per hour. Temperature is maintained, by pyrometer control, at 500° C., as indicated at a point between the two rows of retorts on the outside. Dust is removed during passage over 5 Hummer screens, equipped with 70-mesh wire cloth (0.073 in.), the undersize being sold. The product of the kilns passes over a magnetic pulley before going to the screens.

Low-density liquors—light sweet water—are inspissated in a series of five Kilby evaporators, each with 1,152 brass steam tubes. The flow varies from 6,000 to 9,000 gallons of raw material per hour, passage being continuous, through all five units in series, the first being under pressure, the last under vacuum. Concentration of the incoming liquor varies from ½ to 40 Brix, of an average of about 18 Brix; it leaves at 67 Brix, or thereabouts. Regulation of density, and work performed in these evaporators, is controlled by steam pressure and rate of flow. The production of concentrated sweet water varies from 35,000 to 40,000 gallons per 24 hours. This goes to the filtration and decolorizing units, then to the low-grade vacuum pans.

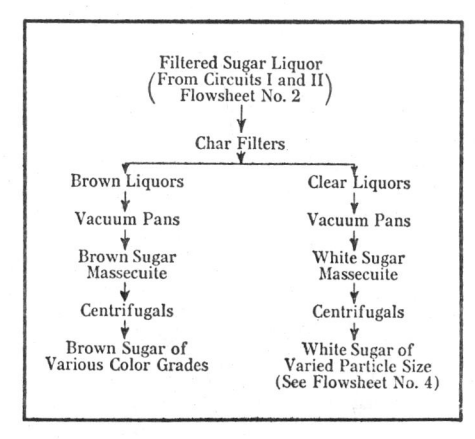

```
            Filtered Sugar Liquor
          ( From Circuits I and II )
              Flowsheet No. 2
                    ↓
               Char Filters
           ↙               ↘
    Brown Liquors         Clear Liquors
         ↓                     ↓
    Vacuum Pans          Vacuum Pans
         ↓                     ↓
    Brown Sugar          White Sugar
    Massecuite           Massecuite
         ↓                     ↓
    Centrifugals         Centrifugals
         ↓                     ↓
    Brown Sugar of       White Sugar of
    Various Color Grades Varied Particle Size
                         (See Flowsheet No. 4)
```

FLOWSHEET No. 3.—Evaporation, decolorization, and crystallization

Fourteen single-effect vacuum pans are in service at Crockett, from 6 to 14 ft. diameter, the load varying from 12 to 86 tons of "massecuite," as the crystal-syrup product is termed. Eleven of the pans are of the coil type; three are equipped with calandrias. Some of the pans are set aside for the production of a low-grade sugar, which is again remelted and refined. Bronze or copper pans are used entirely for the production of fine sugar of the highest grades. The cycle of operations in a vacuum pan is essentially as follows: Concentration, by evaporation at low temperature and high vacuum, is continued until a point is reached at which crystallization will occur throughout the pan on the addition of a bucket of "seed," or small dry sugar crystals of the appropriate size. According to the character of the product required, the growth of the crystals is continued by the addition of more liquor to the pan while evaporation continues. Temperature control, of course, is an important factor.

Centrifuging and Drying

The mixture of crystallized sugar and syrup from the vacuum pans is discharged into a V-bottom bin, from which it is drawn as required into a battery of 44 centrifugals, of American Tool & Machine type. The regulation of wash is effected by means of an electrically operated mechanism, developed by the company's engineering department. Electric current is used to operate a relay that, at the termination of a definite number of seconds after maximum speed has been reached in the centrifugal, makes connection which opens a water valve and allows it to remain so for a predetermined period of time. The centrifugals are discharged by hand-operated scraper, the product, containing about 1½ per cent moisture, going to two revolving drum driers in series, each 6 ft. diameter and 30 ft. long. The first, locally known as the sweater, is fitted with baffles to lift the sugar and sift it through the hot air which is provided by heater coils and a suction fan. Moisture is reduced to about 0.1 per cent in the sweater; and to an inappreciable amount, about 0.06 per cent, by passage through the second drum, which contains a steam-heated cylinder, about 24 in. diameter, placed in the center of the drum and revolving with it, against which the sugar comes in contact. The dust from the "granulators," as the driers are termed, is collected by water spray and returned to the evaporation circuit.

The dried product, granulated sugar, passes over an electromagnet forming the tail pulley of a belt conveyor, then to twelve Hummer screens, each with two sieves, 3 ft. by 4 ft. 9 in. Three products result, known, respectively, as "Berry," "Standard," and dust. The dust is collected by a suction system, remelted, and returned to the evaporation circuit. Special 15-cycle, alternating current is provided for the vibration of the Hummer screens.

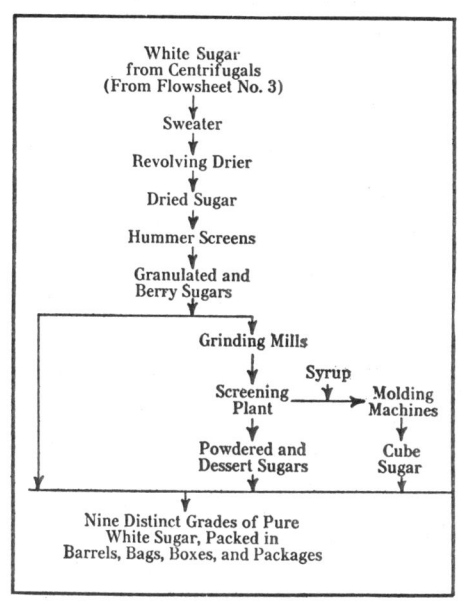

```
              White Sugar
           from Centrifugals
          (From Flowsheet No. 3)
                   ↓
                Sweater
                   ↓
            Revolving Drier
                   ↓
              Dried Sugar
                   ↓
            Hummer Screens
                   ↓
             Granulated and
              Berry Sugars
                   ↓
            Grinding Mills
                   ↓      Syrup
              Screening ────→  Molding
                Plant           Machines
                   ↓              ↓
             Powdered and        Cube
             Dessert Sugars      Sugar
                   ↓              ↓
         Nine Distinct Grades of Pure
           White Sugar, Packed in
       Barrels, Bags, Boxes, and Packages
```

FLOWSHEET No. 4.—Drying, grading, and grinding white sugar

The finest sizes of California and Hawaiian sugar, "Powdered" and "Dessert," are prepared by grinding "Berry" or "Standard" sugar in Mead disc mills. The product is screened through silk cloth, and the oversize is returned to the grinders. A suction system removes the dust, which is melted in a wet dust collector and returned to the main liquor circuit. The grinding plant is situated at a considerable distance from the main refinery building, beyond the warehouses and shipping department. This provision indicates that the company is awake to the danger of dust explosion, and has taken every precaution to eliminate the possibility of it. Electric light fittings are protected with double globes, and provision is made against the ignition, by sparking or overheating, of those parts of the equipment where the atmosphere is laden with sugar dust, which is well known to be explosive.

The refinements in processing at the California and Hawaiian plant make possible the production of several varieties, with particular reference to the size of the crystal, to serve all conceivable purposes and tastes. Local prejudice must be taken into account; and it is a significant fact that sections of the United States show marked preference for sugars of a certain grain size. Moreover, the manufacturer cannot dictate the character of the package in which the sugar is supplied. In spite of obvious disadvantages in that type of container, the barrel—from which the customer's requirements are dipped and weighed, with concomitant loss, contamination, unnecessary labor and expense—is still popular in some places; but bags, varying in weight from 2 to 100 lbs., are becoming more and more popular, and the bulk of the output is sold in these containers.

The coarsest products made at the Crockett plant are known as Confectioners' "A" and Confectioners' "AA." Each type is produced by special manipulation of operations in the vacuum pan. The Hummer screens, taking the product from the granulators, produce "Berry" and "Standard Granulated," the former being the finer grained of the two. Among the so-called brown sugars, the following varieties are prepared: "Extra C," light brown; "golden C," medium brown; and "yellow D," dark brown. These sugars are prepared in the customary manner, but from syrups that have not been decolorized completely in the char filters.

"Cubes" and "cubelets" are made from a special granulated white sugar to which is added a sufficiency of pure syrup to act as a binder. The Hersey machine used to fashion the cubes is ingenious and complicated; when ejected they are friable and moist. Drying, on galvanized-iron sheets which pass continuously through a steam-heated oven, results in the cementing of the mass and the formation of the characteristically hard "lump" sugar.

The power plant acts as a pressure reducing system for the steam needed for heating, evaporation, and other purposes in the refinery. It consists essentially of four 1,500-kw. Curtis turbo-generator units, of General Electric manufacture. The average total load is 3,900 kw., with an occasional peak load of 4,200 kw. About 1,000 motors are in use. All except those operating the Hummer screens take 60-cycle, 3-phase alternating current at 440 volts. Three of the turbines are operated at 10 lb. and one at 70 lb. back pressure, any reduction below this minimum being adjusted by the addition of high-pressure steam to the main going to the plant.

The boiler plant consists of eighteen boilers, the control of which is accomplished by the use of an automatic oil regulator,

THE REFINING DIVISION

damper controllers, and feed-water regulators. A CO_2 recorder and a soot blower have been installed for each boiler. The auxiliary plant consists of two 1,000 g.p.m. turbine-driven feed pumps, two horizontal steam-driven fuel oil pumps, two 1,000 g.p.m. motor-driven service pumps and two feed-water heaters, each with a capacity of 250,000 lb. water per hour, and two oil heaters, each of 600 sq. ft. heating surface. A feed-water treatment plant has been provided, and each set of two boilers is connected with a fuel economizer.

Mention has already been made of the attention paid at the Crockett refinery to neatness and cleanliness, as essential prerequisites to smooth operation and the avoidance of waste. In every department, even where bone char is handled, it would seem to the casual arrival that a visitor of critical observation had been expected; but as a matter of fact the record of impressions gained during three visits, several months apart, indicate that order is the rule, to which all employees must subscribe. This fine influence is carried, insensibly, into the township.

4. TECHNICAL OR CHEMICAL-CONTROL DEPARTMENT

This department is in charge of the technical superintendent of the plant. Generally speaking, this department is in charge of the formulation of rules and practices governing methods of manufacture. It writes chemical specifications, checks technological manipulations, and watches the results. The department has a line staff of its own, which operates beside and parallel to the supervisory personnel of the operating department.

In general, the work of the technical department may be divided into three main classifications: chemical control, operating control, and special investigations. *Chemical control* covers the simpler laboratory analytical work which is carried on, to some extent at least, in all sugar refineries. This is the portion of the chemical work without the elements of which one would hardly attempt to operate a sugar refinery. *Operating control* covers work which, for the most part, can hardly be considered chemical in nature, but which concerns itself directly with the operations of the plant. This control has been developed in this plant because of the technical nature of the operations and the consequent necessity for detailed technical assistance in supervision. *Special investigations* is a term which is self-explanatory.

CHEMICAL CONTROL

1. *Analyses of incoming and outgoing products.*—All raw sugars entering the plant are carefully analyzed and weighed, and the same is done with all the final products—white sugars, soft sugars, and molasses. This makes it possible to keep a record showing the disposition not only of all sugar, but also of the individual non-sugar substances involved in the process. Through this system of recording it is possible not only to measure yields and losses, but also to some extent to locate the sources of the losses and take steps toward their reduction.

2. *Control of losses.*—There are a number of places in the plant where it is necessary to take out certain waste products—for example, waste water from the char filters, which is sent to the bay, and kieselguhr from the cloth filters, which is salvaged. In all of these places, of which there are quite a large number, there is danger of sugar being lost with the wastes unless a careful control is exercised. In order to prevent such losses, the laboratory makes frequent routine analyses of all products going to waste, recording the results, and of course sounding an immediate warning if anything unusual is found.

3. *Laboratory control of operating details.*—A number of operations throughout the plant can be properly carried out only when a knowledge is had of the composition of the products involved. This is true of such operations as the washing of raw sugar, the separation of liquors and sweetwaters from char filters, and the mixing of syrups for soft sugar production and for boiling of remelt

sugars. Analyses are continually being made by the laboratory for such purposes, some of them being regular and routine, and others being made as occasion requires.

4. *Laboratory control of general methods of operation.*—As the rate of melt, the quality of the raw material, and the methods of operation gradually change, the results are reflected in the quality of the output, the purity of discard molasses, and the efficiency of various processes of manufacture. Most of these effects can be measured by the changes in the composition of refined products and by the intermediate products while in process. In order to study such changes, many routine analyses are made and recorded so that results of different periods and of different ways of working may be compared.

OPERATING CONTROL

1. *House control.*—In the refinery there are a great many valves—some two hundred or more—through which sugar may be lost to the bay, or through which erroneous mixtures of high- and low-grade products may take place if the valves are not handled correctly. In order to centralize responsibility, these particular valves have been placed under lock and key, the keys being handled only by the "house controllers." While these controllers have a number of other miscellaneous duties, the handling of these valves is by far the most important. In this way the possibility of serious losses or bad mix-ups is practically eliminated. This work is considered one of the most useful and important functions of the department.

2. *Alkalinity control.*—The maintenance of correct alkalinity conditions in all products in process is extremely important. If alkalinities become too high, invert sugar, a valuable non-sugar which occurs in raw sugar, is destroyed. This destruction results in the production of objectionable color and the development of operating difficulties. If the alkalinity becomes too low, and acid con-

ditions develop, sugar itself is destroyed. The possible losses from this amount to hundreds of thousands of dollars yearly. For the maintenance of proper alkalinities, therefore, a comprehensive liming system has been provided which reaches all parts of the plant. Alkalinity controllers are employed, whose sole duty it is to make rounds of the plant, testing all products for alkalinity, and seeing that proper alkalinity conditions are maintained by the operators.

3. *Instrument control.*—A large number of indicating and recording instruments are required in the refinery for many purposes. For example: The maintenance of proper temperatures is of great importance in the same way as proper alkalinity. If temperatures in liquors get too low, operating difficulties and even fermentation may occur, while if the temperatures get too high, sugar is destroyed. To control temperatures, therefore, a great many indicating and recording thermometers (about two hundred) are used, as well as a number of regulators which automatically regulate the temperatures of products.

Flow-meters are used, not only to measure products and materials for record but, to a large extent, to regulate the whole rate of operation of the plant. A great many pressure and vacuum gauges are indispensable for the physical operation of the many pieces of equipment. Altogether, over one thousand instruments of various kinds are in use in the plant. In order to care for these instrument, an instrument shop has been built for this department. The work of this shop includes the testing and repairing of instruments, the changing of charts, and all other work in connection with the instruments.

4. *Supervision of technical phases of process.*—Because of the many technical problems involved, a small corps of specialists has been developed among the chemists. For example, one chemist is continually studying the problems connected with cloth filtration, another those

connected with char filtration, another those connected with char burning, and still others the problems connected with pan boiling, centrifugal work, crystallizer work, etc. These "specialists," however, do not merely study the larger problems in connection with the various stations, but each one spends a certain amount of time each day going over the work of the station he is particularly interested in, keeping in touch with the operators and foremen, making criticisms and suggestions regarding the work, and helping to clear up any unusual difficulties which may arise.

5. *Clerical and administrative control.*—The work handled by the technical department office relates to many activities. Much of it bears directly upon operating work in the plant generally classed under the head of operating control. These activities may be divided into four classes:

a) Preparation and distribution of operating rules.—In a technical process, such as the refining of sugar, in which new developments are continually taking place, the variety of operations may become very great and their details quite intricate. In order to secure the greatest efficiency, the methods evolved must be followed up in the strictest detail. In order to keep operators and foremen properly informed, to keep the details of the methods before the eyes of old employees as well as new, and to fix the responsibility for the proper observance of correct operating methods, a system of issuing written "Plant Rules" has been developed. These rules prescribe in detail the methods to be followed throughout the plant, a separate "Rule" being drawn up for each operation. These have been drawn up in the course of a number of years as the need for them has arisen, or as new methods have replaced old ones; and as new rules are issued, obsolete ones are rescinded. Copies of each rule are distributed to all persons involved or interested. Arrangements are now being made to have at each station a loose-leaf binder containing all the rules applicable to that station—the book being accessible to all employees.

The drafting of these rules is done chiefly by the various "specialists" in the technical department, working in collaboration with various members of the operating, engineering, and other departments. It is the function of the technical office to mimeograph and distribute these rules and to see that all sets throughout the plant are kept up to date.

b) Recording of technical and operating data.—It is important that quite a number of calculations and records of operating and technical nature be kept up—figures relating to sugar melted, output, yields, losses, materials consumed, analytical results, and other details regarding the operation of individual stations and of the plant as a whole. These records are of importance in order to keep the management and the supervisory force properly informed regarding conditions and efficiency of operations, and in order to provide comparisons with previous periods. The calculations and maintenance of these records, then, is another important function of the technical clerical force.

c) Distribution of technical and operating information.—A considerable number of reports on special investigations, together with routine reports embodying some of the data referred to above, are continually in preparation. It is the policy of the company to distribute these rather widely, not only among department heads, but also to foremen and many others who will derive benefit, both for themselves and for the company, from the information. The preparation and distribution of these reports is naturally a function of the technical department office.

One feature of this function is the preparation and distribution of the daily "Refinery Notes." This is a daily bulletin, giving all the vital figures of the previous day's work in the plant and also a discussion of conditions, irregularities, or difficulties experienced at the various stations. It is drawn up by the various "specialists" in the department and published by the technical clerical force. About fifty copies are distributed daily, to all who may benefit by it. The "Refinery Notes" serves as a valuable aid to department heads and others, enabling them to keep in touch with the many problems continually arising in the plant.

d) *Maintenance of library.*—An extensive library of technical books on sugar manufacture is maintained in the technical department office. These books are available to all employees of the company. In addition, a number of technical journals are subscribed to, and these are systematically distributed to all who can make use of them.

SPECIAL INVESTIGATIONS

Since much of the technical progress of the plant depends on investigative work, this may be considered one of the most important functions of the department. To this work are devoted its greatest energies. However, owing to the complexity and continually changing nature of the work, only a brief description of this function will be given.

Roughly, the investigative work may be divided into three classes:

1. *Raw-sugar investigations.*—These cover routine and special studies of the quality and operating characteristics of the raw sugars received from the different plantations, and studies relating to storage of raw sugar. The results of these studies are reported to the Hawaiian Island planters to aid them in improving the quality of their sugars, for the mutual benefit of the plantations and of the refinery.

2. *Operating investigations.*—The corps of "specialists"

is continually engaged in making special investigations of improved methods or equipment in the plant. Almost all phases of operation are studied and experimented with in the plant itself at one time or another. Practically all improved methods now in use have been tried out experimentally in this way before being finally adopted.

3. *Laboratory investigations.*—The line between laboratory and operating investigations cannot be clearly drawn, as the two often merge and one is often used to assist the other. However, certain investigations which are carried on primarily in the laboratory may be classified as laboratory investigations. These include such research work as theoretical work on the properties of bone char, studies on such little-understood impurities as colloids, development of improved methods of testing and analysis, and, to a large extent, the preliminary phases of investigations which are ultimately completed on large scale within the refinery.

This investigative work, which corresponds to the research maintained by other large companies, has been much emphasized in recent years because it became clearly apparent that the progress of the plant in securing greater sucrose recoveries, improved quality of output, and lower costs was so greatly dependent upon it.

5. OPERATING DEPARTMENT

The operating department is in charge of the physical operation of the plant. The department is managed by the operating superintendent, with three principal assistants, one to each shift, known as shift superintendents. All planning of production and of personnel is done in the office of the operating superintendent.

This department manipulates the refinery equipment and working personnel to carry out planned schedules each day, in accordance with the schedule for various grades and packages. The chemical control department

THE REFINING DIVISION

determines the technological and chemical procedure to be followed, and the inspection department passes upon the acceptability of the refined sugars, weights, and containers.

The operating department receives its raws from, and returns the refined product to, the warehouse. The five principal subdivisions of the operating department are: melting, filtration, refining, packing, and container manufacture. A sixth department is known as "Transfer—Powdered, Dessert, and Brown." Each of the six sections is in charge of a general foreman who reports directly to the shift superintendent.

The organization of this department is shown on the chart (Fig. 4) which follows on page 50.

This department, handling as it does the major part of the working personnel and equipment, has to work in close contact with the industrial relations or personnel department and with the department of engineering and maintenance.

A detailed description of the refining processes, that is, of the operations of the various subdivisions of the operating department, except that for the manufacture of containers, is given on pages 29–41 of this study. The following is a brief description of the work of the container department.

The container department.—This department is in charge of a foreman who receives his orders and instructions from the planning section of the superintendent's office. The main function of this department is to provide the requisite number of containers, in accordance with definite specifications, for each day's pack of sugar. There is a great variety of containers, which vary from the wax-lined cardboard boxes holding one pound of powdered sugar, to the cloth-lined burlap sack holding one hundred pounds, and the paper-lined barrel holding, on the average, 335 pounds of sugar. The average day's output re-

50   THE C & H SUGAR REFINING CORPORATION

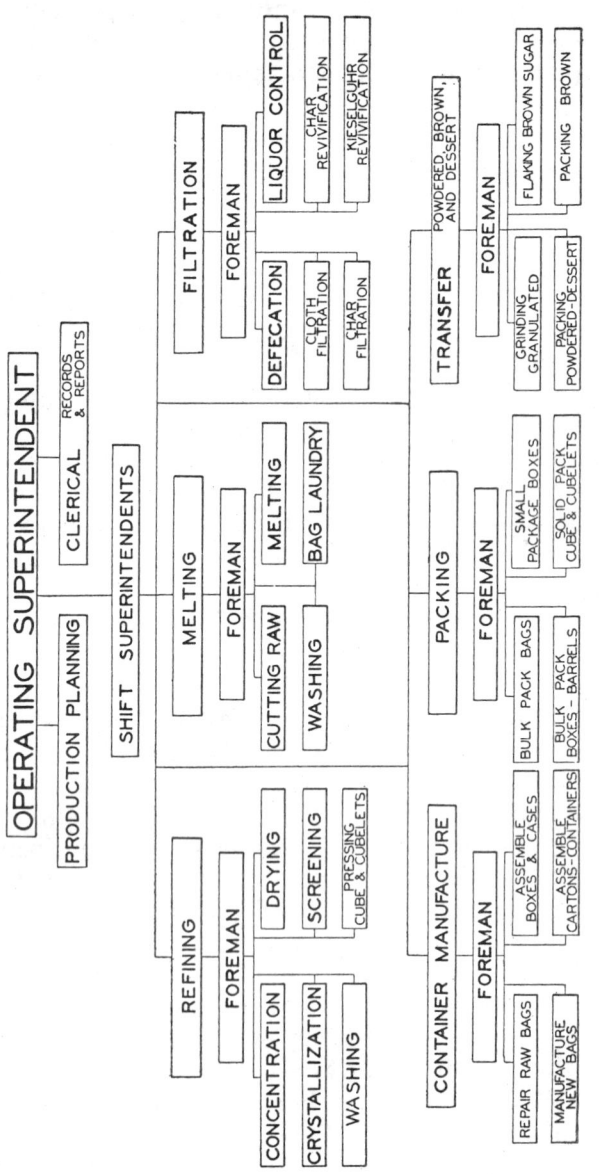

Fig. 4.—Chart of Operating Department

quires from one hundred and fifty thousand to two hundred thousand containers.

The burlap bags in which the raw sugar was received are washed, dried, lined with cotton liners, and used for the packing of refined sugar. About one per cent of the bags from the Islands are damaged beyond repair, and are sold as seconds. The raw sugar is received in 125-lb. bags, sixteen to the ton. The refined sugar goes out in 100-lb. bags, twenty to the ton. This means that the container department has to manufacture daily a certain number of new bags. The new bags are made up (according to definite specification as to size and weight of burlap), printed, lined with a cotton liner, and forwarded to the storage bins just as are the washed raw sugar bags.

As stated elsewhere, the Refinery operates for twelve consecutive days and shuts down for two days. The problem of synchronizing the work of the container department, operated largely by women, with the general operating schedule of the refinery was quite a complicated one because of the California law which forbids the employment of women for more than six consecutive days of eight hours each. A schedule is now in operation whereby the work period of the container department parallels that of the refinery proper; yet the shift management is such that no woman works more than six consecutive days of eight hours each.

Both time-work and piece-work methods of compensation are applied in this department. Women time-workers receive 46.5 cents per hour or $3.72 per 8-hour day. The actual working time for women per 8-hour day is 7 hours and 40 minutes, as they have two ten-minute rest periods during the day. The women working by the piece average 51.9 cents per hour or $4.15 per day. The following operations are done on the piece-work basis: sewing burlap bags, sewing cotton liners, printing burlap bags, lining burlap bags, and mending.

6. PLANT SANITATION AND CLEANLINESS

Plant sanitation is taken care of by a crew of twenty-seven cleaners, assisted by the various station operators. Each station operator is charged with keeping his station clean and orderly at all times. Cleanliness enters into every operation performed in the refinery and warehouse, and extends even to the freight cars in which the refined sugar is shipped. These cars are all thoroughly cleaned and lined with clean building paper before any sugar is placed in them. In fact, everything possible is done to insure a clean, healthful product reaching the consumer.

When a man is hired he is impressed with the fact that he is going to work in a plant producing a food product, which must be perfectly clean and free from all impurities at all times. Hands never touch the sugar during the entire process. As stated elsewhere, newly hired employees are required to pass a physical examination to avoid the hiring of infected persons.

While in the liquid stage all the sugars are purified by being filtered through cloth and then through thick layers of char, which filter out all impurities of the raw sugar before it is crystallized into white sugar.

The containers in which the refined sugar is placed are very rigidly inspected for cleanliness, so that no foreign matter may find its way into the sugar.

The plant is always kept in such condition that visitors are welcome to inspect it at any time and are free to go into any part of the plant to see the various phases of the process.

7. INSPECTION DEPARTMENT

This department operates as an independent unit, reporting directly to the plant manager. Because of the emphasis on quality of sugars, proper packaging, and correct weight, the policy of this department is upheld to the utmost. The principal function of the department is to maintain quality of output, and the scope of its activities includes:

1. Sugar standards
    a) Quality
    b) Weights

2. Container standards
    a) Quality
    b) Strength
    c) Economy

3. Storage and handling methods
    a) Refinery warehouses
    b) Outside warehouses
    c) Transportation

So far as quality is concerned, whether it be that of sugar, of containers, or of workmanship, there is but one standard—the very best practicable. There is no grading of output according to quality. If it is either equal to or better than the standard, the product goes on to the trade; if it is below standard, it is ordered reprocessed.

Standards are selected after careful consideration of the requirements of the trade and the possibilities of the plant equipment. These tentative standards, after a thorough discussion and approval by both production and sales departments, are adopted as official standards below which the quality of production must never fall. It is the responsibility of each station operator and of each foreman to see that the required quality of product and workmanship is maintained while the product is in his care. While the inspectors maintain a careful watch over production in order to detect any carelessness which might have taken place, the important function of the inspection department is to follow operations in an effort to prevent the production of sugars below standard.

The following is a more detailed description of the activities of this department:

Sugars.—To the experienced operator or inspector, the color and grain of a sugar are reliable indicators of its quality. For this reason, constant sampling of the sugars is carried on in the packing rooms and at other points in the process. A slight lowering of the color toward the low-limit standard is usually detected in time to warn the station foreman and shift superintendent that more careful work is necessary to avoid subsequent reprocessing. Detection of poor grain indicates improper boiling or separation, and permits speedy correction.

Weights.—The most accurate automatic commercial scales obtainable are used in weighing the product. The scales are kept in the best possible condition by capable mechanics skilled in scale maintenance and repair. Half-hourly or hourly checks are made by competent checkers using super-sensitive check scales. The inspectors make intermittent checks to see that the routine checking is conscientiously carried on. Once each month an outside inspection bureau makes an independent survey of scales and filled packages, and periodically a similar check is made by the California State Department of Weights and Measures.

Containers.—In addition to maintaining careful watch to see that the containers are in accordance with approved specifications, studies are constantly being made to learn ways of securing containers of satisfactory appearance and ample strength at lower cost. Containers constitute one of the largest single items of cost in the refinery.

Storage and handling.—Handling methods in the refinery and warehouses are carefully supervised so as to make sure that the product leaves the premises in perfect condition. In addition to local inspection, many outside trips are made to observe conditions to which the sugars are subjected while in the hands of transportation companies and the trade, and improper conditions are called to the attention of those concerned. As a result of this outside work over a period of years, sugars are now treated with a noticeable improvement while enroute to the customer. Much work has been done in co-operation with the railroads and steamship companies along the lines of damage claim prevention. This activity has proved profitable to the carriers, to the refinery, and to the customers.

Complaints.—All complaints are routed through the office of the plant manager to the inspection department, where they are studied. Where technical analysis is required, assistance is secured from the chemical laboratory. Wherever possible a comprehensive report is rendered on each complaint. It is too often true, however, that not enough facts accompany the complaint to permit a correct analysis of the difficulty. When the Refinery is found to be at fault, a candid admission is made. When the customer is at fault, an effort is made to show him tactfully wherein he may be in error.

8. INDUSTRIAL RELATIONS DEPARTMENT

One of the most outstanding features of the operations of the Corporation, responsible for much of its growth and success, is the prevailing morale of its men and women. The maintenance of proper relationship between the Corporation and its employees is a subject of daily concern to the management, and has been for many years. Constant efforts are being made to understand the workman and his point of view, to avoid arousing discontent, and to insure effective co-operation and mutual confidence.

The management contends that good wages often mean low production costs. The base wage paid, therefore, is somewhat higher than that paid for similar work elsewhere in the region; it is considerably higher when the fact is considered that the cost of living is somewhat less in Crockett—a town of 5,000—than in the larger cities and towns of the San Francisco Bay Region.

In the opinion of the management, a workman has six prime interests. These are: (1) a reasonably good annual income (that is, a good base wage and continuous employment throughout the year); (2) security of employment (that is, freedom from arbitrary discharge); (3) insurance against loss of earnings due to sickness or disability; (4) absence of managerial arbitrariness; (5) good and reasonably cheap housing; and (6) interesting community life.

All of these problems are being met by the Corporation, with much success. This fact registers itself in a progressive stabilization of the working personnel, as shown further below in this study. The relative satisfaction of the employee can be measured by his willingness to remain in the Corporation's employ—a fact easily apparent upon an examination of the extent of voluntary separations. The relative satisfaction of the Corporation with its men can be measured by the extent of discharges and in terms of lower unit costs, fine quality of product, and good service, incidental to a stabilized working force.

Judged by the last named yardsticks, the industrial relations policy of the Corporation has met with much success. A detailed analysis of the extent of labor turnover, as well as of production costs, given elsewhere in this report, bears out the contention that the Corporation's labor policy has been very effective from a business point of view.

In its industrial relations policy the Corporation steers clear of anything which might smack of paternalism. No so-called welfare flavor is attached to any of its labor policies. As one of the chief executives puts it, "We do it because it is good business and because it produces our sugar cheaper and better."

Organization of industrial relations department.—At the commencement of this company's operations in 1906, what is now the industrial relations department consisted only of an employment clerk. Several years later the responsibility for plant safety was given to this department and a safety inspector added. Either the safety inspector or the employment clerk rendered all necessary first aid. The functions of the department gradually increased under the designation of Service. Responsibility for the Community Center Club, the Girls' Club, Hotel Crockett, plant protection (including supervision over gatekeepers and watchmen), and the entertainment of plant visitors, was gradually added.

The industrial relations (or personnel) department as now constituted is under a manager who reports directly to the plant manager. The chart on page 58 (Fig. 5) shows the present organization and principal functions of the department.

The work of the department falls into the following seven major groups: I. Employment and personnel; II. Safety; III. Health and sanitation; IV. Training and education; V. Housing and community activities; VI. Public relations and publicity; VII. Records and research.

The following outline shows the numerous ramifications of each of these major activities:

I. *Employment and personnel*
 1. Labor supply
     a) Outside sources
     b) Within plant
 2. Recruiting
     a) Interviewing
     b) Job classification
     c) Investigation of past records of applicants
     d) Physical examinations
     e) Assignment to work
     f) Badges, clock cards, tool checks, locker keys

58   THE C & H SUGAR REFINING CORPORATION

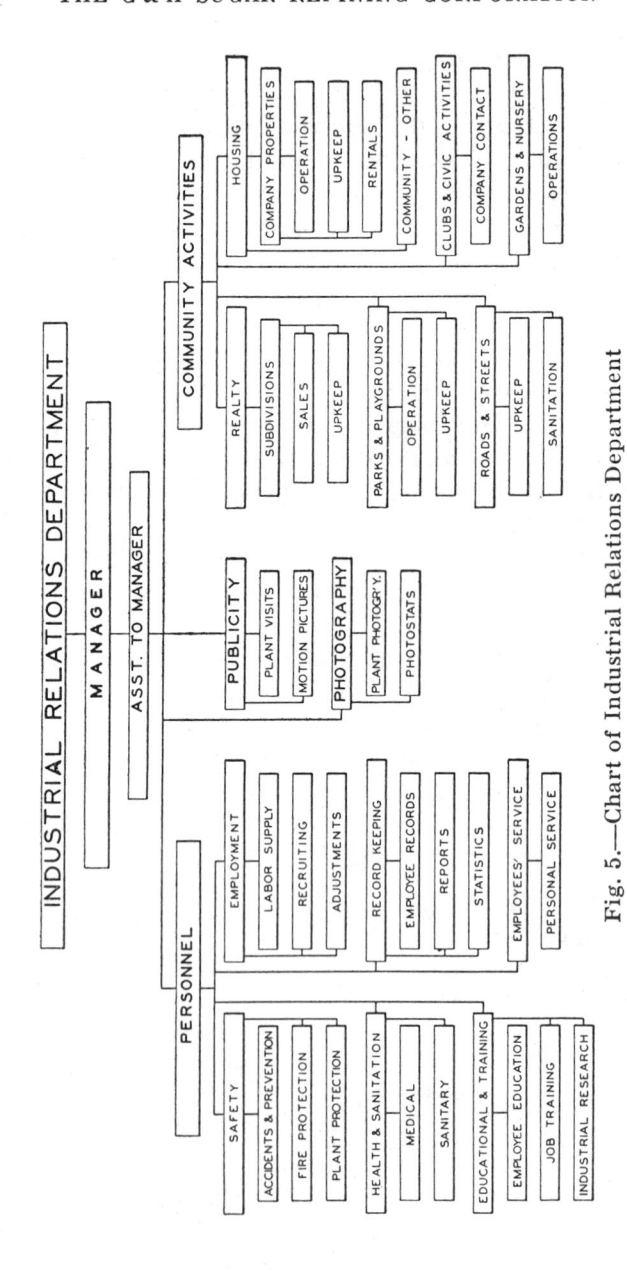

Fig. 5.—Chart of Industrial Relations Department

3. Adjustments
   a) Promotions, demotions, transfers
   b) Discipline
   c) Grievances
   d) Discharges and permanent lay-offs
   e) Interviews with employees who terminate service
4. Personal service
   a) Legal advice
   b) Alien aid
   c) Americanization
   d) Recreation and amusements
   e) Rest rooms and smoking quarters
   f) Parks and playgrounds
   g) Employees' homes and gardens
   h) Promotion of thrift and savings
   i) Lost and found
   j) Company gardens and greenhouses
   k) Miscellaneous (too numerous to mention)

II. *Safety*
  1. Accidents and their prevention
     a) Safety committees
     b) Safety standards
     c) Mechanical safeguards
     d) Safety posters and literature
     e) Inspection and report on plant hazards
     f) Investigation of accidents which cause loss of time
  2. Fire prevention and protection
     a) Co-operates with engineering department in—
        i. Organization of brigades
        ii. Drills
        iii. New installations to prevent fire hazards
     b) Inspection and report on plant fire hazards
  3. Plant protection
     a) Watchmen
     b) Gatekeepers

III. *Health and sanitation*
  1. Medical
     a) Physical examination on entrance
     b) First aid and hospital work
     c) Follow-ups of sick and injured employees
     d) Co-operation with local health officers

2. Sanitation
    a) Clean-up of grounds
    b) Clean-up of buildings
    c) General sanitary conditions
    d) Toilets and locker rooms
    e) Lunch and rest rooms
    f) Drinking water
    g) Heat and ventilation
    h) Lighting

IV. *Training and education*

   The training and educational activities of the company cover two separate and distinct fields: (1) The training and education necessary to induct a man into the organization and into the job, Americanization activities and co-operation with community, state, and national educational agencies. Also lectures and movies, suggestion system, library, bulletins and posters. (2) Systematic training of employees for positions of minor and sub-major executives.

V. *Housing and community activities*
   1. Housing
       a) Supervision of rentals
       b) Maintenance of buildings
       c) Listing of available houses, apartments, and boarding-houses
       d) Hotel Crockett
       e) Supervision of subdivisions, sales and maintenance

   2. Community activities
       a) Parks and playgrounds
       b) Gardens and nursery
       c) Health and sanitation
       d) Fire protection
       e) Local celebrations
       f) Men's and Women's Clubs
       g) Boy Scout movement
       h) Public Library
       i) Miscellaneous civic activities

VI. *Publicity or public relations*
    a) Plant visitors
    b) Motion pictures and lectures
    c) Luncheons and entertainment

VII. *Records and research*
   a) Personal records
      i. Individual reference
      ii. Progress record
      iii. Accident and attendance record
   b) Report of daily and monthly numbers of employees at work
   c) Employment, transfers, and terminations
   d) Daily absentee reports to department heads; semimonthly absentee payroll authorization report (monthly employees); monthly time balance report (monthly employees)
   e) Monthly analysis of employees on roll
   f) Labor turnover report
   g) Files

Normal force of refinery.—The total working force as of February 1, 1928, including supervisory employees, was 1,519. Of this number about 12 per cent were women. The number and percentage of total employed by departments, is shown herewith.

Department	Employees	Percentage
Warehouse	196	12.9
Operating	779	51.4
Inspection	5	.3
Technical	50	3.3
Engineering	356	23.4
Personnel*	45	3.0
Plant stores	24	1.6
Plant Manager's office	3	.2
Plant office	28	1.8
Miscellaneous	5	.3
Hotel Crockett	28	1.8
Totals	1,519	100.0

* Watchmen and gatekeepers.

Racial distribution of employees.—In the placement of new employees an attempt is constantly made to consider

62 THE C & H SUGAR REFINING CORPORATION

physical fitness, since much of the work in the refinery, particularly in the warehouse, is of the heavy type. It is the opinion of the management that the Portuguese laborer, with his broad, heavy shoulders, is particularly fitted for trucking and the handling and piling of bags of sugar in the warehouse. Mexicans are said to be particularly adapted to work in the charhouse, where high temperatures prevail. A certain type of Italian, it is believed, fits best on the centrifugal machines. Native Americans usually begin their service with the Company in the packing house.

The following table shows the proportions of the five major racial groups among the employees, also changes in racial composition of refinery force between July 26, 1923, and February 3, 1928:

MAJOR RACIAL GROUPS

Country of Birth	Percentage of Total Force	
	1923	1928
1. United States	39.19	41.8
2. Italy	23.61	20.3
3. Great Britain	7.58	6.8
4. Portugal	6.79	8.6
5. Mexico	5.66	7.7

The most significant facts shown in the above table are: (1) A slight increase, about 2 per cent, in native born; (2) a correspondingly larger decrease, about 3 per cent, in Italians; (3) a considerable increase in Portuguese, from 6.79 per cent to 8.6 per cent; and (4) a significant increase in Mexicans, from 5.66 per cent to 7.7 per cent.

The following table (p. 63) shows relative changes in extent of Americanization in four of the largest groups of foreign born:

PERCENTAGE OF ALIENS, NATURALIZED AND DECLARANTS, 1923 AND 1928

Racial Group	Alien 1923	Alien 1928	Naturalized 1923	Naturalized 1928	Declarant 1923	Declarant 1928
Italy	55.77	53.8	24.23	28.0	20.00	18.2
Great Britain	36.84	37.3	40.35	44.1	22.81	18.6
Portugal	89.22	91.4	6.86	4.7	3.92	3.9
Mexico	97.65	99.1	2.35	....	.....	.9

The Italian group shows some increase in proportion of naturalized from 24.23 per cent to 28.0 per cent. The British contingent shows an increase in naturalized of about one-tenth—from 40.35 per cent to 44.1 per cent. The Portuguese show a drop in proportion naturalized (from 6.86 per cent to 4.7 per cent), and no appreciable change (only .02 per cent) in declarants. The Mexican group is overwhelmingly alien—99.1 per cent—without a single naturalized person.

Americanization.—The Company has been instrumental in having the local high school develop courses in Americanization. This Americanization work, directed by especially capable and well-trained supervisors, has produced gratifying results.

Employment.—The initial contact with the prospective employee is made through the receipt of an application, on a special form which calls for all necessary personal information and the record of former employment. As a rule, applications for work are made by personal appearance at the gate of the refinery, although an appreciable number of applications are received through correspondence, particularly from men with technical training and experience. At the present time the number of applicants at the gate is much larger than the number of openings for employment, which makes it possible to select men well-fitted for the vacancies.

The selection is made by the employment officials. An applicant is required to pass a physical examination. No man or woman fifty years of age or over is hired; the policy is to prefer applicants several years under this maximum age.

All newly hired male refinery employees except those in the warehouse are started at the base rate of 58½ cents per hour. Warehouse employees receive a minimum of 62 cents per hour on account of the greater physical exertion required.

New employees usually start in the packing department, regardless of educational preparation for technical work or of prior sugar experience. While this policy results in a failure to attract as many graduates of techcal or business schools as may at times be desired, it has the advantage of giving assurance to employees of longer standing that, all things considered, the Corporation does not make it a practice to take on new men in positions of advanced work.

Placement and follow-up.—Employees with special qualifications in education, experience, or native ability are entered in a follow-up record, and such supervisory employees as are concerned are notified of the employment of these men with information as to their special qualifications. Promising men are thus placed under special scrutiny so that opinions may be formed as to their fitness for various branches of work. These opinions form the basis for advancement, as promotions are made more with reference to capability, adaptability, and merit than with reference to length of service. Length of service is considered only when two or more men are equally well qualified for the same position, the man with the longest service record being preferred in such cases.

The industrial relations department has a woman assistant who acts as supervisor for the female help. In addition to occupying clerical and stenographic positions, women are found in the following departments of the refinery: sugar packing, container manufacture, laboratory, and in clerical positions.

Transfers.—An endeavor is constantly made to transfer employees found wanting, for one reason or another, to other departments or jobs where they may give satisfactory service.

Overtime pay.—Hourly employees working in excess of their regular time are paid time-and-a-half for overtime. Monthly employees working overtime are credited in an overtime allowance account, and are given equivalent time off. Each account is kept at all times as nearly at a balance as possible for the department concerned to permit. Monthly employees who take time off for reasons of their own, are required in the absence of an overtime credit, to make up the time lost by an equivalent amount of overtime, if the nature of the work permits of useful overtime employment.

All the overtime rules apply only to men, as the California law does not permit the employment of women in excess of eight hours daily.

Vacations.—A vacation of twelve consecutive working days with full pay (equivalent to two calendar weeks) is given to every employee who has been on the monthly payroll for one year or more. About one-fourth of the employees are entitled to this privilege at present. Plans are being studied now for instituting vacations for all employees.

Christmas bonuses to employees.—It has been the custom of the company for many years to present Christmas bonus checks to every employee, according to the following schedule: a full month's salary to monthly employees earning $200 or more, and one-half month's salary to monthly employees earning less than $200. These bonuses are paid after the employee has served a full year. Proportional payments are made for each month less than a year's service. Hourly employees receive a flat bonus of ten dollars each.

Working hours.—This refinery was the first in the United States to abandon operations on a two 12-hour shift basis, substituting for that a three 8-hour shift plan. The plant operates on an alternating shift basis of three 8-hour shifts, 8:00 A.M. to 4:00 P.M., 4:00 P.M. to 12:00 midnight, and 12:00 midnight to 8:00 A.M. Operations continue over a period of twelve days and nights, and terminate in a two-day week-end shut-down every other week. The personnel of each shift changes every third week. The refinery closes down completely each year about the month of December for the cleaning of machinery, alterations, installation of new equipment, etc.

Lay-offs during annual shut-down.—It is the policy of the company to give its employees steady and continuous employment, provided some useful work can be had. The only exceptions to this rule are in the cases of mechanics employed for temporary work such as special construction, and in cases where unusual operating conditions arise.

The company's goal has been to provide work for all employees during the annual shut-down period. In early years this goal was only partially achieved, it being necessary to lay off several hundred men between the beginning of the shut-down work and the resumption of refinery operations. In more recent years, however, careful accumulation of necessary work such as the installation of new machinery, repairs, and general clean-up have made it economically possible to utilize all male employees. The length of the shut-down period is gradually being lessened because of the increased volume of business and because of an increased efficiency of the maintenance work through the operating year.

Method of wage payment.—Table 8 following outlines the methods of wage payment in existence in the refinery, by showing the number and percentage of employees paid by the month, by the hour, by the piece, and under the premium classification. (The latter is a system of collective premium payment.)

TABLE 8

METHODS OF WAGE PAYMENT

Method	Men No.	Men Percentage	Women No.	Women Percentage	Total No.	Total Percentage
Monthly	350	27.1	37	20.5	387	26.2
Hourly	813	62.8	93	51.3	906	61.4
Piece work	...	....	51	28.2	51	3.5
Premium	131	10.1	..	....	131	8.9
Totals	1,294	100.0	181	100.0	1,475	100.0

The tabulation above is as of October 1, 1927, and does not include employees attached to Hotel Crockett.

Almost 90 per cent of all male employees are paid by the month or by the hour. Of the men 10.1 per cent work under the premium system of collective bonuses. The system of collective responsibility operates in the belt gang and the shipping gang of the warehouse. Of the women employees 71.8 per cent are employed on a time basis by the month or hour.

Sanitation, ventilation, lighting, and employees' conveniences.—The management provides facilities which tend to contribute to the health, convenience, and the pleasant working conditions of an employee. To this end problems of sanitation, ventilation, lighting, heating, locker rooms (individual metal locker for each employee), shower rooms, lunch places, rest rooms, drinking fountains, and toilet facilities have been the subject of careful consideration and extensive improvement from time to time. Continuous improvements are made to insure the maintenance of the nearest possible degree of perfection in these respects.

Absenteeism and tardiness.—Because only the minimum number of men and women are employed to carry on the operations of the plant, every absence on the part of an employee handicaps the efficiency of the organization. Continuous attention is therefore given by the supervisory staff to the promotion of the regularity of attendance. Advice and suggestions are given to minimize the duration of sickness or disability. Each department head is kept informed of the reasons for absences and is advised weekly of the condition and prognosis in cases of prolonged sickness.

Attendance is checked carefully. Late comers find their time cards missing and have to see their immediate superiors before they can go to work. Regular attendance is insisted upon, and enforced. Unless specifically excused by his immediate superior, unwarranted absence subjects the employee to a warning in the first place, a three-day disciplinary lay-off in the second place, and a seven-day disciplinary lay-off for a third offense. A fourth offense results in a permanent lay-off.

An analysis of reasons for discharges during 1926–27, discussed in detail elsewhere in this report, shows that 58 per cent of all permanent lay-offs was due to "excessive absenteeism."

Disciplinary procedure.—Certain offenses result in discharge; others, in permanent lay-off. In all involuntary separations the company distinguishes between discharge for a grave cause—such as smoking, threatening or attacking a superior, or willful destruction of property—and permanent lay-offs, for reasons not as grave. The idea is to avoid blackening a man's record in a manner which might prevent him from securing another job. Permanent lay-offs are usually made only after two disciplinary lay-offs, and after final warning. The major offenses which result in discharges and permanent lay-offs are:

Discharges, offenses causing:
1. Smoking within refinery
2. Threatening or attacking superior
3. Willful destruction of company property
4. Stealing

Permanent lay-offs, offenses causing:
1. Fighting while on duty
2. General undesirability caused by improper personal conduct, such as frequent drunkenness
3. Repetition of objectionable conduct for which two temporary disciplinary lay-offs and final warning have been given
4. Excessive absenteeism

When the conduct of an employee involves an offense less serious than those enumerated under "Discharge," a three-day disciplinary lay-off (without pay) is given for the first offense, and a seven-day lay-off (without pay) and final warning for the second. The third offense subjects the employee to permanent dismissal. Discharged employees are not rehired.

Disciplinary action is usually taken when an employee shows repeated carelessness in his work. In such instances, a third offense sometimes results in a demotion rather than in a permanent lay-off. All contributing circumstances are considered carefully before final disciplinary action is taken.

Employees who voluntarily leave the employ of the company, or are laid off for lack of work, receive a work rating of from 1 to 4 to indicate the following degrees of desirability for rehiring: (1) "excellent service and conduct"; (2) "satisfactory service and conduct"; (3) "unsatisfactory service or conduct, or both; not to be rehired"; and (4) "extremely poor service or conduct, or both; not to be rehired."

The suspension leading to a lay-off is made by the immediate superior of the employee. Lay-offs must, however, have the sanction of the department superintendent; no discharge or permanent lay-off becomes effective without the additional approval of the plant manager.

Every effort is made by the management and the supervisory force to make better men and better workers of those found deficient. Good judgment, much patience, and a considerable degree of human kindness are used in the handling of such cases in a manner that will accomplish the object in view while preserving the proper regard for discipline and efficiency. The results of this policy have thus far been very gratifying, and many rather unreliable young men have developed into steady and valuable employees.

First aid.—A registered nurse is on duty during the business day. Her duties consist of rendering first aid and checking up on the sick and injured. She also keeps the records pertaining to her work. To provide first aid on the night shifts, when the nurse is not on duty, three fully equipped first-aid cabinets are located at points of convenience in the refinery and warehouse. Foremen trained to render first aid are assigned to care for all injuries occurring in the various parts of the plant. Detailed instructions as to methods of locating plant officials and doctors are furnished to all concerned. Physicians must be notified in all cases of injuries requiring treatment beyond that which the first-aid foreman can render.

It is customary to conduct a class in first aid during the annual shut-down. This class is composed partly of men who have not previously taken such a course, and partly of men who have already received first-aid training and wish to review it. This course has been presented from year to year by a representative of the United States Bureau of Mines. It is also customary to conduct, under the leadership of the Company's dock maintenance foreman, a course in water-rescue training, since the refinery premises extend for more than half a mile along the water front. The plant thus has a large contingent of employees qualified to render first aid on practically all parts of the premises.

The company is planning to arrange for the employment of a company physician. In the meantime, all physical examinations and other work requiring the services of a physician or surgeon are performed, in rotation, by three of the physicians residing in Crockett, except when circumstances require the selection of an out-of-town doctor.

The company physician, when employed, will have immediate supervision over all first-aid work, make regular periodical physical examinations of all employees, give attention to sanitary problems in the plant and in the community, and advise employees generally in matters of health. Some part of the physician's time may be given, it is said, to the certification of disabilities for the Employees' Mutual Benefit Association.

Accident prevention.—A full-time safety inspector is vested with authority to enforce all proper safety rules and practice. During the annual shut-down for repairs his work is supplemented by that of three assistants, because of the abnormal volume of unusual and heavy work involved in major repairs, demolition, transfers, and the setting up of various installations.

Every new employee meets the safety inspector for the purpose of receiving instructions regarding safety requirements. When possible, a number of men are grouped together for these instructions.

Workmen's and foremen's safety committees make plant inspections each month. The membership of each committee rotates every four months. The workmen's committee consists of eleven members and the foremen's committee of seven. The members of both these committees are paid a special fee for each inspection, in addition to being reimbursed for time lost from regular work. All recommendations of these two committees are referred to the engineering department for execution, rejection, or reference to the central safety committee.

The central safety committee directs the safety program. This committee, which meets once a month, is made up of the following members from among the supervisory staff: Plant Superintendent, Plant Engineer, Assistant Plant Engineer, Warehouse Superintendent, Assistant to Warehouse Superintendent, Chief Chemist, Personnel Manager, Assistant to Personnel Manager, Shift Superintendent, Dock Maintenance Foreman, Safety Inspector, Storekeeper.

As a result of the continuous emphasis on safety in refinery and warehouse operations, little remains to be done as far as physical safeguards are concerned. The company recognizes, however, that it is far short of the goal in the education of employees to practice safe working methods at all times. Much of the effort of the above-mentioned committees is now directed toward this end.

It is the duty of the personnel manager to see that injured employees are properly treated and properly represented at all hearings before the Industrial Accident Commission. Except in instances where deliberate fraud appears to be involved, the company looks out for the employee and seeks to obtain full justice for him. Hospitalized, sick, and injured employees are visited from time to time by members of the staff of the Industrial Relations Department.

Active and constant attention is given by the management in providing safe working conditions. The company expects that its accident-prevention program will receive the serious and constant co-operation of every employee. Employees with a record of frequent injuries due to carelessness are classified either as incompetent for greater

THE REFINING DIVISION 73

responsibility, or as disqualified for continued employment by the company.

The effectiveness of the work described in this section in reducing the frequency of accidents and in diminishing their severity may be seen in the following paragraph.

Workmen's compensation.—Workmen's compensation insurance is carried by the Corporation through a participating-stock insurance company. The premiums are based upon various payroll classifications established by the California Inspection Rating Bureau. Premium costs are reduced by an annual dividend to policy-holders, dependent in amount upon the year's accident experience of each policy-holder. The best commentary on this company's persistent efforts toward accident prevention and accident reduction is embodied in the following record of its gradually reduced minimum base rates:

Year	Rate
1920	$2.24
1921	2.24
1922	2.20
1923	1.67
1924	1.52
1925	1.83
1926	1.67
1927	1.56
1928	1.35

To provide employees with an income during periods of disability not due to industrial accidents, as well as for the purpose of providing employees with insurance protection in cases of death, a special organization known as the Employees' Mutual Benefit Association is in operation. This organization is described more fully on pages 90–99 of this chapter.

Housing.—In the early years of the company's operations in Crockett a number of dwellings were erected to be occupied by supervisory employees on a rental basis. These are still maintained. Congested housing conditions during the War brought about the erection, by the company, of an additional group of twenty small, temporary cottages. These continued in use under the rental plan for several years after the War.

In 1920 the company discontinued its policy of erecting rental cottages, in order to encourage the building and purchase of homes by employees. Under this plan, houses are erected principally by contractors selected by the company, usually in concerted building campaigns which obtain the benefit of quantity prices. Large tracts of land are subdivided and improved with sewers, curbs, streets, etc., and are sold for the most part for less than the cost of these improvements.

Where desired, lots are sold on the same basis to employees who desire to employ private contractors, and even to non-employees who desire to contribute to the community housing. A portion of one new subdivision has been divided into half-acre lots to encourage agricultural pursuits, in a small way, by workers who often have ample spare time during daylight hours, owing to their shift employment. This plan has proved popular with the employees.

Homes are sold to employees upon a cash payment of 10 per cent of the total cost of the house. The banks of the community finance such projects to the extent of 60 per cent of the value of the home, by means of a first deed of trust, and the company finances the remaining 30 per cent under a second deed of trust, to a maximum of $1,500. Both deeds of trust carry interest at the prevailing commercial rate. Payments on both deeds are required in a minimum amount of one per cent monthly on the total cost of lot and house.

Homes of from four to nine rooms have been built under this plan with shingled, rustic, clap-board and stucco exterior finishes, with shingled, composition, and gravel roofs, and with wall-board, plaster, and papered interior walls. Houses may be had with or without hardwood floors, fireplaces, sleeping porches, breakfast rooms, built-in baths and showers, garages, and many other special features. Expert supervision and inspection of construction of all houses financed by the company is extended by the company's engineering staff, without charge. Under the company's plan of beautifying the community, an ample supply of attractive trees, shrubs, and plants is furnished each owner without cost.

Most of the desirable construction has been done under a policy put into effect in 1920. Under the 1920 building program and policy 163 dwellings have been erected, of which 121 (or 74 per cent) were built for employees with financial assistance from the company, 22 (or 14 per cent) were built for employees who did not require company financial assistance, and 20 (or 12 per cent) were built by non-employees on company lots without company financial assistance.

The building of new houses under the company's plan has actively continued throughout 1927, during which year seventeen houses were constructed. The number of applications pending at the close of the year indicated considerable activity in 1928 as well.

Plant protection.—The industrial relations department is responsible for the protection of the company's property both inside and outside of the plant (except fire protection, which is a function of the engineering department), and has a staff of gatekeepers and watchmen for this purpose. For the most part this staff is made up of dependable, intelligent men of long service who have become incapable of performing the more active duties of their former positions.

Educational Activities

Various efforts have been made in the past to provide a general and practical educational program for employees. In the past few years educational opportunities for the employees have been confined to the facilities of the Crockett High School. The company frequently suggests desirable courses not previously given, and encourages its employees to enroll and to attend regularly.

A technical library is maintained at the plant for general reference and for the use of employees. Several series of industrial posters are used to call the attention of employees to various necessary phases of conduct and caution in industrial employment. The general policy of the company is to confine its notices and posters to subjects immediately significant, rather than to dull the edge of the meaning of a message by the continuous display of posters.

The above plan is practical and useful only to the general run of employees. For this reason the company has, during the summer of 1927, instituted a comprehensive and rather unique program for the technical training of supervisory employees.

Technical and operating education.—This educational program is separate and distinct from the general educational work for the average run of employee, described in the preceding paragraph, and is designed to train executives, from head operator (a minor supervisory job) to shift superintendent. The object is to build up a corps of understudies for many of the supervisory positions in the refinery.

The new plan is unique in three ways: (1) Final qualification for a job is obtained by actually running it. (2) Advancement in pay is proposed for those qualified for new positions but still remaining in old jobs because of temporary lack of vacancy. (3) The training is done while the men are on the job and while actually discharging the duties of their positions.

The following represents a condensed summary of the work.

1. *Purpose of educational work.*—The aim of training is twofold: (a) to give promising young men an opportunity to pass through the different stations in the plant so as to gain such co-ordinated knowledge of the entire process as will fit them to assume positions of greater responsibility; (b) to broaden their general education by recommending courses of study at night school or by correspondence instruction, and by recommending books or magazine articles pertaining to some phase of their work.

It is expected that as a result of such training the company will have a more efficient and flexible organization.

2. *Present status and methods employed.*—Catalogues of all non-fiction books available in the Crockett Public Library, the Community Center Club Library, and the plant library were gone over. A list of books worth recommending to the men was then made up, an effort being made to correlate the reading matter with the work the men were doing. The men were encouraged to take up work at the local night school. Arrangements were made in the English course to have a class late in the afternoon, so that the men on the 4:00 P.M. to 12:00 P.M. shift might attend classes.

A complete survey of all the men in the operating department was made, with the aid of the shift superintendents. A list of promising men was then compiled, the candidates being segregated into six groups according to their estimated capabilities and rates of pay.

Group No. 1 consisted of eight men on monthly pay already in supervisory positions, who were to be trained as char-house and refinery foremen. Members of this group were subsequently to receive additional training for the work of shift superintendent if they demonstrated that they were capable of filling positions of greater responsibility.

The training of this group consists of:
1. Station training in charhouse and refinery
2. Pan floor and general boiling experience
3. Technical training
    a) Prescribed reading
    b) Laboratory and control work
4. General training for position of shift superintendent

Group No. 2 consisted of twelve men on monthly pay who were holding minor supervisory or station positions. These men were to receive training on other stations to develop any latent executive ability they might have and to give them a further insight into the sugar-refining business.

The men in this group were to be trained on the following stations and positions, if they had not had previous experience on them:

- a) Melt centrifugal operator
- b) Main melt operator
- c) Head operator in melt house
- d) Sweetland Press operator (all presses)
- e) Receiving-tank operator
- f) Oliver operator
- g) Head Oliver operator
- h) Regenerator operator
- i) Regenerator operator's helper
- j) Blow-up operator
- k) Sweetland fireman
- l) Liquor man, No. 1 house and Nos. 2, 3, and 4 houses
- m) Liquor-gallery operator
- n) At least one month on the pans and evaporators

Such men as had demonstrated that they were capable of filling the positions of refinery foreman or charhouse foreman were to be given the following additional training:

- o) Remelt centrifugal head operator
- p) White-sugar centrifugal foreman
- q) Packing-house foreman
- r) Cut-in foreman
- s) Specialty foreman
- t) Container-department foreman
- u) Charhouse foreman
- v) Refinery foreman

Also technical training, as follows:

- a) Prescribed reading
- b) Alkalinity control
- c) Raw-sugar control
- d) House control
- e) Special research and laboratory

Group No. 3 consisted of four men on monthly pay who were on station positions and who were considered capable and reliable station operators, but who lacked directive ability. The men in this group were to be trained on stations other than those they were then managing. They were to be trained on the following stations:

THE REFINING DIVISION

a) Main melt operator
b) Blow-up operator
c) Regenerator operator
d) Liquor man, No. 1 house and Nos. 2, 3, and 4 houses
e) Liquor-gallery operator
f) Evaporator operator
g) Pan-floor—thorough training as a sugar boiler

If any of these men broadened out through training and developed latent leadership qualities which would justify placing them in Group No. 2, they would be moved into this group and given its training.

Group No. 4 consisted of ten summer students, who were in the plant primarily to give a day's work for a day's pay. These men were to be given as much insight into the industry as could be given while getting value received for the wages paid them. These students were taken on a complete tour of the plant, and all stations and functions were explained to them. All questions asked by them were carefully answered, and additional information was given.

Group No. 5 contained eleven men on daily pay who had shown directive ability and who, it was felt, would develop into executive material. These men were to be given the same training as the men in Group No. 2, with the exception of the three last-namd positions under Group No. 2, viz.:

Container-department foreman
Charhouse foreman
Refinery foreman

Some of the men in this group are now on monthly pay, and may therefore be classed in Group No. 2 as eligible for training on Group No. 2 stations.

Group No. 6 comprised twenty-one men on daily pay who were considered capable of advancing to station operators with a possibility that some of them might develop into executive material during the training period, or as a result of the training. These men were being trained for the following positions:

1. Melt operator
2. Evaporator operator
3. Head operator, bag laundry
4. Head operator, remelt centrifugals
5. Sugar boiler
6. Blow-up operator
7. Regenerator operator
8. Head Oliver operator
9. Liquor man, No. 1 house
10. Liquor man, Nos. 2, 3, and 4 houses
11. Liquor-gallery operator

3. *Future program.*—The following educational subjects are under consideration at the present time:

A. *Organization of classes,* under the direction and with the assistance of the various heads of departments, on their respective fields of work. Such instruction should lead to a better understanding of what the other fellow's problems are, and of what is being done in other departments.

B. *A foremen's training conference* for a group to be composed of the following men, together with such men as have been trained for these positions:

>Refinery foremen
>Charhouse foremen
>Container-department foremen
>Specialty foremen
>Powdered-sugar station foremen

By the holding of a conference this year for the above-named group, the management should be able to form a more definite opinion of the value of subsequent similar conferences. If the men in the initial conference demonstrate by their work during the coming year that they are better foremen as a result of the conference work, the management could conduct other conferences for the remainder of the supervisory force.

C. *Inspection trips* by foremen to other plants. This should give them a broad general view of industry which would be of value both to the company and to the employee. Such trips would tend to increase individual efficiency and would perhaps lead to constructive suggestions for improvements in the plant. Such trips would also tend to efface the complacency of some of the foremen who have never worked in another plant, by showing them different and perhaps better methods of handling men and materials in use elsewhere.

D. *"Get-together" dinners* about once a month for the major foremen of the different departments. At these dinners the several executives of the company would give talks on some phase of the sugar business or on some problem of the refinery. These get-together dinners would tend to break down departmental friction and lead to a more co-operative organization.

E. *A system of measuring or rating* men in supervisory positions to indicate the benefit of the educational work carried on. Such a record would be of value for purposes of promotion and in making transfers.

F. *A special wage-rate schedule,* above base pay, for those men on daily pay who have demonstrated through their training that they are capable of advancing but for whom no openings are as yet available.

Community Activities

General.—The community adjacent to the refinery is principally dependent upon the sugar refinery. Crockett may therefore be referred to as a one-industry town. The population approximates 5,000 persons. About 1,400 employees of this company live within the community, while the remaining hundred commute to Port Costa, Martinez, Pinole, Rodeo, Vallejo, Richmond, Berkeley, and elsewhere.

When the company started operations in March 1906 living conditions in Crockett were in many respects deplorable. Housing facilities were extremely limited and such dwelling places as were available were unsatisfactory from the standpoints of convenience, sanitation, and health.

The management immediately gave its attention to the problem of improving living conditions, with the result that a consistent, constructive community program has been followed through the ensuing twenty-two years. Crockett is often referred to as a model community, offering very attractive housing and fine surroundings.

The development of the community has not been without its problems. Because of the company's desire to accomplish maximum results in the early years, there developed on the part of the townspeople a sense that no civic responsibility existed for them as individuals or as a group. The Refinery, they thought, should attend to all necessary community matters. This tendency has since been much modified and largely overcome. For several years past, community improvements have been conducted on a co-operative basis between the property owners and the company. Where possible, the county, too, contributes its share.

There has been a historic division between the east end of town, known as Crockett, inhabited principally by American families, and the west end of the town, known as Valona, which comprises the foreign colony. The rivalry has at times been bitter. Each end of town has, for many years, had its separate volunteer fire department, with no thought of co-operation for the interests and protection of the entire community. In 1926, however, a standing agreement was entered into under the terms of which each fire department stands ready to assist the other in case of second-alarm fires. A single lighting district, too, now serves the entire community.

Much still remains to be done, of course. The company has a community improvement program to be carried out during the coming years, as funds for such work become available.

Community Center Club.—The Corporation has provided for the use of the men of the community a large clubhouse equipped with a spacious lobby and sun porch, a gymnasium with bleachers, a handball court, a swimming pool with bleachers, showers, and dressing rooms, a pool and billiard room, a library and reading room, and card and committee rooms. The club has a dormitory consisting of thirty-one rooms. Management of the club's activities was first directed by the Y.M.C.A., but owing to that organization's policy of not permitting the use of athletic facilities on Sunday (at that time the one day when the company's employees could benefit most by these facilities), it was found desirable to change the plan of management. The company then attempted to direct all club activities by employing a manager. Fair success was achieved until 1922, when a reorganization was effected whereby the company released its control of the club and placed the responsibility in the hands of a Board of Directors selected by the membership.

The Club frequently provides for its members dances, smokers, wrestling and boxing exhibitions, card parties, motion pictures, swimming meets, etc. It maintains both boys' and girls' basketball, football, and baseball teams. During the summer months the club provides a swimming instructor for children and adults.

Under the company's agreement with the directors of the Club, the use of and responsibility for the Community Center Club building, the Community Auditorium, the tennis courts, the athletic field, and the putting green are placed in the hands of the Club directors. The company maintains the buildings and grounds, pays the taxes and insurance, provides heat, and contributes the manager's salary. The rest of the cost is contributed in dues or services by members.

All men of good standing within the community, whether employees of the company or not, are eligible to full membership in the Community Center Club. Boys of from sixteen to eighteen years of age are eligible to junior membership. Women having no male relative in the community, and men residing outside of the community, may enjoy the Club's social privileges under associate membership.

Parks and playgrounds.—As a part of the program to develop and maintain an attractive community the Corporation has planted several parks and equipped two playgrounds and a large athletic field. The parks are planted with a fine variety of plants, trees, shrubs, and lawns, and the resulting beauty is accentuated by streams and fountains. Under stimulation of the company, an increasing number of owners of private property have undertaken a plan of planting gardens and sidewalk parkings consistent with the company's town beautification.

The trustees of both the local high and grammar schools have developed the school grounds in harmony with the general town plan. The general beautification through gardening has been encouraged by the fact that the company maintains a propagating nursery where a large variety of plants are grown from seeds and cuttings and distributed without charge to any persons residing in the community.

The largest park, located on the main highway, is known as Alexander Park. In this park is located the Community Auditorium (built by the company at a cost of over $40,000), which is the center of the community's social life. Nearby are located tennis courts with locker and shower accommodations. The courts are lighted for night playing. A smaller park known as Rithet Park is located in the center of town on the main business street, and is in the form of a sunken garden. An area in the east end of town, which the company had reserved for ultimate parking purposes, is at present at the disposal of the Camp Fire Girls.

Women's Club.—The Women's Club House is owned, maintained, and managed by the Corporation. The company provides a matron who resides in the building. This Club House is the center of women's activities in the community. The Carquinez Women's Club, a branch of the State Federation of Women's Clubs, makes its headquarters here and directs its program of educational, civic, and charitable work from this point.

The Camp Fire Girls' and Blue Birds' activities are likewise centered here. The building, located close to the railroad and stage depots, serves as a convenient and comfortable meeting place and waiting place for women.

The building is equipped with library, reading, lounging and billiard rooms, kitchen, and Camp Fire Girls' Rooms. Girls of the community frequently entertain at this clubhouse.

Hotel Crockett.—In 1890, a large frame hotel building was erected on Crockett's main street, adjoining land now occupied by the Corporation's main plant office building, to meet the acute housing needs of that time. Upon commencement of operations the hotel was taken over and has since been operated by the Corporation. Additions were made in 1914 to provide a total of 146 rooms, and until the last two years the hotel has been filled to its capacity of about 280. During the period of the World War and the years immediately following, it was taxed beyond its maximum capacity. The company has taken an annual loss of many thousands of dollars on this hotel in order to provide adequate living accommodations for some of its employees.

With the rapid expansion of housing facilities by reason of the company's housing program and the construction of private hotels, apartment houses, and single dwellings, the time is approaching when the company will consider itself justified in abandoning the hotel business.

Boy Scouts and Wolf Cubs.—Ten years ago the Corporation sponsored the first Boy Scout activity within the community, and there has been a constant program among the boys ever since. There are at present two full troops of Boy Scouts and a large organization of Wolf Cubs (boys below the minimum Scout age).

About three years ago the company donated a building (which had been moved from another part of town to a location next to the Community Center Club) to serve as a Boy Scout Center. Many carpenters, plumbers, and other builders donated their time in fitting up the buildings as an up-to-date Scout quarters.

Sanitation.—A number of sewer mains throughout the town have been installed by the Corporation and a number by private owners. Practically all of these mains have been made use of by owners of property subsequently improved.

Another problem met in unincorporated towns such as Crockett is the disposal of garbage. Up to 1925 there had been no organized system of collection. A mass meeting was then called by the General Manager of the company in order to call to the attention of the citizens the unsatisfactory sanitary conditions. At this mass meeting, plans for a garbage collection service were formulated and approved. Of the total number of householders in the community 88 per cent took advantage then of the new service; at the present time 95 per cent of the householders avail themselves of this service. The above-mentioned mass meeting appointed a permanent Sanitary Commission for the town.

At the request of the Sanitary Commission, the County Board of Supervisors appointed one of the company's employees as a deputy health officer to serve in Crockett without remuneration from the county. As a result of that appointment, it is now possible to make occasional inspections of the premises of non-subscribers to the garbage collection service, in order to see that all garbage disposal is being handled in a satisfactory manner.

Streets and roads.—The State Highway running through the town is maintained by the State Highway Commission and the county roads in the community are maintained by the County Board of Supervisors. There are many other streets, however, the maintenance of which is borne by the Corporation and the owners of the abutting property.

Christmas Festival.—A traditional Christmas Festival is conducted each year. It started about twenty years ago with a Christmas tree and the distribution of presents to a limited number of children, and has gradually grown into an extensive community celebration.

MISCELLANEOUS

Contemplated pension plan.—The company has no pension plan in operation at the present time. It is, however, vitally interested in the development of some plan which will protect its aged employees. The management has now under consideration a plan which is designated to solve this problem.

In spite of the fact that the Corporation is but twenty-two years old, its proportion of relatively old employees is rather great. This is probably due to the fact that in the earlier years of the life of the Corporation, and particularly during the period of the World War, when labor was very scarce, little consideration was given to the age of newly hired employees, and also because of the fact that some of the present employees were taken over from the old beet-sugar company.

As bearing upon the pension problem, the two following tables (Tables 9 and 10), one showing age distribution of refinery employees and the other their length of service classification, are pertinent:

TABLE 9

AGE DISTRIBUTION OF EMPLOYEES
(As of October 1, 1927)

Age	Number	Percentage of Total
Under 18	3	0.2
18–20	70	4.7
21–25	229	15.4
26–30	301	20.3
31–35	271	18.3
36–40	251	16.9
41–45	161	10.9
46–50	83	5.6
51–55	55	3.7
56–60	22	1.5
61–65	19	1.3
Over 65	18	1.2
Total	1,483	100.0

TABLE 10

Length of Service of Employees

(As of October 1, 1927)

Years of Service	Number	Percentage of Total
Less than 1	321	21.6
1	177	11.9
2	139	9.4
3	99	6.7
4	150	10.1
5	123	8.3
6–10	301	20.3
11–15	93	6.3
16–20	45	3.0
Over 20	35	2.4
Total	1,483	100.0

Cost of Industrial Relations activities.—The cost incidental to the carrying on of all industrial relations activities of the company is shown in the following table (Table 11) in dollars and cents per man on the roll. The total cost is subdivided into the costs of (*a*) personnel work, (*b*) community activities, and (*c*) fixed and other charges.

For 1927 the total cost of all industrial relations activitives was $98.75 per man on roll. Of this amount about 28 per cent was expended in personnel work, 56 per cent in community activities and the remainder in so-called fixed and other charges. Assuming an average annual earning per man of $1,400, the cost of industrial relations activities was equivalent to 5.30 per cent of the cost of wages in 1925, 6.27 per cent in 1926 and 7.06 per cent in 1927.

Between 1925 and 1927 the cost of personnel work per man on roll increased from $24.55 to $28.86, or slightly over 15 per cent. The cost of community activities during the same period increased from $39.84 to $56.64, or almost 40 per cent.

TABLE 11

COST OF INDUSTRIAL RELATIONS ACTIVITIES

Function	Cost per Man on Roll
Personnel	
1925	$24.55
1926	27.72
1927	28.86
Community activities	
1925	39.84
1926	49.88
1927	56.64
Fixed and other charges	
1925	11.06
1926	10.03
1927	13.25
Totals	
1925	75.45
1926	87.63
1927	98.75

Public relations and publicity.—The public relations work of the industrial relations department concerns, among other things, with the reception and entertainment of visitors to the plant. For this purpose the department has under its charge a group of thirty-five experienced guides who escort visitors over established routes through the refinery. Guides are selected from among men in the company's employ who have had a thorough training in the various parts of the plant and who are therefore competent to explain the refinery processes and answer such questions as visitors may ask.

The department is also in charge of making arrangements for the showing of films depicting the community, the refinery, and the refinery processes. The manager of the department frequently represents the company at public and semi-public conferences.

Employees' Mutual Benefit Association

The present Employees' Mutual Benefit Association, which came into existence on March 1, 1924, is an outgrowth of the old "Mutual Hospital Association," which operated for about ten years prior to 1924. The M.H.A. charged dues of 50 cents per month, in return for which it paid a death benefit of $75, and a disability (non-industrial) cash benefit of $8 per week for a period not exceeding twenty weeks. No benefits were paid for the first seven days of disability. This old Association confined its membership to employees of the refinery at Crockett. The Corporation made contributions from time to time during the few years of the Association's existence. At the time of its liquidation in 1924, the M.H.A. had a membership of 309, or 21 per cent of the total employees of the Refinery, and a surplus of $3,337.87.

The initial fund for starting the present Employees' Mutual Benefit Association consisted of the balance on hand in the M.H.A. on February 29, 1924, and a contribution of equal amount from the company. The E.M.B.A. began to operate on March 1, 1924. Its two main objects are (1) to provide benefits for non-industrial disabilities equivalent to two-thirds of the normal earning capacity of members, and (2) to make up the difference in industrial accident disabilities between the maximum allowance under the State Compensation Law and two-thirds of the normal earnings of the disabled member.

Disability Division.—As already pointed out, in cases of disability due to industrial accidents, the E.M.B.A. makes up the difference between the maximum allowed by the State Compensation Law and two-thirds of the employee's normal earnings.

The non-industrial disability benefits consist of cash benefits and medical, hospital, and surgical operation allowances.

Cash benefits.—Two-thirds of actual average earnings are paid to disabled members for a period of twenty-six weeks. No benefits are paid for the first three days of disability, the payment beginning with the fourth day. (In cases of monthly employees, the company compensates the disabled for the first three days.) A member who receives the maximum benefit of twenty-six weeks is not entitled to further benefits in the succeeding twelve months, unless he has returned to work and has been continuously employed for one full month before the disability occurs.

Medical and hospital benefits.—A hospital benefit up to $150 in any one year is paid in the case of bona fide hospital internment. Operation expenses are paid to the maximum aggregate amount of $75 in any one year, for one or more operations, in accordance with a special schedule provided for. The amounts actually allowed under this provision vary with the specific nature of the operation, from as low a figure as $10 in the case of a tonsil operation up to a maximum of $75 in abdominal cases.

Sources of Revenue.—The financing of the organization is based upon a contribution by members at the rate of 77 cents per month for each $100 of earnings. The aggregate income thus collected is matched monthly with a like amount by the company. Membership is optional with the employee, provided his minimum earnings are less than $300 per month.

The E.M.B.A. is administered by a Board of Managers of seven. Five of these are selected by the employees (four from among employee-members at Crockett, and one from among employee-members of the San Francisco office) and two by the company. The representatives of the company are appointed by the President, one from among the company's staff at Crockett, and one from among the company's staff at the San Francisco office.

Representatives of the company on the board need not be members of the E.M.B.A.

Within two years of its founding the E.M.B.A. accumulated a surplus of about $25,000. (In reality the actual accumulation was only about $18,000, as the E.M.B.A. started with a fund of almost seven thousand dollars.) The payment of additional benefits was therefore authorized on June 1, 1926. These benefits consisted of additional hospital expense payments and surgical expense allowances, both under an established schedule.

Mortality Division (Group Insurance).—Group insurance was introduced in 1926 on an optional basis, for all employees of the company, under a policy issued by the Aetna Life Insurance Company. The group insurance premium, however, is paid in addition to the previously described disability dues.

The E.M.B.A. acts as the agent in the collection of premiums for group insurance and in the settlement of claims. Membership in the Disability Division does not mean, necessarily, participation in the benefits of the Mortality Division or group insurance; one may belong to one of these without joining the other. The premium paid by members of the Mortality Division runs now at the rate of 60 cents per month for a policy of $1,000. The company contributes the difference between the total of the premiums paid in by members and the actual cost of the insurance.

Group insurance is allowed in amounts ranging from $1,000 to $10,000 per member, in accordance with the earning capacity of the individual. The group insurance policy provides, in addition to death benefits, a cash benefit for total disability prior to the age of sixty.

Membership of E.M.B.A.—The table on the following page (Table 12) shows the membership in both divisions— the Disability Division (p. 93) and the Mortality Division (p. 94)—as of December 31, 1927. The table also shows for each division the percentage of eligibles who have actually taken advantage of these privileges.

In the Disability Division, out of a total of 1,358 eligibles, 1,324 actually belong to the Association. The most numerous department—that of operating—shows a membership of 99 per cent of the eligibles. Among significantly important departments, the warehouse department shows the lowest percentage of members, 90.17 per cent of eligibles.

The average percentage of eligibles who joined the Mortality Division was 92.94 per cent, which is less than in the Disability Division. The operating department shows a percentage of 96.03 per cent in the Mortality Division.

TABLE 12

Membership of Employees' Mutual Benefit Association as of December 31, 1927

Department	Disability Division						Not Eligible
	Total Employees	Number Eligible	Number Members	Percentage of Eligible	Eligibles not Members		
					Number	Percentage	
Operating	659	625	618	98.88	7	1.12	34
Personnel	25	25	25	100.00	..	....	..
Gardeners	19	19	19	100.00	..	....	..
Mechanical	361	321	316	98.44	5	1.56	40
Accounting	28	27	26	96.30	1	3.70	1
Plant manager's office	2	2	2	100.00	..	....	..
Stores	24	24	24	100.00	..	....	..
Warehouse	192	173	156	90.17	17	9.83	19
Technical	41	38	38	100.00	..	....	3
Construction	1	1	1	100.00	..	....	..
Department heads	8	...	...	......	..	....	8
Miscellaneous	12	9	8	88.89	1	11.11	3
Hotel Crockett	26	19	17	89.47	2	10.53	7
Community Center	6	5	4	80.00	1	20.00	1
San Francisco	107	70	70	100.00	..	.....	37
Totals	1,511	1,358	1,324	97.50	34	2.50	153

94   THE C & H SUGAR REFINING CORPORATION

TABLE 12—Continued

Department	Mortality Division					
	Number Eligible	Number Members	Percentage of Eligible	Eligibles not Members		Not Eligible
				Number	Percentage	
Operating	629	604	96.03	25	3.97	30
Personnel	25	22	88.00	3	12.00	..
Gardeners	19	18	94.74	1	5.26	..
Mechanical	329	311	94.53	18	5.47	32
Accounting	27	26	96.30	1	3.70	1
Plant manager's office	2	2	100.00	..	....	..
Stores	24	24	100.00	..	....	..
Warehouse	173	132	76.30	41	23.70	19
Technical	40	37	92.50	3	7.50	1
Construction	1	...	.....	1	100.00	..
Department heads	8	8	100.00	..	....	..
Miscellaneous	11	10	90.91	1	9.09	1
Hotel Crockett	20	15	75.00	5	25.00	6
Community Center	5	4	80.00	1	20.00	1
San Francisco	105	95	90.48	10	9.52	2
Totals	1,418	1,308	92.24	110	7.76	93

Taking into consideration the optional character of the E.M.B.A., one is greatly impressed with its popularity as shown by the proportion of eligibles who have joined. The records of the E.M.B.A. show that since its inception, in 1924, the membership in the Disability Division has ranged from 96 per cent to 99 per cent while the Mortality Division membership has varied from 90 per cent to 92 per cent of the eligibles. In the Disability Division, departments of an administrative nature show a membership of 100 per cent of eligibles. In the Operating Department 98.88 per cent of the eligibles actually joined. In the Warehouse the proportion joining was only 90.17 per cent. This fact is attributable, largely, to the greater labor turnover in the warehouse.

Financial status of E.M.B.A.—Table 13 presented below gives a statement of the revenues, expenses, assets, liability, and surplus of the E.M.B.A. (Disability Division only) for the year ending December 31, 1927.

TABLE 13

STATEMENT OF REVENUES AND EXPENSES OF E.M.B.A., DISABILITY DIVISION, FOR YEAR ENDING DECEMBER 31, 1927

	YEAR TO DATE	
	Detail	Total
Revenues (dues)	$35,152.16	
Less dues rebated	43.12	
Total revenue		$35,109.04
Expenses		
Benefit claims—sickness and disability	$25,547.96	
Benefit claims—medical fees	3,413.40	
Benefit claims—hospital fees	3,317.40	
Salaries	2,801.58	
Stationery and supplies	72.11	
Traveling expenses	201.36	
Doctors' fees	152.05	
Miscellaneous	168.30	
Total claims and expenses		$35,674.16
Total operating profit [loss]		$ 565.12
Interest earned on savings and investments	$ 1,269.76	
Interest paid on investments		$ 1,269.76
Net gain		$ 704.64

STATEMENT OF ASSETS AND LIABILITIES AS OF DECEMBER 31, 1927

ASSETS		LIABILITIES	
Cash on hand—Commercial	$ 3,866.20	Accounts payable	$ 220.00
Cash on hand—Savings	3,803.36	Insurance premiums payable	16.17
Investment bonds	19,146.25	Unclaimed sick benefits	221.97
		Surplus	26,357.67
Total	$26,815.81	Total	$26,815.81

SURPLUS

December 31, 1926	$25,724.08
Plus write off, estimated 1926 income tax liability	540.00
Less 1926 income tax—paid quarterly, 1927	346.05
1926 stationery bill—paid 1927	225.00
1924–1925 capital stock tax	40.00
Plus net gain above	704.64
December 31, 1927	$26,357.67

Revenues and expenses.—For the year 1927, the Association showed an operating loss (that is, an excess of benefits paid over dues collected) of $565.12. When the year's income of $1,269.76 from interest on savings and investments is taken into consideration, the Association shows a net gain for the year of $704.64. The percentage of the total annual expense for 1927 consumed by the various items of cost is shown herewith:

NATURE OF EXPENSE AND PERCENTAGE OF TOTAL COST

Nature of Expense		Percentage of Total Cost
Cash claims—sickness and disability		71.6
Benefits—hospital, medical, and doctors' fees		19.2
Administrative costs—		
Salaries	7.9	
Stationery and supplies	0.2	
Traveling expenses	0.6	
Miscellaneous	0.5	9.2
		100.0

The table above shows that out of every dollar of revenue, more than 90 per cent was paid out, in cash or medical benefits, to the members. Less than 10 per cent was consumed by the cost of administration.

Average cost per member.—The total revenue from members' dues and from the pro-rata contribution of the company was $35,109.04. Of this amount half, or $17,554.52, was contributed by the members. The average membership for the year was 1,324. This would make the annual cost of the society to each member-employee $13.25, or about $1.10 per month.

Surplus.—On December 31, 1927 the cumulative E.M.B.A. surplus was $26,357.67. The financial success of the Association was very gratifying up to the middle of 1926, when increased benefits were decided upon as a permanent policy. As shown elsewhere, the Association really had a small deficit in 1927. Since the middle of 1926, the surplus of the E.M.B.A. has increased by only $1,600, as against an average increase of almost $9,000 per annum between 1924 and 1926.

Those familiar with the experiences of organizations of this type know that, in order to cover special contingencies which frequently arise, organizations such as the E.M.B.A., with a limited dispersion of risk, must have progressively increasing surpluses.

Two reasons may be given for the present status of the Association. First comes the liberality of the additional benefits allowed in 1926. The second reason is the method followed in the verification of claims, with particular reference to the time of beginning and time of termination of disability. Under the system now in vogue, the verification of claims is made by local private physicians. None of these physicians has any particular interest in the stability and welfare of the Association. The physician is closer to the individual claimant than he is to the interests of the Association. The benefit of the doubt is thus automatically given the claimant.

There is only one remedy for this situation—the employment of an Association physician. If possible, the physician should spend some of his time in the refinery. This would give him a practical understanding of the psychology and of the real needs of individual claimants and perhaps a better idea of the frailty of human nature. (As stated in the preceding pages the employment of such a physician is now under contemplation.)

In addition to a tightening and a systematization of benefit payment procedure, a careful analysis should be made of the actual disability and cost experience of the E.M.B.A. since its inception, to bring out the following: (1) the proportion of the members who have drawn benefits of one sort or another, by sex, department, age, length of service, racial origin, and marital condition; (2) the number of individuals who have drawn benefits more than once each year, and the total amount drawn by them; and (3) the nature of the disabilities for which benefits were paid and the amount for each, in terms of money paid and in terms of days lost. Many other questions of vital importance to the continued development and financial solidity of the Association would naturally suggest themselves as the survey progressed.

Extent of group insurance as of January 1, 1928.—The following table shows the status of group insurance as of January 1928:

TABLE 14

GROUP INSURANCE IN FORCE

Policy Denomination	Number	Percentage	Amount	Percentage
$ 1,000.........	153	10.67	$ 153,000	5.75
1,500.........	910	63.46	1,365,000	51.27
2,000.........	143	9.97	286,000	10.74
2,500.........	124	8.65	210,000	7.89
3,000.........	18	1.25	54,000	2.03
4,000.........	33	2.30	132,000	4.95
5,000.........	13	.91	65,000	2.44
7,500.........	1	.07	7,500	.28
10,000.........	39	2.72	390,000	14.65
Totals	1,434	100.00	$2,662,500	100.00

The table shown on page 94 gives the number of members in the Mortality Division as 1,308. The difference between this figure and the number of policies shown in the last table, 1,434, is due to the fact that a number of members of the executive personnel of the company are participating in group insurance, though ineligible for E.M.B.A. membership.

The following table shows the relative cost of group insurance to the employees and to the company:

TABLE 15

DISTRIBUTION OF COST OF GROUP INSURANCE

Year	Percentage Paid by Corporation	Percentage Paid by Employees	Total
1926	24.6	75.4	100.0
1927	23.2	76.8	100.0

On the average, as shown by the actual record for 1926 and 1927, one-fourth of the cost of group insurance was paid by the company and the remaining three-fourths by the employees.

9. ENGINEERING AND MAINTENANCE DEPARTMENT

The work of the engineering department falls into four main classifications: (1) engineering, (2) mechanical operation, (3) maintenance and repairs, and (4) new construction.

(1) ENGINEERING

The staff consists of the plant engineer and his assistant, a group of engineers, and the master mechanic who is the field executive supervising the work of the department foremen.

In the supervision of all departmental activities the authority of the assistant plant engineer is coextensive with that of the plant engineer. As a rule, the assistant plant engineer devotes his attention to the routine detail of mechanical operations, maintenance and repairs, while the plant engineer confines his attention to engineering and to new construction. The two consult freely with each other, the assistant plant engineer keeping the plant engineer continuously advised as to the general situation in connection with the work he is handling.

With the exception of one or two who are concerned with the supervision and direction of labor, the staff engineers exercise no direct control over labor. They act in the capacity of consultants, engaged largely in studies of the various phases of departmental work. Their work is supplemented by special consultants from the outside whose services are engaged from time to time as required.

Each engineer on the staff specializes along some definite lines. Final decisions, however, are usually reached in staff conferences, thus securing the advantage of the combined talent of the staff.

As part of the regular routine the engineers are expected to keep in close touch with plant operations, and to co-operate with the members of the other departments toward the solution of operating difficulties. Through co-operation with the maintenance organization the engineers are continuously studying maintenance and repair work, with a view to a better selection of materials, improvement in design, reduction in cost of maintenance and repairs, minimization of interruptions to operations through failure of equipment, and prolongation of life of equipment.

Because of depreciation and obsolescence, there is a continuous necessity for the replacement and renovation of plant equipment. Each such replacement calls for careful investigation and study. In addition to this there is continuous study, in co-operation with the technical staff, of changes in equipment which will result in a saving in labor, or in economies in consumption of fuel, materials, and supplies.

There is a civil engineer on the staff, who attends to all engineering work which the company undertakes in the community—surveying; construction, maintenance, and repair of outside structures; construction and maintenance of roads and sewers; all work in connection with the sub-divisions and the company's housing program; and all other outside activities which require engineering direction.

Valuation of properties.—In 1922 the company arranged for a re-valuation, to (1) ascertain the correct fixed charges for accounting purposes, (2) determine a basis for insurance and taxes, and (3) lay a foundation for perpetual valuation with proper accounting for future betterment and additions.

This valuation was made in detail rather than by groups. It embraced the complete description, specifications, and value of each building and unit of equipment. Reference to these units was made by number, and was supported wherever possible by photostat copies of construction and equipment drawings. Historical cost values were compiled from field sheets showing exact measurements, listings, and notes. The computation of reproduction values was based on historical costs. From the reproduction values, depreciation was deducted to arrive at the depreciated or present values. Insurable values were arrived at by the elimination of all non-insurable items from present values.

Briefly, values were determined in the following manner:

Quantities were gathered in the field by careful measurement and count, and recorded on working sheets. Weighted average unit costs for each quantity or groups of quantities were developed, for the greater part historically, from Corporation records. With historical costs as a basis, the reproduction (new) values were computed by graphical analysis giving relations (for materials and labor costs on combined gradients) between the historical value and the cost of reproduction. Provision for depreciation for all units, except bone coal, was figured on the straight line method. Depreciation rates were fixed only for one year, subject (upon inspection) to variation because of age and condition. The depreciated or present values were arrived at by deducting accrued depreciation from the estimated cost of reproduction.

On the completion of the re-valuation, the work was turned over to a valuation engineer, whose position in the engineering department was created for the purpose of carrying on this valuation work.

From the original valuation set-up the plant ledger system, numbering about 2,500 cards, was developed. The set-up permits the making of all necessary asset and depreciation adjustments to the various units of equipment and buildings, thus maintaining a continuous valuation. These cards have provision for the item, reference number (in case of major equipment), location, account number, asset division, name of vendor, order number, date, and general description—all in addition to twelve columns provided for continuous valuation. As originally set up, these cards contained the valuation date, the reproduction cost as of that date, the depreciation percentage and amount, and the depreciated or present value.

Total annual depreciation is compiled on a depreciation schedule, prepared annually. The schedule shows the reproduction cost, previous annual rate of depreciation, and accrued depreciation. The schedule is subjected to field examination of equipment and buildings and to discussion, before final depreciation rates are arrived at for the ensuing year. Calculations are then made, and after final approval the postings are made to the cards. The necessary adjustment to the present value is thus completed.

The cost of each building is subdivided into the cost of excavation and fill, foundations, and superstructure, with a card for each. Machines each have a card bearing a reference number corresponding to the number shown on the placement diagrams, of which there is one for each floor of each building. These placement diagrams are kept up to date. From the plant ledger cards the insurable values and plant tax values are derived. The plant ledger cards also serve as an equipment and construction record, and are the means for furnishing overhead charges for cost accounting purposes.

All jobs wherein assets are affected are handled through the medium of plant orders. Upon the closing and analysis of these plant orders, the plant ledger cards are adjusted so that the valuation of properties is made continuous.

Standardization.—The engineering staff, by its studies of maintenance and repairs, determines the standard specifications of materials as a basis for purchasing. When a material of a certain quality has been selected for a given purpose, the specifications are adhered to until further study discloses the desirability of a change. There are standard specifications for special conveyor and elevator belts, cast iron pipe, black and galvanized steel pipe, copper pipe, and the like. Packings for valves, pump rods, etc., are standardized.

In the securing of fabricated parts, attention is given to a reduction in the number of shapes and sizes so that the capital investment in the stores department may be held at a minimum. For instance, an effort is made to reduce the number of different gear sets, so that the gears may be interchangeable from one machine to another, and a single spare set in stores may serve as a reserve for a large number of different machines. Whenever a new machine involving the use of gears is designed, an effort is made to duplicate the gear specifications already established.

To insure against delays to operations, a carefully selected list of spare machinery parts is kept on hand and available for immediate use. A Rand file is maintained covering all spare parts carried. These cards are prepared by the engineering office in duplicate so that a complete file may be kept in the main plant office. Each card shows, for the plant as a whole, the number of the particular item installed and the equipment on which used. Complete specifications for ordering are shown, and also the maximum and minimum quantities to be carried in stock.

Purchase requisitions.—The stores department maintains a stock of standard materials and supplies in quantities sufficient to satisfy normal demands. It also maintains the stock of machinery spares in quantities based on the maximum and minimum specified on the Rand file cards. All quantities carried, both of standard stock and of special spares, are originally specified on the basis of judgment. The engineering department co-operates with the stores department so that, through accumulated experience, existing quantities may be reduced as far as is consistent with safety.

As already indicated, continuous effort is being made to reduce the stores inventory through the use of the same material or part as widely as possible throughout the plant. Whenever changes in standards are under consideration, the engineering department co-operates with the stores department toward the reduction of stocks so that material or parts in stores may not be in danger of obsolescence.

As the standard stores stocks are based on normal demands, special orders are necessary in anticipation of extraordinary repair jobs or for new construction. All such purchase requisitions emanate from the engineering office through the medium of a foreman's "Request for Purchase Requisition." These requests may be made by various members of the staff in the engineering office, or they may be made by the department foreman, in which case the request must bear the approval of the master mechanic. These forms are carefully checked to see that they contain all the information which the purchasing department will require, and that the correct charges are shown. Before the requisition is prepared, the possibility of substitution from salvage stock is also considered.

Salvage.—The potential waste in a plant as large as this one may become a serious source of loss. It is not always possible to specify the exact quantities which will be used. If the excess drawn is not properly returned to stores but is allowed to accumulate in out-of-the-way places, not only will the charges against the particular job be in error, but there will be inevitable waste of material.

Whenever installations are removed from the plant, there is left much second-hand material which is of value provided there is an organized effort to take care of rehabilitation and to arrange for its re-use. Certain members of the staff of this department are assigned exclusively to salvage work. All excess new materials and all second-hand materials and equipment removed from the plant are delivered to the salvage section. Materials unfit for further use are placed on scrap piles, properly segregated in order that the best price may be secured when they are sold as scrap.

Non-standard material or equipment which has value and for which a use may be found, is properly segregated and placed on racks. A careful follow-up is provided in order to secure its re-use. Valuable non-standard materials or equipment for which there is no further use are listed for sale.

Accounting.—The engineering staff has grown to appreciate the importance of accounting as an aid in attaining an increasingly higher standard of economy. A continuous effort is being made to educate each employee in the department to an intelligent appreciation of correct accounting, and to a knowledge of accounting sufficient for the requirements of his particular work.

The valuation engineer occupies the focal position in the carrying out of these policies. He is in intimate contact with the rest of the engineering staff from the inception of a job through the period of design, and assists in the preparation of estimates. He is also in close contact with the master mechanic and the departmental foremen. In the same manner, the valuation engineer assists toward securing correct accounting in all of the departmental activities, and in the analysis and interpretation of the final results as reported by the accounting department. The valuation engineer also assists the staff in the preparation of the budgets which control all activities.

(2) Mechanical Operation

All mechanical operations are under the supervision of the master mechanic, with the exception of water towage, steam generation, and fire protection. These are supervised directly by the plant engineer with the assistance of the engineering staff.

Steam generation.—The boiler plant plays a vital part in the operation of the Refinery, as operations demand large quantities of steam for heating, evaporating, crystallizing, drying, etc. This steam must be supplied at a constant pressure and at a rate corresponding to the demands of the refinery. Any interruption in the supply would immediately disturb the uniformity of plant operations.

The boiler plant organization consists of a boiler house foreman and a crew of men. Each shift is composed of one fireman and one water-tender. As operations are continuous throughout the year, a swing fireman is necessary to allow the shift fireman and water tenders their regular days off. There is a crew of five boiler-washers, one of whom acts as a straw boss over the others. One employee is responsible for the handling of the fuel oil supply and related duties, and one man acts as a handy man, or boiler-house mechanic. This man makes repairs to the burners and does other minor odd jobs of a similar nature. The boiler-house foreman is directly responsible to the plant engineer through one of the staff engineers.

The steam generating plant consists of ten water-tube boilers rated at 600 horse power each, operating at 160 pounds pressure. By over-load, there is developed from this plant about 10,000 boiler horse power. There are also maintained eight older and smaller boilers having a total rating of 900 horse power, largely for emergency use.

A large percentage of the steam produced is for the vacuum pans. These units have a wide fluctuation in steam demand. As this fluctuating demand would otherwise require the constant attention of the boiler-house operators, there is provided an automatic control, which increases or decreases the fuel supplied to the boilers in accordance with the demand. This automatic control decreases the number of operators necessary, and also allows the operators to give closer attention to water and fuel supply, condition of fires, and other matters.

To insure against interruptions through failure of equipment, the fuel oil pumps, feed water pumps, heaters, etc., are provided in duplicate.

Fuel oil constitutes one of the heaviest items of expense, as the plant consumes approximately one-half million barrels per operating year. It is therefore of utmost importance to secure the highest possible efficiency through the maintenance of a high standard of operation. Neglect of small details could easily contribute to heavy losses. Within the last year a saving of approximately eight per cent in the total fuel cost was effected by the introduction of a lower grade of fuel oil—a residuum resulting from the "cracking" of ordinary fuel oil. This oil is somewhat more difficult to handle, and requires more expert attention for the best results, but the additional attention required is relatively small in comparison with the lower cost of the fuel.

The present boiler plant is about ten years old. Since the installation was made, great advances have been made in the design of boiler plants; many improvements have been devised which increase efficiency to a degree not possible with the present installation. At the present time, the engineering department is considering the adoption of mechanical burners in the place of steam-atomizing burners, together with larger furnaces, forced and induced draft, and air pre-heaters. These improvements will increase the possible over-loads on the boiler plant, thus increasing available capacity by about thirty per cent. This change is imperative in view of the great increase in demands for steam.

Power generation and usage.—Large quantities of electric power are required in a sugar refinery. Unlike the situation in many industries using electric power, however, large quantities of steam are also required for process use. The relation existing between the power demand and steam demand in a sugar refinery presents an unusual opportunity for economy, as power may be generated from the steam as a by-product. In this case, steam is exhausted from the power plant at pressures suitable for the process requirements, and the heat loss in passing through the turbines is only from three to five per cent. With the demand for steam in excess of the power plant production of steam, power can be generated as a by-product, at a cost of about one-quarter less than the price which would be paid for purchased power.

The power-producing plant and the processing apparatus which utilize steam must be such as to maintain a proper balance between supply and demand of steam. If the steam requirement for production of power exceeds the demand of the plant the excess is exhausted to the atmosphere. In order to secure the maximum over-all economy, the task of the refinery engineer is to search continuously for ways to decrease both the steam consumption of the power plant (that is, the supply of steam to the refinery) and the consumption of steam in the refinery.

The power plant of this refinery consists chiefly of one turbine which takes steam from the boiler house at 160 lbs. gauge and exhausts against a back pressure of 70 lbs. gauge. The rated capacity of this unit is 1,500 kilowatts, but it is capable of carrying a sustained load of 1,750 kilowatts. The exhaust steam at this pressure is used for the boiling of sugar in coil vacuum pans. The production of power by this turbine fluctuates with the fluctuations in demand for steam, at the above-mentioned pressure. Where the demand for 70 lb. steam exceeds the capacity of the turbo-generator unit, the excess requirement is automatically provided direct from the boiler house through make-up reducing valves.

The balance of the power plant consists of three turbo-generators each rated at 1,500 kilowatts each, but capable of carrying a sustained maximum load of 1,750 kilowatts each. Two of these turbo-generators operate continuously when the refinery is at capacity, with the third unit carried for emergency. These three units operate with steam at 160 lbs. gauge, exhausting against a back pressure of 10 lbs. gauge. The exhaust from these units is used for boiling sugar in calandria pans and for general heating and evaporating throughout the plant.

These units operate at a fluctuating rate, determined by the difference between the refinery power demand and the amount of power produced at any given moment by the high back-pressure turbine. Where the demand on these units results in a production of more 10-lb. steam than the simultaneous demand of the refinery, the excess is exhausted through the relief valves to the atmosphere.

The steam balance is, however, so established and maintained that this situation rarely develops. Where the refinery demand for 10-lb. steam exceeds the production by the turbo-generators, the requirement is automatically made up direct from the boiler house through reducing valves.

The power generated in the power plant is distributed by a feeder system to all parts of the refinery buildings, and is the sole source of power for the driving of all equipment, with the almost negligible exception of a few steam-driven pumps. Another comprehensive distributing system from the power plant, with the necessary transformers, serves for plant illumination.

In addition to these two major uses of electric power, the use of electricity has been extended in recent years in manifold ways. The "electric mindedness" of the organization has resulted in many important and interesting electrical developments, which have in some cases made possible major economies and in others greater ease of operation. Electrical control is used in the various operations on sugar centrifugals, so that, for example, the twenty-two washed-sugar centrifugals are now operated by three workmen per shift, instead of five as before this application was made. Another recent development has been a central control station for the conveying systems in the warehouses.

The plant is served throughout by an electric bell signal system operated by motor generator sets. All packages entering or leaving the plant are automatically counted by electrically operated counters designed by the engineering organization.

From motor generator sets low frequency current is supplied for operating the vibrators on sugar screens. From other motor generator sets direct current is produced for magnetically cleansing sugar and char of any iron with which it may be contaminated through the scaling of equipment. This direct current is also utilized for solenoids to operate valves and for many other special applications throughout the plant.

The plant is equipped with a fire alarm system, which, in addition to serving the company's own premises, has one circuit extended to serve the community of Crockett.

Water supply.—One of the most essential requirements for sugar refining is a plentiful supply of fresh water of good quality. While this refinery is ideally situated in every other respect, it lacks a suitable water supply close at hand—a handicap which is overcome by a special water towage arrangement. The plant's freshwater requirements average about two million gallons daily. Any curtailment of supply means an immediate reduction in output, with consequent loss of economy. For delivering this water two steam tugs are provided, with three specially designed wooden barges, each having a capacity of about one-half million gallons of water.

Some of the water is taken from the Sacramento River, and some comes from a reservoir in the hills. When hauling water from the river source, the barges are filled through the simple expedient of opening sea cocks. The water from the reservoir is taken from a pipe line and enters the barges through filling curbs placed in the deck. Each barge is equipped with motor-driven centrifugal pumps and discharge piping ending in a manifold on either side of the deck amidships. When a filled barge ties up at the refinery dock, its pump motors are connected to an electrical supply on the dock. The discharge manifolds are connected by large flexible hoses to the refinery piping systems. The water is delivered into a steel tank having a capacity of 1,600,000 gallons. In addition to this tank, auxiliary storage is provided in three reserve tanks. The four tanks have a combined capacity of 6,900,000 gallons, sufficient to keep the plant in operation for three and one-half days. This reserve storage is provided solely for insurance against a prolonged interruption to water deliveries, such as might be caused by an accident to the water-towing equipment.

Plant fire department.—The plant fire department consists of a fire chief, an assistant fire chief, and an apparatus man, all of whom devote their entire time to inspection of fire hazards and to the maintenance of fire-fighting equipment. The balance of the organization is selected from the general plant organization, and includes three shift brigades, a chemical brigade, hose brigade, ladder brigade, first aid brigade, electrical brigade, tug brigade, fire police, fire messenger, and salvage brigade. The fire chief, to whom, of course, all members of the fire department are directly responsible while on fire duty, is responsible to the plant engineer.

At least once each month a surprise fire drill is called by the turning in of a fire alarm. Each brigade unit also meets once a week for one hour with the fire chief for special drill.

Shift organization.—Under the supervision of the master mechanic a shift organization is provided, with a mechanic foreman for each of the three shifts. It is the duty of the shift organization to maintain a continuous inspection of all equipment and, in co-operation with the members of the operating department, to secure smooth and uninterrupted operation. To this end it is their responsibility to make such adjustments to the machinery as may be required from time to time, and in cases of necessity to make emergency repairs. In this work the shift foreman has the assistance of a refinery engineer and a helper, who patrol the refinery, packing house and melt house buildings, and of a char house engineer who patrols the char house group. These men in turn supervise the work of the oilers.

On each shift there is also a pump attendant who is directly responsible to the shift mechanic foreman. This employee operates the fire pumps, air compressors, condensor pumps, refrigerating plant, and the water-filtering plant. In addition to this, an employee of the electrical department is assigned as a "trouble man" to both the four o'clock and the twelve o'clock shifts. The foreman electrician lays out shop work to occupy the time of his men when they are not required for "trouble shooting."

Mechanical operation budget.—The Mechanical Operation budget is prepared quarterly by the engineering department to cover the expenses of all of the activities under this caption. This budget also covers the salaries of the engineering staff, and all engineering office expenses. In preparing the budget for the boiler plant, the rate of melt scheduled for the ensuing quarter determines the expected or budgeted cost. In preparing a budget for water hauling, not only must the melt schedule for the quarter be considered, but also the distance which the water has to be hauled.

(3) Maintenance and Repairs

For each piece of equipment in the plant, some member of the organization is directly responsible. It is his duty to know the condition of this equipment at all times, and on his own initiative to do all work necessary for its maintenance. As proper maintenance is of the utmost importance in assuring freedom from interruptions to operations, all "red tape" which might interfere with prompt attention has been practically eliminated. Employees in all departments are encouraged to deal directly with the maintenance men, and to report promptly matters which need attention. At the same time there has developed throughout the organization a receptive attitude toward suggestions and criticisms. The maintenance force has come to understand that such criticisms and suggestions do not come in the way of orders, but are a valuable aid to them in the execution of standing orders from their superiors.

In the organization for plant maintenance, the line of responsibility passes from the plant engineer through the master mechanic to the foremen of the twelve principal crafts, which are as follows:

Sheet metal workers	Painters
Pipe workers	Electricians
Boiler workers	Mechanics
Carpenters	Brick masons
Copper workers	Belting workers
Machinists	Dock maintenance

Much specialization has been developed in the work of these mechanics. Under the mechanic foreman there are the following maintenance sub-divisions: centrifugals, pumps, pans, Sweetland and Oliver filters, sewing machines, scales, and powdered and dessert sugar equipment. To each of the foregoing, one or more men are definitely assigned. For the balance of the mechanical equipment, the plant is divided into char houses, packing house, and refinery, with a maintenance mechanic assigned to each.

The present organization for the handling of maintenance work has been developed not alone with a view to fixing responsibility, but also with the object of developing experts for the different classes of work.

The maintenance shops until now have been widely scattered through the plant. Recently these shops have been centralized. This improvement not only affords opportunity for better supervision, but also assists in securing a greater unity of purpose.

Maintenance and repair budget.—All maintenance and repair expense is budgeted annually in advance. In preparing this budget, the engineering staff carefully studies accumulated detail in connection with previous budgets. From this it endeavors to make an intelligent forecast of the probable requirements for the coming year. Consideration is given to the general condition of each of the stations, in so far as it has been possible to determine this by inspections, so that provision may be made for such major repairs as are likely to be needed.

Upon the formulation and approval of the budget, a set of graphs is prepared, one for each account, showing by a straight line curve the budgeted expense for the year. Each month, as the figures are received from the accounting department, the actual expenditures are plotted on these sheets. Throughout the year the staff watches daily the development of this graph in its relation to the budget.

There is also a set of graphs whereon the annual totals for each account are plotted to show the trend of expenditures over a period of years. These graphs as a rule show an expected upward trend. From 1917 to 1922 the plant was more than doubled in size, through the addition of new buildings, machinery, and equipment. Besides this, much of the old plant has been renewed. Another element contributing to the annual increase in the total maintenance and repair costs is the constant addition of new labor-saving devices. A third factor which has also contributed to increased expense has been the annually increasing melt.

To make a long story short, the company has each year been purchasing its economies in plant operation at quite some increase in expenditure for maintenance and repairs. To offset in a measure this tendency toward rising costs, continuous study is carried on to devise ways for reducing expense by improved design and by the proper selection of materials.

(4) New Construction

Reference has been made to the engineering studies carried on in co-operation with the staffs of other departments to meet the need for replacement of equipment because of depreciation and obsolescence as well as the continuous study which is made in the search of plant improvements.

Formerly much of the equipment of new design was built by outside shops. With the passage of time, however, this department has handled more and more of this work, until today little or no work is done outside, except for some stock equipment. Practically all of the equipment is of special design and is built inside at a cost lower than that offered by competitive bidders. There is also an additional advantage in doing this sort of work on the inside; the department is able to build up a larger and more skilled organization, which is of great value in the handling of regular maintenance and repair work.

As another result of this policy the company has been able to afford the addition of a considerable number of tools for the various shops. The expense of some of these would probably not have been justified for maintenance and repair work alone. Through possession of these tools, however, it is possible to carry on the maintenance and repair work at a reduced cost and to much better advantage.

Routine maintenance and repair work, it should be noted, is considered as the first responsibility of the department. Construction work is so planned as to occupy the periods of least activity.

Improvement budget and plant order procedure.—With the assistance of other departments concerned, the engineering department prepares quarterly two improvement budgets—one to cover all improvements within the plant, and the other for all improvements exterior to the plant. All charges to the improvement budgets are made through the medium of "Plant Orders," which are issued by the engineering department, approved by the plant engineer, and countersigned by the plant manager.

One copy of the plant order is sent to the master mechanic's office as his authorization to start work on the job. The master mechanic issues orders to the craft foreman on an "Engineering Department Work Order." The foreman holding such orders from the master mechanic may in turn call for work to be performed on the plant order by other crafts through the medium of a "Foreman's Request for Work to be Performed." On completion of the work, the "Foreman's Request for Work to be Performed" is signed and returned to the foreman issuing it. The "Engineering Department Work Orders" are signed by the foreman and returned to the master mechanic, who checks the jobs for satisfactory completion, signs and dates his copy of the plant order, and forwards it to the engineering office for closing.

The engineering office reports the completed job to the plant manager, the technical superintendent, and the office manager. In due time the engineering office receives from the plant office an analysis showing a recapitulation of charges, labor by crafts, hours, and money, material by stock number, craft using the material, quantity, and money, together with copies of invoices of special order material, and copies of requisitions for spare parts and other material not classed as regular stock.

There is then prepared in the engineering office a form called "Recap of Plant Order Labor and Material by Craft," in duplicate, for the scrutiny of the plant engineer and the master mechanic. At the same time, after careful investigation and analysis, a "Plant Order Closing Voucher" is prepared in duplicate, showing the distribution of charges to assets and expense. The plant engineer approves and signs this and forwards it to the main office for auditing and posting.

All engineering expense is planned in accordance with the budget for mechanical operations. For major improvements, the engineering expense is assembled through the medium of separate plant orders. These plant orders are closed out, on completion, to the proper expense account. If, on analysis, any of the engineering is to be capitalized with the improvement, a separate voucher is prepared which provides for a credit to the expense account, and a charge to the asset.

At the end of each month, after all closing vouchers have been made and posted, a recapitulation of charges by asset accounts is prepared in the engineering office, and the totals are balanced with the main office books. Each voucher on which assets are affected is transferred to "Addition—Betterment—Deduction" sheets and prepared for entry into the plant ledger. The plant ledger detail cards are balanced, and the main account cards are posted to agree with the detail cards and also with the main-office totals. By means of these adjustments to the plant ledger cards the valuation of properties is made continuous.

It seems opportune, at this point, to describe briefly the policies which have been followed in securing and developing the personnel of this department. Since 1922, permanent additions to the organization have been secured so far as possible by adding men for only the lower grades of helpers. The higher positions have been filled by promotion. Also, wherever practicable, men were secured by transfer from other departments, usually the operating department.

There is on file an application list of young men in other departments who wish an opportunity to learn a trade. The experience which such men have had in plant operations is considered an important asset in their service in the engineering department. Because of their contacts with other departments, it is easier to implant in these men the idea of service so essential to the success of the engineering department. In the majority of cases these men have already, during annual shut downs, worked temporarily on mechanical work and their adaptability to this work has therefore been under observation. This makes it possible to select the men best fitted for training. Of the 330 men now working in the engineering department, about one-half have entered the department by transfer.

During the annual shut-down of about six weeks, all mechanical equipment in the plant is completely inspected and overhauled. Between three hundred and four hundred men are temporarily transferred from other departments to assist the engineering department in completing this work within the limited period available. The department is thus more than doubled in size by the addition of several hundred men without confusion and with little loss in efficiency.

This temporary expansion of the personnel demands careful planning and effective organization. Some time prior to the annual shut-down, all work to be undertaken is listed as completely as possible. The planning of this work is then carefully studied and the amount of work to be performed by each of the crafts is estimated. The size of each of the craft groups required for the shut-down is thus determined.

Accurate records are kept of the work of individuals from other departments. These records make possible proper assignment of individuals to the different craft groups. In organizing these groups it is necessary to maintain the proper balance between (1) the number of skilled men already in the group, (2) the number of men available from the other departments who are semi-skilled through experience elsewhere before entering employ (or more particularly, through the experience gained on previous shut-down assignments), and (3) the unskilled men who have not been used before and who can be expected to serve only as helpers. To get an economical balance between skilled, semi-skilled and unskilled for the work which has to be done, it is sometimes necessary to employ temporarily a few skilled men from the outside. The above-described policy for doing maintenance, repair, and improvement work during the annual shut-down has developed within the other departments a large number of men who have had repeated shut-down assignment to the same kind of work and have developed a certain degree of skill.

In addition to its direct advantages in providing continuous work for the employees of other departments while aiding the engineering department in its shut-down undertakings, the pursuance of this policy has strengthened the relations between the departments. Men returning to their regular operating duties have some mechanical experience, which makes it possible for them to use their equipment more intelligently and with greater care.

As stated, additions to the engineering department are now made almost entirely by transfer from one of the other departments to the lower ranks of helpers. Thereafter these men, according to their ability and the spirit which they display, are so shifted from one kind of work to another within the craft that they secure a well-rounded experience. The average young man, if industrious, will advance from the rank of helper to that of full journeyman in the course of about six years.

10. THE WAREHOUSE

The storage facilities herein described are used for the storing of both raw and refined sugar. The main warehouse has a storage capacity of about 115,000 tons of sugar. In addition there is an auxiliary warehouse with a storage capacity of another 20,000 tons. Such extensive storage facilities are required because of special conditions in the company's business as shown in other sections of this study. A constant effort is made, however, to avoid storing in the auxiliary warehouse, for two reasons: (1)

It is not equipped with as fine a conveying system as the main warehouse. (2) Because of the character of its construction, the insurance rates on sugar stored therein are higher than in the main warehouse.

Raw Sugar.—Of the total warehouse storage space, room for about 33,000 tons is allotted for the storing of raw sugar. Beyond that, the raw sugars encroach upon space needed for the storing of the refined product. Raw sugar is taken from the vessel and loaded on stevedore tables. From these tables the bags go into conveyor scales and are weighed while in transit. After being weighed the bags are sampled. As the bags leave the scales they are tallied by an electric bag-counter. This tally is used as a check against the weighers' bag outturn. The bags are then mechanically transferred from the scales to a main distributing belt, from which a given number of bags per minute are delivered direct to the cut-in station, where they are emptied. The balance goes into storage. The bags en route to the cut-in station pass over a mechanical spacing device, which provides a definite interval between each bag in accordance with the rate of cut-in. This spacing permits the organization of a minimum working-crew to open the bags before dumping raw sugar into the cut-in grates.

The bags going to storage are either trucked away and stacked with a portable stacker, or stored by means of gravity from an overhead storage belt.

The rate of discharge of raw sugars varies from 2,000 to 2,850 tons per day. The cost of stevedoring is borne by the steamship line, as raw sugar is delivered F.O.B. the company's docks. The labor complement required for the discharging of raw sugar is used also for the moving of raw sugar from storage piles to the cut-in station.

The warehouse department compiles all initial records and reports on raw sugar, for use in the accounting of and payment for raw sugar.

Refined Sugar.—The receipt of refined sugars from the refinery is a function of the refined-sugar belt gangs or crews. The belt gangs operate over a twenty-four hour period, in three shifts of eight hours each, with twenty minutes off for lunch on each shift.

A storage plan has been adopted for refined sugar, wherein each grade and package has been allotted a definite storage space. It is the function of the refined-sugar belt gangs to receive sugars from the refinery as produced, properly route these sugars over the conveying system units to their destination, properly segregate each grade and package, and store each grade and package in its proper place in accordance with the piling scheme and handling methods that have been adopted as standard—all of the above with a minimum of damage to the containers involved.

In order to save re-handling, sugar from process is used, whenever possible, for making up shipments, in which case the sugar goes directly into cars, or onto the dock for delivery to river vessels. The refined-sugar foreman designates where the different grades and packages are to be stored and what cars and orders are to be loaded direct from production.

The overhead conveying units are the belt gang's main tools. Definite take-off places have been established for delivery of sugar to the floor. This is accomplished by gravity through the use of wooden chutes and step-towers. In a number of cases, the chutes and step-towers have been augmented by the addition of power-driven conveyor tables at the delivery end. Storage beyond the height possible by these means is accomplished by gravity from the overhead storage belts. Sugar from output to shipment is transported by hand trucks, electric trucks, and transveyors.

Shipment of refined sugar from storage.—The function of the shipping gangs or crews is to fill all orders with sugar from storage if unable to fill direct from output. Orders for shipments are received by wire from the order department located in the San Francisco office. The orders specify grades, quantities to be shipped, date of shipment, method of shipping, and routing. Distribution of the various copies of each order is made by the warehouse shipping clerk to the refined-sugar foreman, checkers, delivery clerks, and others involved. The refined-sugar foreman decides what sugars on any particular order shall be loaded direct from the output and what sugars shall be loaded from storage, and assigns the various orders to the various foremen accordingly.

It is the function of the shipping clerk to make the proper distribution of all orders, spot all cars (usually in consultation with the refined-sugar foreman so that the car is conveniently located with respect to the sugar to be loaded in that car), make "on switch" lists, arrange for all switching, supervise billing and checking of all orders, and issue instructions to the delivery clerks and shift foremen for the loading of river boats. In addition to the above, the shipping clerk exercises full supervision over the molasses department—receipts, storage, shipments, billings, and records.

It is the function of the shipping gang foreman in charge of each group to take the proper amount and kind of sugar from storage (in fit condition for shipment) to fill the orders given him, and to transport such sugars from storage into cars or on to the floor in accordance with the Standard Practice and Rules. In the case of car loading, the sugar must be so stowed and braced that it will go through to its destination without damage. The shipping gang foreman carefully checks each car or order as completed, and enters upon the copy of the order all the information necessary. All cars are checked as to grades and packages for the shipping clerk by a car checker. This check is the official record for future reference.

The hand truck is the principal means of transportation employed by the shipping gang. This means is augmented to a large extent by the use of electric trucks with and without platforms, and also by the use of transverse conveyors.

Facilities for car loading.—The train shed on the premises of the company permits the loading of thirty

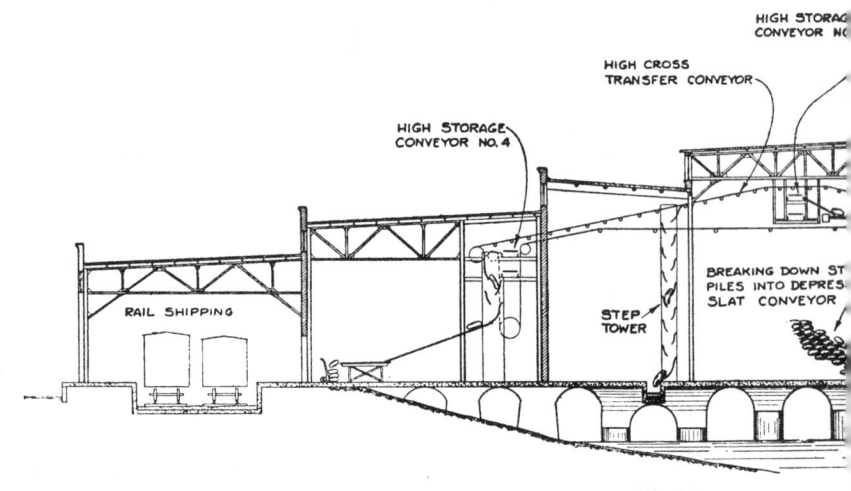

Fig. 6.—Diagram o

cars simultaneously, seventeen on the inshore track and thirteen on the offshore track.

Automatic conveyor system.—The conveyor system in the warehouse is of the most modern type, being automatic and controllable by means of a central switchboard. It is difficult to describe this conveying system, with all of its interlocking features so that it may be clearly grasped. The diagram of Fig. 6 gives a cross-section of the warehouse conveyor system and will greatly assist the reader in understanding it.

There is a complete system of mechanical transportation within the warehouse. This system is connected with the refinery by means of two belt conveyors, which serve the double purpose of taking the raw sugar to the refinery and of returning the refined product to the warehouse for distribution to storage or to shipping points. In addition, there is a separate mechanical arrangement for transporting barrels and boxes to the warehouse.

Within the warehouse there are four belt conveyors,

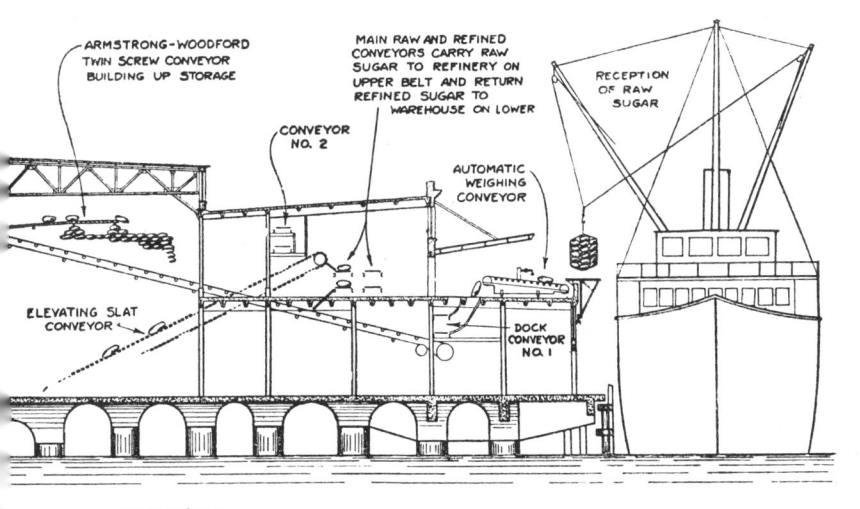

se conveyor system

and two depressed slat conveyors in the floor. These in turn are served by four cross belts, two inclined slat conveyors, and miscellaneous portable and semi-portable conveyors and chutes which transfer the product from one to another of the main conveying units.

Conveyor No. 1, shown in the illustration as "Dock Conveyor" is located on the water front to receive the raw sugar from the steamers, and is so arranged that both the upper and the lower, or return, sides may be used, thus providing transfer facilities in both directions. All belt conveyors are similarly designed for use on both sides. Conveyor No. 2 is used largely for the movement of the refined product. It delivers sugar to any desired point on the waterfront, either for trucking to the steamers or for storage. In an emergency this conveyor may be used for the transfer of raw sugar to the refinery or to storage on the second floor. Conveyor No. 3, known as a "high storage" conveyor, is used for delivering either raw or refined sugar to storage piles. Conveyor No. 4 ("High storage") is used for the distribution of refined sugar for rail shipments.

A control operator, in charge of an electric switchboard, is stationed at a point where the conveying system converges for delivery to the two main raw and refined conveyors leading to the refinery. This control station is located at a strategic point which affords to the control operator an uninterrupted view of all the conveyors in this section. All other parts of the warehouse are connected to the switchboard by telephone and bell signals. The entire system of thirty-two conveyors is thus under a centralized scheme of quick, almost automatic control.

On the bench of this switchboard are located the remote-control start and stop switches for all units. The control automatic starters are of the transformer or "across the line" type, and are mounted on centrally located panel boards in each section of the warehouse. At each switch a red light shows operation and a green light the fact that a particular conveyor is idle. Specially marked rubber caps which fit over the remote control buttons indicate the combination of conveyors in a complete train.

Above the bench are the signal and instrument panels. The operating signals are given by colored lights behind transparencies, supplemented by bell alarms. Throughout the system are located emergency push buttons. When a unit is stopped a red light automatically illuminates the transparency for that unit and a bell alarm sounds. Also, the red light on the bench goes out and the green light comes on. To prevent blockades, the control operator, when necessary, stops the conveyors which feed the unit affected and stands by to restore operation on signal.

Provision is made on the panels for adding ammeters which will act for the control operator as "periscopes" as they will show normal or abnormal operation, thus making it possible to arrange for the correction of improper conditions before serious trouble develops.

11. REFINERY OFFICE

This office, although working in conjunction with the operations of the refinery, is an integral part of the Finance-Accounting Division. The refinery office is directed by a manager who reports to the Treasurer. The work of the office is subdivided into four main parts: (1) cost accounting, (2) sugar-production and stock records, (3) tabulating, and (4) payrolls and labor distribution.

Cost Accounting

In its relationship to the various departments of the refinery office and to the refinery management, this department may be likened to the general accounting department of the general office. It maintains the records and prepares all the detailed statements of refinery costs and expenses. Each month the costs and expenses are summarized, reconciled with controlling accounts, and reported to the San Francisco office by journal voucher.

The refinery cost ledgers control all subsidiary records of operations, as follows: (1) stores investment; (2) rents receivable; (3) construction in progress; (4) maintenance and repair orders; (5) factory costs and expenses.

The classification of manufacturing cost accounts has been made along functional lines, following the processes of refining. Functional expenditures thus obtained are further classified by objects of expenditure, such as labor, materials, supplies, and expenses. Allocation of fixed charges to operating departments is made only in totals. It is not considered worth while to subdistribute fixed charges to the detail functions or stations.

Costs and expenses on construction, maintenance, or special work are controlled, in co-operation with the engineering department, through a system of plant orders and standing station maintenance and repair accounts.

As outlined elsewhere in connection with a description of budgetary procedure, the refinery office co-operates with all departments in the preparation of budgets of production and costs, by supplying statistical data on past performance. It makes comparisons between expenditures and budget appropriations, and prepares periodical progress statements of expenditures, encumbrances, and unexpended balances.

This office uses electric tabulating machines for the gathering of costs and production data. Posting data, for the most part, come to this section in the form of tabulated summaries of labor, material, and expense distributions from the tabulating department.

The following list gives briefly some of the more important statements issued by this department:

1. Closing monthly voucher to San Francisco
2. Detail monthly and cumulative statement of costs
3. Fuel oil and water—costs and consumption
4. Comparative, object-of-expenditure statement
5. "Construction in process" reports
6. Budgets versus actual performance

Sugar Production and Stock Records

This section of the office maintains all records, other than those of a technical nature, concerning raw sugar, refined sugar, and molasses. All technical data is in the custody of the technical control department. Monthly reconciliations of production and stocks are made between this office and the technical control department.

THE REFINING DIVISION

Raw sugar.—A daily stock record is kept of raw sugar—the outturn of raw sugar from vessels, deliveries to the refinery, and stock on hand in warehouses and in process of refining.

Refined sugar.—A detail record is kept of refined sugar, segregated by grades and the various packages in each grade. Daily summaries are prepared in the tabulating department and forwarded to this department for entry. The daily summary covers: (1) output—grades and packages; (2) remelts—damaged stock from the warehouse and the trade; (3) transfers—powdered-sugar ground from granulated; (4) shipments—grades and packages. Daily stock balances of refined sugars are checked with warehouse records. This dual operation is designed to avoid errors in the clerical segregation of stocks.

Molasses.—There are two kinds of molasses at the refinery, one a by-product of the refining process, and the other "plantation" molasses or "blackstrap." The latter is handled and sold through the molasses department (see pages 152–53) for the account of the plantations and in no way affects refinery operation or results.

From its record books, this section furnishes the various departments of the refinery and the San Francisco office with essential daily, weekly, monthly, and annual reports. The three main statements thus made relate to—

Mill Run—A statistical statement of refinery operations, days operated, segregation of employees, output, melt, shipments, stock, etc.

Raw Sugar—Receipts, melt, on hand and in process (inclusive of molasses).

Refined Sugar—Output, remelts, shipments, and stocks.

Because of the large scale of production and the existence of a varied assortment of grades and packages, the records must be accurate. Electric counting devices are relied upon to get correct figures. To verify the stock sheet totals periodical inventories are taken of refined stocks. The tonnage adjustments as a result of these physical inventories are comparatively small. However, errors in segregation between packages and grades frequently do occur. The problem is to eliminate or minimize these.

TABULATING

This section uses automatic electric listing machines and one sorter, and serves each of the other sections of the refining office by accumulating and summarizing posting data. In addition to the above equipment, electric key punches are used for punching cards preliminary to sorting and tabulating.

The major tasks of this section relate to—

Sugar production and stocks.—Production, remelt, and transfer reports come to this section from the control department; cards are cut, checked, and tabulated, and the summary, by grades and packages, is forwarded to the sugar production and stock section. Shipping orders from the warehouse are likewise tabulated and reported.

Payrolls and labor distribution.—Individual employee timecards, after being verified for rates and distribution to accounts, are forwarded to this office. The time cards are then perforated for employee number, hours worked, and total amount earned, and are tabulated by departments to arrive at the total daily payroll. From the job or account distribution shown on the time card, labor distribution cards are punched. The tabulation of job and account distribution, hours worked, and amount, must balance with the predetermined total of the daily payroll. To cover the matter of absent employees, absentee card is punched giving the employee number, reason for absence, and number of hours lost. Before the cards are filed away, a list of the day's absentees is made for the operating departments. A tabulation is also made of the number of men on the roll and the day's labor cost, for departmental checking against standard labor costs of stations.

The time-cards are then filed by employee number—for the computation of payrolls and labor distribution cards; by both job and account numbers—for the making of weekly tabulations for the cost accounting section. Pay checks (on tabulating card forms), after being made up in the payroll department, come to this section, where they are cut and a check register is made, to balance with departmental rolls. The tabulating equipment is also used for sorting checks in effecting bank reconciliations, and in preparing employee earnings statements for the United States Treasury.

Stock control and material distribution.—Stores requisitions, after being priced and extended by the stores accounting department, are forwarded to the tabulating section, where dual cards with distinctive marking are punched, each showing requisition number, quantity used, account number, and amount. One of these cards is filed by account number and tabulated weekly for the cost accounting section. The other card, which is used for stock control purposes, is filed by commodity or stock number, for use in the analysis of material and supplies consumed. This data is used in the preparation of budgets, in buying, and in analysis of stock investment.

Vendors' invoices, checked for quantity, price, and extension by stores accounting department, are forwarded to this office and subjected to the same tabulating procedure as that of stores requisitions.

This division also serves the industrial relations department and the E.M.B.A. by the compilation of statistical data from cards punched in their respective departments.

Pay Rolls and Labor Distribution

The payrolls of the refinery cover the employment of about 1,500 operatives. The work of this division covers payroll records, timekeeping, and actual payments.

Payroll records.—All employees enter upon their employment through the personnel department, which has authorization to place employees on the payrolls by means of "On Roll" slip. Likewise all severances from the rolls reach this department through the industrial relations department, which handles all details in connection with clearance records.

The payroll record shows employee number, hours worked, rate of pay, gross earnings, deductions, and the net amount due. This payroll record, with the exception of postings of deductions and extensions of net earnings, is compiled twice a month from daily time cards by means of electric tabulating machines. Supporting the payrolls, files are maintained of all time cards, authorizations of "On Roll" and "Off Roll," "Transfer Slips," and "Rate Changes."

Two series of employee numbers are used, one known as the badge number, for identification purposes and for the gathering of payroll records, and the other known as the employee's serial number, for the tabulation of statistical data. Badge numbers frequently change as employees are transferred from job to job; the serial number, however, remains the same throughout the term of employment.

Timekeeping.—Time clocks are located at the entrance to the plant, with racks holding each employee's daily time card. Each employee checks in and out, and accounts for the number of hours on duty and the distribution of time to various jobs. All cards are approved for time worked and correctness of account segregations by foremen or field timekeepers. Time cards are checked for rate, hours worked, and extensions made, and then sent to the tabulating section for punching and filing.

At the close of each payroll period, time cards are tabulated on the payroll form, giving employee number, hours worked, and gross earnings. The cards are then transferred to storage files by employee number, for use by auditors and for the compilation of any statistical data which may later be required.

The total semi-monthly departmental payrolls are verified before certification for payment, and audited against daily cumulative balances of gross earnings and against predetermined totals of deductions. Deductions from employee's earnings are made for rentals of cottages, hotel room and board charges, Employees' Mutual Benefit Association dues, and group insurance premiums.

12. STORES ACCOUNTING

Records and Reports.—This section, referred to elsewhere as the Stock Control section, is in charge of a specialist in materials and stores accounting, who reports to the office manager. The section is closely associated with the stores department, whose function is primarily that of physical handling of materials. Stock control here deals with the recording, financial, and economic phases of material handling.

For proper control, the section is equipped with adequate records, the most essential of which is the stores stock record. This record, covering some 8,000 units of materials and supplies, is maintained in standard visible-record cabinets. For each item of stock, a card, in addition to a general description and code number, shows quantities on hand and on order, receipts, withdrawals, allotments, and unit price. Provision is also made for showing requirements and minimum, maximum, and "order when" quantities. The use of visible records has made it possible to use colored celluloid markers, which furnish a graphic picture to the stock control clerks in their constant follow-up of the movement of materials.

The stores ledger, subdivided in accordance with the major classifications of material and supplies, controls the values and investment in each group. This subsidiary record is in turn controlled, for totals, by the refinery ledger. Values are extended monthly on major stock items and, at longer intervals, on others, and each is verified with classification controls of the stock ledger. At the close of each month a stores balance report is compiled showing the investment by classes of material and the changes which have taken place. These figures are plotted graphically to follow the trend of investment.

Subsidiary to the above, records and files are kept of special order material (non-standard stock), purchase requisitions and purchase order records, receiving records, vendors' invoice register, and purchase order and commodity files.

In addition to the stores balance report referred to, various reports and tabulations are compiled and distributed to operating units, such as: consumption reports—fuel oil, kieselguhr, containers, chemicals, etc.; insurance reports—location and values for insurance coverage; container reports—"on hand," "on order," requirements; and statistical—investment and turnover.

Classification and code numbers.—A thorough analysis was made of materials and supplies and a classification and numerical coding adopted. Stock numbers are made up of seven digits, the first two or prefix numbers representing the stock or commodity controls, and the five following digits, individual item numbers. The five digits are further separated to designate class of material and sizes. For materials having a wide range of dimensions, uniform interchangeable dimension charts are compiled, as for example: bolts and screws—diameter and lengths; pipe fittings—diameter of threaded openings; iron and steel sheets—gauge. Cross-indexed registers are kept of numbers assigned to materials where charts are not applicable.

To illustrate the application of stock numbers, a 2″ 45-degree galvanized iron elbow would bear the number 43-31320, developed as follows:

    43-00000—Commodity control for pipe fittings—galvanized
      -31000—45-degree elbow
      -00320—2-inch size
    ―――――――
    43-31320

Inventory control—Stores.—It is the function of this section to maintain its investment at the lowest point consistent with operating demands. For its guidance in placing purchase requisitions for replenishment of stores, it has the production budget, showing requirements monthly and three months in advance. Maintenance and repair material control is effected by careful analysis of past consumption, and through co-operation with the engineering department to cover anticipations of unusual requirements which occur from time to time.

The plant improvement budget and engineering department plant orders serve this section in its follow-up of material requirements for all construction and improvement. The section in co-operation with the consuming departments, has established maximum and minimum stocks to be maintained, and standard specifications for major items and equipment parts. All requisitions on the purchasing department from the operating departments are cleared through this section, affording further control of materials.

This co-ordination of the purchase routine has had the effect of reducing the stores investment, increasing its turnover, and effecting a material decrease in dead and slow-moving stocks.

The above-described stock-control system was installed in the fall of 1925, simultaneously with the inauguration of budgeting practice. The two subjects are closely allied, and each serves the other in the achievement of better planning and in lowering of costs.

Complete cycles of physical inventories are taken, for checking against stock-control records. This is a function of the stock-control section, and serves as a physical check on the storekeepers. Upon approval of the stock-control clerk, inventory adjustments are made to conform with results of actual counts. Inasmuch as a minimum of two cycles is completed annually on small-investment groups, and as often as monthly on major controls, the amount of these adjustments has been nominal.

Operation of stores records.—As materials and supplies are received in the plant they are identified and placed in stock under specific number. A card is punched for the invoice, indicating purchase order number, stock number, quantity of item received, the main and sub-account number, and the total of the invoice.

These cards are tabulated on a "Stores Materials and Supplies Receipts" sheet, from which the main controls receive their debits for incoming items and the clearing account receives credits for charges made on the general books at San Francisco.

The invoice is recorded on a visible index as a receipt and checked against "on order" items. Disbursements and withdrawals from stores are made by requisition on the stores department, properly signed by foremen authorized to withdraw material from stock. These requisitions are forwarded to the accounting department for a credit to stock records.

The requisitions on stores department are checked for correctness by field men from the department issuing them. After this approval, requisitions are forwarded to the accounting machines where stock control cards are punched in duplicate. Requisitions thus completed are filed according to requisition number.

Duplicate stock control cards make a complete cross index possible; one card is filed according to the stock number, and the other by the account number on which the material has been used. Complete and readily available analyses are thus to be had. From cards filed by stock number one may readily see on what stations or accounts a certain class of material has been used, while those filed by account number readily determine what materials have been charged.

13. PHYSICAL INVENTORIES

Periodic physical stock taking, as a check on existing book records, is essential to good business. A brief description is therefore given of the methods used and the results arrived at in the taking of the physical inventory at the end of 1927.

Physical inventories are taken under the direction of Accounting Department. In a refinery of the magnitude of this one and with a policy of refining for storage pending demand, the taking of physical inventories is a large task, involving the physical count of thousands of tons of sugar, both raw and refined, the latter in a large assortment of grades and packages. The rapidity with which the count has to be made, and the necessity for final reconciliation with the stock records, call for careful planning in advance of stock taking, as well as for uniform methods of piling commodities.

During October 1927 a definite storage plan was adopted, providing for definite standard tier counts. All sugars coming from the refinery were piled in accordance with these plans. All odd piles were broken down and re-piled in accordance with these standards. When a pile was completed and checked, a tag bearing a description of the pile and its total count was attached to its topmost bag. Large piles covering many bays are made up of several standard units as outlined above.

Inventory procedure.—The form of inventory procedure of 1927 was as follows: Four teams of three men each were organized, two from the warehouse and the third from the accounting department. Each team was provided with the necessary forms and storage maps as follows: (1) inventory sheets, for recording counts; (2) floor diagram of each section, indicating bay numbers and letters; (3) reference sheet, showing location and count of tagged piles.

Before starting the count all teams were called together to receive instructions as to methods to be followed and as to the use of the forms. Each team worked its section through each bay, then doubled back through the next bay, and so on. Where piles overlapped, great care was taken to avoid duplicate counts. Each bay was counted individually by each member of the team and the count agreed upon before entry on inventory blanks. One member of the team carried a floor diagram and marked off each bay as its count was taken.

In the case of standard piles, verification of the tag count was made by getting the tier formation. In cases where the outside of a pile could be seen, the tiers were counted and the pile calculated and compared with tag computation. All other sugars, piled or in dumps, were actually counted.

All inventory sheets were numbered prior to stock taking and accounted for upon completion. After the completion of counts all inventory sheets were summarized. A special tabulating card was then perforated for each item, to show inventory sheet number, grade and package, and number of each container. These cards were then checked by clerks (other than those who did the actual punching) to verify the correctness of punching. The cards were sorted by grade and package; they were then passed through the tabulating machine, and a printed statement of the complete inventory was obtained.

The next step was to compare the actual count results with the book count, to determine "overs" and "unders." The books were then adjusted to the net totals of the physical count, upon authority of the Treasurer.

III. THE SALES DIVISION

Sugar is so nearly uniform in quality, regardless of its source of manufacture, that the marketing problem is somewhat different from that involved in the sale of other foodstuffs. As has been said, "sugar is sugar."

It is the custom of refiners to transact their business with their customers through sugar brokers. Rolph states[1] that the sale of sugar by the refiner direct to the consumer has not been found practicable, as an organization complete enough to keep in touch with consumers in every city, town, and village of the country would be top-heavy and too costly to maintain.

The brokers keep in constant touch with jobbers, wholesalers, chain stores, manufacturers, and other large consumers and distributors of sugar. While the brokers are paid by the refiner, their ability to hold the jobbers and other customers depends to some extent upon the brokers' service in buying for their trade.

1. CENTRAL SALES ORGANIZATION

The brokers make delivery contracts with their customers, subject to confirmation as to quantity, terms, and credit by the central selling organization of the Corporation in San Francisco.

The central selling organization is headed by the vice-president in charge of sales, or sales manager. The sales manager has an understudy who acts as his assistant. Under the sales manager are two district managers, one for the Eastern sales territory, and the other for the Western or Coast territory. The present assistant to the sales manager is also the district manager for the Coast. The Coast district has a corps of six men who promote sales by visiting customers and by keeping in general touch

[1] George M. Rolph, *Something about Sugar*, p. 95. San Francisco: John J. Newbegin, Publishers, 1917.

140   THE C & H SUGAR REFINING CORPORATION

with the trade. Under the sales manager there is also a small staff in charge of promotion and publicity.

2. VARIETIES OF PRODUCT

The following varieties of product are offered at the present time:

Fine Standard
Berry
Coarse { Confectioners' "A"
         Confectioners' "AA"
         Confectioners' "AA" Special
Cubes { Cube
        Cubelets
Soft { Extra "C" (Light Brown)
       Golden "C" (Medium Brown)
       Yellow "D" (Dark Brown)
Powdered

3. VOLUME OF SALES

No readily available figures of the company's sales tonnage are to be had prior to 1914. The following table shows the sales tonnage each year since 1914 in terms of a percentage of 1914:

TABLE 16

RELATIVE VOLUME OF SALES, 1914–1927

Year	Percentage of 1914 Tonnage	Year	Percentage of 1914 Tonnage
1914	100.0	1921	155.7
1915	109.4	1922	205.4
1916	134.8	1923	205.0
1917	146.2	1924	232.0
1918	126.4	1925	282.5
1919	157.1	1926	264.5
1920	163.0	1927	291.0

All figures on volume of business given in this study refer to the production of cane sugar, which is the only sugar refined by this company. However, as an accommodation to the trade, the company purchases and sells beet sugar amounting to ten or twelve thousand tons a year.

The volume of sales has constantly increased although during certain years it has declined slightly as compared with the year immediately preceding.

Average tonnage per customer invoice.—The increase in volume of sales since 1923 has been accompanied by a decrease in the number of tons of sugar sold per customer invoice, as follows:

TABLE 17

AVERAGE TONNAGE OF SUGAR PER CUSTOMER INVOICE

Year	Coast	East	Entire Sales Territory
	Tons	Tons	Tons
1923	12.0	14.8	13.3
1924	12.3	11.8	12.0
1925	9.6	9.3	9.4
1926	9.7	9.5	9.6
1927	10.8	7.9	9.0

The table above shows a constantly decreasing average tonnage per invoice, ever since 1923. The average for the entire sales territory has dropped from 13.3 to 9.0, or more than a third. This fact has complicated the sales problem and has brought about an increase in the distribution costs and general office expense.

The change in average tonnage per invoice is accounted for by (1) the general tendency on the part of wholesalers and manufacturers to buy "from hand to mouth," (2) the expansion of the sales territory as a result of increased production and competitive conditions, and (3) the replacement, in the larger markets, of quantity buyers by smaller ones. The number of customers has more than doubled since 1925. Unethical competitive conditions resulted in special secret concessions to large users on the part of competing sugar refiners. One is informed on reliable authority that this Corporation has at no time made any concessions which failed to appear on its printed price lists.

4. SALES TERMS: COAST AND EAST

The sales activity of the company covers thirty-six states. For purposes of sales administration, and because of the differences in marketing conditions, the entire sales territory is divided into two districts, one comprising the West (or Coast) territory and the other the East and South. The Coast territory comprises the eleven western states, the other district being all east of the Rocky Mountains.

The Coast territory is the so-called "natural" market of the company. The company's sugar on the Coast is sold F.O.B. San Francisco, the consumer paying the freight between San Francisco and the ultimate point of destination. Competition with Eastern and Southern sugars makes the sales problem of the Eastern territory more difficult and more costly. In the Eastern territory the company is forced to absorb the difference between the freight rate from Crockett to the destination and the rate from New Orleans or New York, whichever is lower. Sugar for this territory is priced F.O.B. Crockett *plus* a charge equal to the freight to the destination from one of these two Eastern points; but it is actually delivered to the destination *from Crockett* at this price.

In addition to the element of freight absorption, some of the other terms and conditions of sale are different in the Eastern territory from what they are on the Coast. The contract terms run 21 days on the Coast and 30 days in the Eastern territory. In the Eastern sales territory the company guarantees all sugar against drop in price, while in transit up to the ultimate destination point. In no case, however, does this guarantee extend beyond twelve days over normal transit time. The guaranty against price reduction does not extend to the West, except in instances of spot orders withdrawable within seven days.

In all territories, the base price is per 100-lb. bag. Container differentials above or below the base, at so much per 100 lbs., are provided for in accordance with grade and packaging. All terms are 2 per cent off seven days after delivery date, except for Alaska, Guam, and Hawaii, where they are 2 per cent off on date of invoice.

Purchases are expressed in terms of a specific number of 100-lb. units, and in figuring the weight equivalent, all containers (bags, boxes, cases, tins, barrels, and half-barrels) are applied at actual net weight.

Eastern territory sales involve a considerable amount of Eastern warehousing, as Crockett is too far away to permit prompt delivery in this territory. The warehousing within the Eastern territory is done in licensed public storage places. The company may thus switch shipments as needed to any point within the territory, without losing the advantage of the initial hauling rate. This gives an opportunity to regulate Eastern-territory distribution by taking advantage of the diversion privileges at focal points. Local warehousing of the type herein described is known in the sugar industry as "consignment."

Table 18 shows the increase in percentage of total Eastern sales shipped on consignment since 1922.

TABLE 18
SALES ON CONSIGNMENT, 1922–1927

Year	Percentage of Total Eastern Sales	Year	Percentage of Total Eastern Sales
1922	31	1925	68
1923	41	1926	67
1924	50	1927	60

144   THE C & H SUGAR REFINING CORPORATION

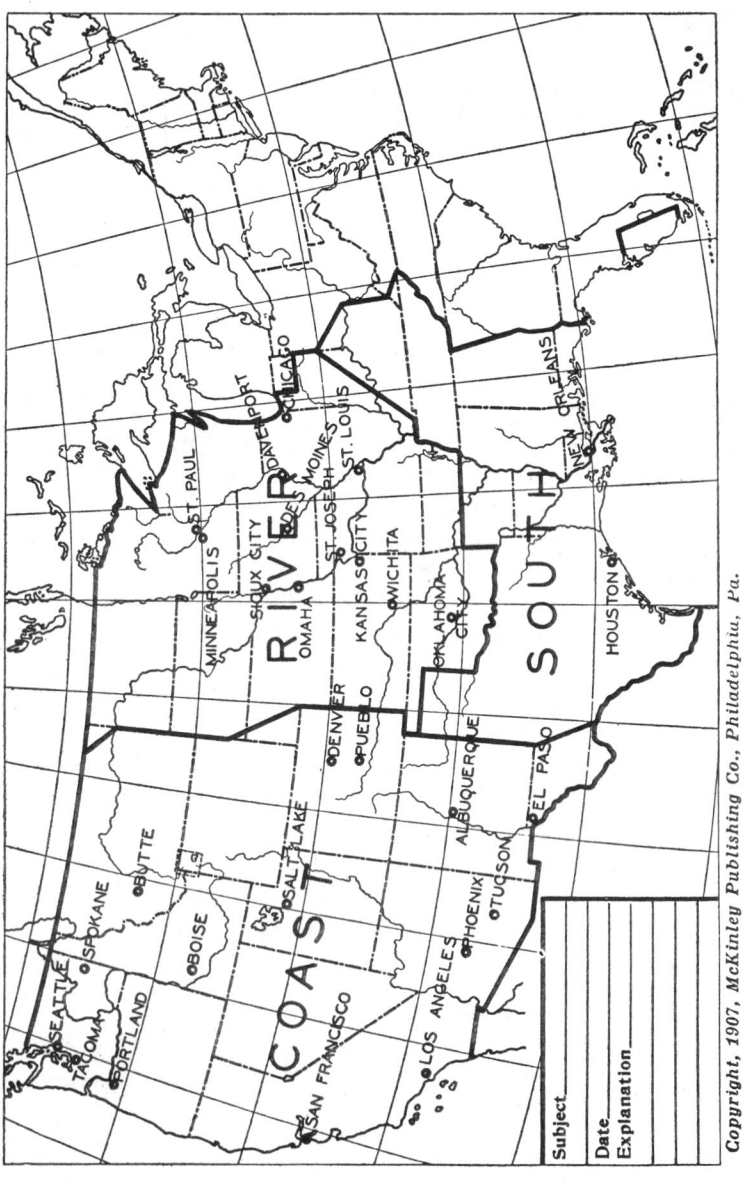

Fig. 7.—Geographical distribution of brokers' offices as shown by the name of the city in which each is located

THE SALES DIVISION

Consignments in the Eastern territory increased from 31 per cent in 1922 to 60 per cent in 1927 (that is, consignments were twice as great in 1927 as in 1922 in relation to total sales). The map on the opposite page (Fig. 7) shows the geographical distribution of brokers' offices handling the company's sugar.

5. GEOGRAPHICAL DISTRIBUTION OF BROKERS' OFFICES

Coast and Eastern direct selling costs.—The following table (Table 19) shows the difference in the average

TABLE 19

COMPARISON OF DIRECT SELLING EXPENSE, COAST AND EAST, 1927

Item	Percentage of Total Coast	Percentage of Total East
Fixed expenses		
Brokers' commission	35.00	13.00
Controllable expenses		
Storage and handling		
Drayage	9.70	.09
Storage—storage allowance	1.24	6.72
Loading	1.52	4.16
Switching	.13	.12
Insurance on storage	.35	.53
Taxes on storage	.42	.16
Total storage and handling	13.36	11.78
Transportation		
Local freight and toll	50.66	
Freight absorption	.49	75.12
Local marine insurance	1.44	
Total transportation	51.59	75.12
Total controllable expense	64.95	86.90
Total direct selling expense	100.00	100.00

direct selling expense, per 100 lbs. of sugar, on the Coast and in the East. The various items entering into the classification of "direct selling expense" are shown for each of the two sales territories in terms of a percentage of the total direct selling expense. In comparing relative costs of various items in the East and West, note should be taken that the total cost in the East is 3.8 times as great as on the Coast.

6. CUSTOMER CLASSIFICATION

The following table (Table 20) gives the classification of sales by types of customer, and shows the relative importance of each group in terms of a percentage of total sales:

TABLE 20

SALES BY TYPES OF CUSTOMER—TOTAL TERRITORY

	Percentage of Total Sales			
	1924	1925	1926	1927
Jobbers and wholesalers	83.51	83.39	82.72	76.63
Chain stores	.01	.44	.72	6.44
Canners and preservers	4.44	4.18	4.62	4.03
Confectionery, ice cream } Soft drinks and syrups	4.45	4.83	5.08	6.81
Bakers and baking supplies	2.63	2.61	2.80	2.93
Miscellaneous	4.96	4.55	4.06	3.16
Total	100.00	100.00	100.00	100.00

The most interesting fact shown in the above tabulation is the increase in proportion of total sales made to chain stores. Up to 1926 chain stores were required to buy their sugar from jobbers, instead of buying direct from brokers. In 1926 the company accorded to the chain stores the privilege heretofore accorded only to wholesalers. For all practical purposes, the chain store *is* a wholesaler. It maintains a warehouse from which it distributes to its various units. Although it has no salesmen in the ordinary sense, it has an overhead control organization which functions toward the retail units in practically the same manner as do the salesmen of the ordinary wholesaler.

In this connection it should be noted that a reduction in the percentage of the total sold to a particular group does not necessarily mean a reduction in the *tonnage* sold, for the reason that the total sales have increased appreciably from year to year. For instance, although the percentage of the total sold to jobbers and wholesalers was less in 1927 than in 1926 (76.63 per cent and 81.59 per cent, respectively) the actual tonnage sold to them was greater in 1927.

The following table (Table 21) shows the customer classification in all territories.

TABLE 21

SALES BY TYPES OF CUSTOMER, IN PERCENTAGES

	1924	1925	1926	1927
Jobbers and wholesalers	82.77	82.56	81.70	75.95
Chain stores	.01	.38	.64	6.96
Canners and preservers	4.81	4.93	5.22	4.61
Confectionery and ice cream, soft drinks, and syrups	5.28	5.57	6.02	6.69
Bakers and baking supplies	2.46	2.39	2.59	2.81
Miscellaneous	4.67	4.17	3.83	2.98
Total	100.00	100.00	100.00	100.00

The tabulation reveals interesting changes in the character of distribution between 1924 and 1927. The total sales to jobbers and wholesalers decreased from 82.77 per cent to 75.95 per cent of the total sales. Sales to chain stores (so negligible in 1923 as not to warrant a separate customer classification) rose in 1927 to a total of 6.96 per cent of all sales. In the Eastern territory the percentage of total sugar sold to jobbers and wholesalers changed but slightly in 1927. Because of greater volume of sales in 1927, the actual tonnage increase in sales to jobbers and wholesalers was considerably greater.

7. SALES BY GRADES OF PRODUCT

During 1927, 56 per cent of the total sales consisted of "fine standard" granulated sugar; "berry" sugar accounted for 29 per cent of total sales, coarse sugars for 5.17 per cent, softs for 4.13 per cent and powdered for 4.05 per cent. The sales of cubes and cubelets were ¾ of 1 per cent of the total sales. Between 1922 and 1927 the proportion of total sales accounted for by powdered sugars more than doubled.

The following table (Table 22) shows the percentage of total sales of each grade or variety of sugar, by years, since 1922:

TABLE 22

SALES BY GRADES OF PRODUCT, TOTAL TERRITORY, IN PERCENTAGES

Grade	1922	1923	1924	1925	1926	1927
Fine Standard	53.21	51.22	50.73	52.90	49.92	56.00
Berry	33.05	35.10	35.16	33.28	35.00	29.90
Coarse (Confectioners' "A," "AA")	6.73	7.16	6.57	6.15	6.12	5.17
Cubes	0.89	0.86	0.87	0.75	0.76	0.75
Soft (Extra "C," Golden "C," Yellow "D")	4.11	3.07	3.64	3.78	4.18	4.13
Powdered	2.01	2.59	3.03	3.14	4.02	4.05
Total	100.00	100.00	100.00	100.00	100.00	100.00

Table 23 shows the grade distribution for all territories, in terms of a percentage of total sales of each grade, for 1927:

TABLE 23

SALES BY GRADES OF PRODUCT—ALL TERRITORIES, 1927, IN PERCENTAGES

Grade	Percentage of All Sales
Fine Standard	43.83
Berry	42.34
Coarse (Confectioners, "A," "AA")	4.89
Cubes	.79
Soft	4.10
Powdered	4.05
Total	100.00

The table above shows that "fine standard" accounted for 43.83 per cent of all sales, and "berry" for 42.34 per cent of sales. "Coarse," "cubes," and "powdered" sugars accounted for between four and five per cent, each, of all sales.

Changes in the proportion of various grades (to total sales) between 1922 and 1927 are shown in Table 24 presented herewith.

TABLE 24

SALES BY GRADES OF PRODUCT, ALL TERRITORIES, PERCENTAGES

Grade	1922	1923	1924	1925	1926	1927
Fine Standard	47.10	48.21	46.64	46.45	45.31	43.83
Berry	39.02	38.16	39.36	39.91	39.85	42.34
Coarse	6.42	6.91	6.30	5.74	5.80	4.89
Cube	.97	.90	.92	.83	.82	.79
Soft	4.24	3.12	3.63	3.79	4.16	4.10
Powdered	2.25	2.70	3.15	3.28	4.06	4.05
Total	100.00	100.00	100.00	100.00	100.00	100.00

Between 1922 and 1927 the proportion of total sold as fine standard has been gradually declining from year to year. From 47.10 per cent in 1922, it declined to 43.83 per cent in 1927. Simultaneously, the volume of berry sugars has gradually increased, from 39.02 per cent in 1922 to 42.34 per cent in 1927. The proportion of total sold as coarse has declined from 6.42 per cent in 1922 to 4.89 per cent in 1927. Soft sugars just about held their own. Powdered sugars have, however, become much more popular. The proportion of powdered sugar sales increased from 2.25 per cent in 1922 to 4.05 per cent in 1927.

8. INCREASES IN "SPECIALTY" SALES

The proportion of the total sugar sold in straight 100-lb. bags has been on the decrease of late. The proportion sold in various assortments of grades and packages has been increasing rapidly. The statistical department of the company estimates the average number of various grade items per invoice at the present time to be at least five.

The following summary shows percentage increases over 1922, according to the several packages and grades:

PERCENTAGE INCREASE IN 1927 OVER 1922

Solid pack 100
Boxes, all grades 44
Bales, "Fine Standard" and "Berry"... 224
Cartons 810*

* Over 1923.

9. SALES FORECASTS AND BUDGETS

Inasmuch as the company refines all the raw cane sugar that may be shipped to it by the planters, the first problem to be determined is how much sugar will be available for sale within the year. After this, each broker is assigned a quota, and as brokers are segregated by geographic groups, totals for these groups are thereby obtained. The brokers are classified into three main classes, the Coast group, the River group, and the Southern group. An estimate is then made of the quantity of each grade which will go to make up the total to be shipped to each of these groups. The estimates for the three groups are combined to determine what tonnage of each grade will be sold and its percentage in terms of the total of sales.

After the annual estimates are prepared, monthly sales forecasts for each grade and package are made. This is necessary because the grades are affected by different seasonal influences. So far as possible, the production budget is calculated on the annual grade percentages, despite this seasonal influence, in order that a uniform rate of production may be maintained. Some variations are necessary, however, because the proper balance of the inventory is of major importance.

At the first of each month a revised sales estimate is prepared for each grade and package. This estimate is checked with the production budget and stocks on hand, and if conditions have so changed that stocks will not be available to meet sales requirements, revisions are made.

At the close of each quarter, sales are analyzed and compared with past indices to determine whether revisions in the annual grade and package ratios will be necessary. Irregular fluctuations in consumption from month to month are encountered, but these tend to equalize over the longer periods of time such as three, six, or nine months, necessitating only slight revisions, if any, in the ratios.

The first sales budget period of the year covers the months of December, January, February, and March. The following table (Table 25, p. 152) shows percentages of the annual quota actually sold in each territory between December 1, 1927, and March 31, 1928.

The column of Table 25 above entitled "Percentage in 1928" denotes the percentage of the total annual sales budget sold during this four-month period of the present season. The meaning of the figures in this column becomes more readily apparent when the figures shown in the other column, entitled "10-year Average," are inspected. This column refers to the ten-year average of the per cent (of the total for each year) sold during the first four months.

TABLE 25

PERCENTAGE OF QUOTA ACTUALLY DELIVERED IN EACH TERRITORY

December to March

Territory	Percentage in 1928	Percentage for 10-Year Average
Coast	31.2	25
River	29.4	25
South	42.7	..
Total Eastern (River and South)	31.5	25
Grand Total	31.5	25

The table shows that during the first four months of the current fiscal year, 31.2 per cent of the annual budget for the Coast and 31.5 per cent of total annual budget for the East were sold. The grand total of both territories shows sales amounting to 31.5 per cent of the budget for the year, as compared with 25 per cent, which was the average for the preceding ten years, for this four-month period.

10. MARKETING OF MOLASSES

A department was organized in April, 1925, with the object of centralizing the sale or distribution of molasses produced by the island plantations as well as molasses produced at the refinery at Crockett. This department has sold, since 1923, an average of about 82,000 tons of molasses per annum.

The trade name for the molasses produced in the Islands is Hawaiian Plantation Feed Molasses. It is used in the manufacture of alcohol and in the preparation of feeds for beef cattle, dairy cattle, sheep, hogs, and poultry. The molasses produced at the refinery is known to the trade as Blackstrap Molasses. It is of a higher commercial value than the Island Molasses and used primarily in the manufacture of alcohol.

The Hawaiian molasses is marketed by the company for the account of the plantations. The proceeds of the sales of the refinery molasses are credited to the refinery.

11. ADVERTISING

Brands.—A part of the refinery output has been standardized into various brands and special packages, such as the one-pound packages of powdered, dessert, and brown sugar. These cartons are prepared in an attractive manner and labeled "C. & H. Pure Cane Sugar," to carry the "C. & H. message into the kitchens of the housewives."

"Something about Sugar."—For several years the company has been confronted with the necessity of answering inquiries from school children and other persons interested in sugar-refining processes. For this reason the company in 1921 published an illustrated booklet called "Something about Sugar," describing the processes of manufacture of sugar at Crockett. The booklet aroused a good deal of interest throughout the country, and has gone through many editions. It is given wide distribution through the territory in which the company does business. The management has been successful in its efforts to place this booklet in many of the public schools.

"Personality" advertising.—The company has men on the road throughout the year in the Pacific Coast territory. These salesmen do not sell a pound of sugar; their sole duty is to visit the retail dealers and familiarize them with C. & H. sugar and service. They introduce brands, adjust complaints, and do anything which in their judgment is necessary to popularize the product with the middleman.

Plant visitors.—Many visitors are received at the refinery in the course of each year. Any person above grammar school age may go through the plant, accompanied by a guide. These guides are competent, and capable of answering a layman's questions about refinery process. More highly technical men are assigned to guide visiting sugar technologists, brokers, and special guests. The immaculate cleanliness and orderliness of the huge plant make a fine impression. On the average about four thousand visitors inspect the refinery in the course of a year.

Motion pictures.—The Corporation has prepared a four-reel motion picture which illustrates the growing and milling of cane sugar in the Hawaiian Islands, the transporting of the raw sugar to the mainland, and the refining, packing, storage, and shipping processes at Crockett. The picture also gives a view of the community development work in Crockett. The showing of the picture is accompanied, as a rule, by a lecture given by the chief guide of the company. Twenty copies of the film are in the hands of the United States Bureau of Foreign and Domestic Commerce in Washington. These films are shown throughout the United States to thousands of people annually.

The question of direct advertising is discussed frequently in the councils of the company. Since considerable amounts of the sugar are now put up in distinctive packages, the possibilities of special C. & H. brands become apparent. After all, from a merchandising angle, sugar is not "just sugar." Although the chemical purity may be the same, the uniformity of the product is not always constant in all refineries. The question of reliable and continuous service to the customer is of great importance. Few refiners, it is said, have had as consistent a record of service performance and uniformity of product as the C. & H. Corporation. Again, the name of the company contains two magic words—California and Hawaii.

THE SALES DIVISION

This psychological advantage, though perhaps of minor importance, should also be considered in discussing the value of direct advertising.

12. SEASONALITY OF DEMAND FOR SUGAR

In this section of this study an attempt is made to reveal the seasonality of the demand for sugar. The basic information consists of monthly tonnages of sales for a period of six years, 1922-1927. Before proceeding farther, however, a description should be given of the methods used in computing the seasonal index.

Method used to show seasonality of sales.—The most satisfactory arithmetical process for determining seasonal variation is the median-link-relative method. In this method of computation the first operation consists of computing, from the actual data, the so-called link relative for each month. The actual figure of each month is expressed as a percentage of the month immediately preceding. In this instance, the link relatives show the manner in which tonnage sales vary from month to month throughout the six-year period under examination. They show, for instance, how each of the six Novembers is related to the preceding Octobers. These link relatives appear in Table 26 (p. 156).

In order to find the seasonal index it is necessary to ascertain how, for instance, November is related to October, on the average, throughout the six years under scrutiny, and similarly how, on the average, each of the other eleven months is related to the preceding month of the year. Many averages could be used in this connection. The important point, however, is that the six relatives, December divided by November, constitute a series. The appropriateness of the average to be used, in this instance, depends upon the form of distribution: questions of dispersion and skewness have therefore to be considered. To exhibit the essential features of the twelve

TABLE 26
LINK-RELATIVES FOR MONTHLY TONNAGES OF SALES, 1922–1927

Year	Dec.	Jan.	Feb.	Mar.	Apr.	May	June	July	Aug.	Sept.	Oct.	Nov.
1922..	...	158	75	113	88	115	188	87	61	86	154	43
1923..	120	87	241	52	167	104	30	341	90	186	41	90
1924..	62	174	109	110	101	102	248	53	103	103	66	106
1925..	84	105	154	137	46	142	185	106	110	77	107	121
1926..	42	120	121	98	152	109	70	128	98	107	81	68
1927..	110	76	123	98	206	94	89	102	121	99	66	98
1927..	95	...	...	...	...	...	...	...	...	...	...	...

distributions, one for each month, a frequency distribution of the six relatives should be made for each month. To facilitate comparisons between successive months, the twelve frequency series should be arranged in adjacent columns, according to a single scale of class intervals. The class interval is usually taken as 1 per cent and the centers of intervals as integers. The range of the per cent scale is determined by the high and low relatives of Table 27, with the understanding that a small number of the relatives for any one month may fall in the "over" and "under" group. The twelve frequency series arranged in this way form the Multiple Frequency Distribution presented herewith:

TABLE 27
MULTIPLE FREQUENCY DISTRIBUTION OF LINK-RELATIVES OF MONTHLY TONNAGE OF SALES

Link Relative	Jan. Dec.	Feb. Jan.	Mar. Feb.	Apr. Mar.	May Apr.	June May	July June	Aug. July	Sept. Aug.	Oct. Sept.	Nov. Oct.	Dec. Nov.
Over												
190		1		1		1	1					
188						1						

THE SALES DIVISION

TABLE 27 (*Continued*)

Link Relative	Jan. / Dec.	Feb. / Jan.	Mar. / Feb.	Apr. / Mar.	May / Apr.	June / May	July / June	Aug. / July	Sept. / Aug.	Oct. / Sept.	Nov. / Oct.	Dec. / Nov.
186					1				1			
184												
182												
180												
178												
176												
174	1											
172												
170												
168				1								
166												
164												
162												
160												
158	1											
156												
154		1								1		
152				1								
150												
148												
146												
144												
142					1							
140												
138			1									
136												

TABLE 27 (*Continued*)

Link Relative	Jan. / Dec.	Feb. / Jan.	Mar. / Feb.	Apr. / Mar.	May / Apr.	June / May	July / June	Aug. / July	Sept. / Aug.	Oct. / Sept.	Nov. / Oct.	Dec. / Nov.
134												
132												
130												
128							1					
126												
124		1										
122		1						1			1	
120	1											1
118												
116					1							
114			1									
112												
110		1	1		1			1				1
108									1	1		
106	1						1				1	
104					1			1	1			
102				1	1		1					
100									1			
98			2					1			1	
96												1
94					1							
92												
90						1		1			1	
88	1			1			1					
86									1			
84												1

TABLE 27 (Concluded)

Link Relative	Jan. / Dec.	Feb. / Jan.	Mar. / Feb.	Apr. / Mar.	May / Apr.	June / May	July / June	Aug. / July	Sept. / Aug.	Oct. / Sept.	Nov. / Oct.	Dec. / Nov.
82									1			
80												
Under 78	1	1	1	1		2	1	1	1	3	2	2

This table shows how, in each column, the items for a particular month are distributed, and therefore indicates how typical a particular average is for the series of that column. The *closeness of cluster* of the scores within each column is of chief importance in this connection.

A second important feature of the distribution is the *deviation from normal,* for each of the twelve months. By inspection of the table, it may be seen whether the group of scores for a particular month tends, on the whole, to lie above or below 100 per cent, and roughly, how great the deviation from 100 per cent is. The importance of this consideration is apparent; as these are link-relatives, the tendency for the entire group of links, for a particular month (say May) to lie above 100 per cent must reflect the fact that such a month is seasonally above the preceding month (April).

The next step is to arrive at an estimate of the *displacement* between adjacent columns. Because the scores represent link relatives, the displacement (difference in level of the groups each considered as a whole) indicates approximately the rate of change in the seasonal movement. The direction and amount of displacement between pairs of adjacent months indicate, then, the changes in direction or the rate of seasonal shift.

These attributes—closeness of cluster, deviation from normal, and displacement—must be considered simultaneously in examining the multiple-frequency table. The object is to determine whether a seasonal movement exists and can be measured precisely. A seasonal variation may be presumed to exist if there is a clear deviation from the normal for some or all of the months. Whether it is measurable depends upon the structure of the table as a whole. If the cluster is very close, determination is precise, even if deviations from normal are not very large. If deviations from normal are large, good precision is attained, even if the cluster is not very close. If the cluster is not close, and deviations from normal are inconsiderable, measurement cannot be precise.

In this connection, it seemed warrantable to assume the existence of measurable seasonal variations. To get the relation which holds, on the average, between November and October, some summary of individual ratios was necessary. The arithmetic mean (or average) was considered objectionable because the frequency series was of the type in which the mean was subject to considerable discrepancy. The median was therefore taken.

An Adjusted Index of Seasonality was then computed as the final step. Table 28 and its accompanying text show the mathematical procedure resorted to in computing the adjusted index.

Each median gives the average percentage relation of a particular month to the month preceding for the whole six-year period. Hence the twelve medians present a picture of the average seasonal movement. The fact, however, that this presentation involves a comparison of each month with that immediately preceding is a serious practical obstacle to the use of this picture in the actual study of seasonal fluctuations. It is therefore desirable to derive from the twelve medians a new set of twelve numbers which will indicate the relation between production in each month and the normal for the year. This new set of numbers is the final adjusted index of seasonal variation.

The several columns in the table indicate the steps

taken in deriving the adjusted index from the medians. The second column presents the logarithms of the twelve individual medians. This conversion to logarithms is used merely as a convenient device for multiplying the medians together successively. If there were no elements of

TABLE 28

COMPUTATION OF ADJUSTED INDEX SHOWING SEASONALITY OF SALES FOR COMBINED YEARS OF 1922–1927

Month	Median	Logarithm	Corrected Logarithm	Cumulative Corrected Logarithm	Anti-logarithm	Index, Percentage
	(1)	(2)	(3)	(4)	(5)	(6)
Jan. ...	1.125	.05115	.03153	.03153	1.075	72
Feb. ...	1.220	.08636	.06674	.09827	1.254	84
March ..	1.040	.01703	9.99741	.09568	1.247	84
April ...	1.265	.10209	.08247	.17815	1.507	101
May ...	1.065	.02735	.00773	.18588	1.534	103
June ...	1.370	.13672	.11710	.30298	2.009	135
July ...	1.040	.01703	9.99741	.30039	1.997	134
Aug. ...	1.005	.00217	9.98255	.28294	1.918	129
Sept. ...	1.010	.00432	9.98470	.26764	1.852	124
Oct. ...	0.735	9.86629	9.84667	.11431	1.301	87
Nov. ...	0.940	9.97313	9.95351	.06782	1.169	79
Dec. ...	0.895	9.95182	9.93220	.00002	1.000	67
		.23546	.00002		17.863	
Monthly correction .01962			Average for year ... 1.489			

error in the medians the total of the twelve logarithms should be zero. The fact that this total does not come out to zero implies an error, and one-twelfth of this error is assigned to each month.

The items of column 3 are obtained from those in column 2 by deducting the monthly error. In column 4 the items of column 3 are cumulated or added successively. By a principle of logarithms this is equivalent to multiplying the medians together cumulatively. The items of column 5 are the numbers whose logarithms are the corresponding items of column 4. If the items of column 5 totaled exactly to 12 the adjustment would be complete.

162 THE C & H SUGAR REFINING CORPORATION

The fact that they do not total to 12, and have an average different from 1 involves an additional and final step to yield the result of column 6 (plotted in Fig. 8 to show the seasonality). Each item in column 6 is obtained by dividing the corresponding item of column 5 by the average of all the items in column 5. In accordance with custom these results in column 6 are stated in percentage rather than in decimal form. This is not, however, an essential element in the method of adjustment.

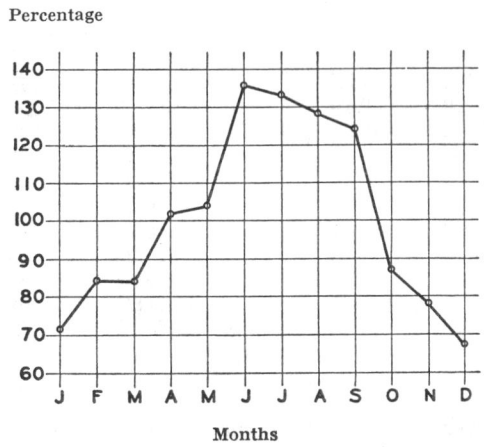

Fig. 8.—Graph showing seasonality of demand for sugar based upon actual monthly sales tonnages, 1922–27. Computed by Link-Relative Method

The seasonal distribution of demand for sugar is very obvious from an inspection of the chart. Each individual year has, of course, its minor variations. These variations do not relate as much to the general trend, as to the specific point of a year when the curve begins to swing up or down. The upward swing in 1927, for instance, was slightly earlier than that shown on the chart. Aside from minor variations of the type mentioned, the graph represents correctly the seasonal movement of sales.

IV. THE FINANCE AND ACCOUNTING DIVISION

1. ORGANIZATION OF DIVISION

As stated in an earlier part of this study in connection with a description of the general character of the business organization, the Finance and Accounting Division is one of three major divisions of the business, under the direction of one of the Vice-Presidents, who is also the Secretary and Treasurer of the Corporation.

The chart (Fig. 9) on the following page shows graphically the detailed organization of this Division.

The principal assistant of the Vice-President in charge of Finance and Accounting is known as the Assistant to the Treasurer.

The main departments of the Division concern themselves with finance, records and accounting, and purchases and stores. In addition to these, there are an insurance and tax department, an auditing department, a traffic department and a department of commercial and statistical research. The functions and operations of the principal departments and functions of the Finance and Accounting Division will be discussed in the following pages.

Records and accounts.—The functions of record-keeping and accounting have been divided between the general office and the refinery. All of the general accounting and the making of financial statements covering sales, finance, production costs, and expenses are centered in the general office. As the refinery is situated some thirty miles from San Francisco it is impractical to centralize in the general office all subsidiary records of refinery costs, payrolls, material distributions, and production.

The general office is under the direct supervision of an office manager, who reports to the Treasurer. The refinery office is in charge of an office manager responsible to the assistant to the Treasurer.

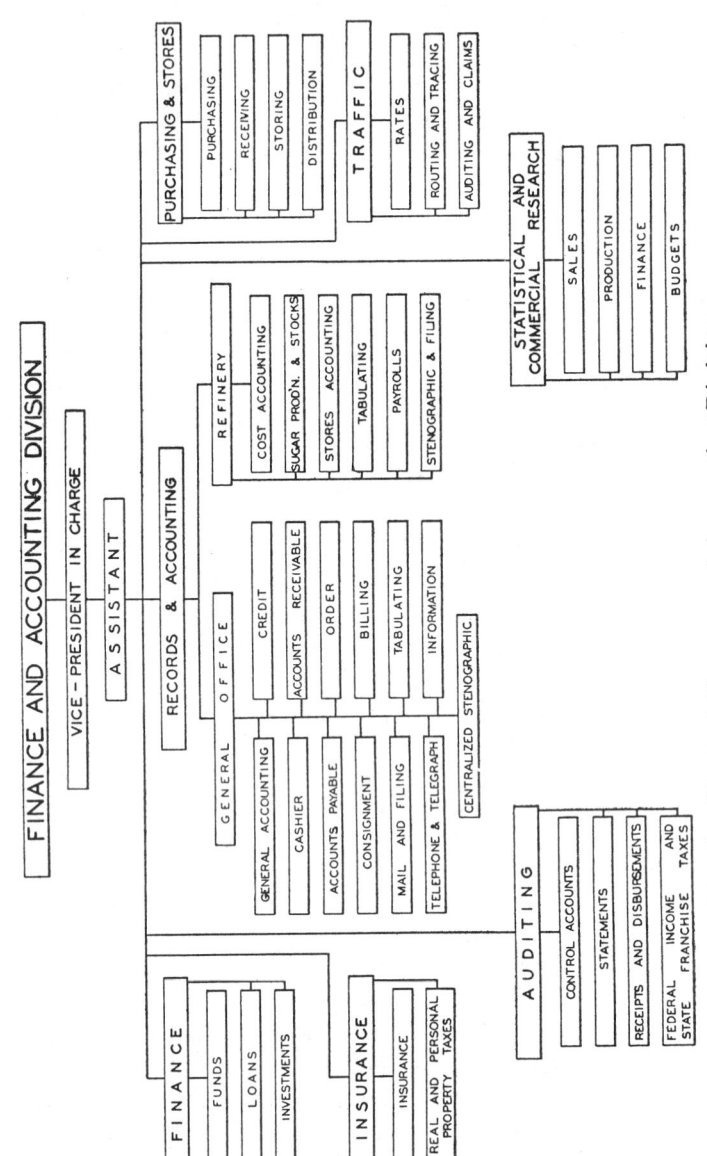

Fig. 9.—Chart of Finance and Accounting Division

The division of each office into departments has been developed along natural lines to form logically functioning units. Most of these units or subdivisions are in charge of minor executives or department heads responsible to the office manager. While the duties of each department are more or less clearly defined, no department is entirely independent. In fact, the effective functioning of each unit requires close co-operation with the others.

2. FINANCIAL OPERATIONS AND ACCOUNTING RATIOS

There is little general corporate financing at present, with the exception of the financial operation incidental to the annual retirement of $700,000 of the outstanding bond issue, through a special sinking fund. The principal day-to-day financial operations are therefore confined to the profitable placement of surplus funds during certain seasons of the year, and to short-time borrowings during others.

The seasonality of raw-sugar receipts from the Islands and the seasonality of the demand for sugar on the mainland cause corresponding fluctuations in the amount of available funds. The peaks of the sales season bring forth large accumulations of money not necessarily payable to the planters until December 15. These temporary funds (which run frequently into several millions) are made interest-bearing. The practice of the company is to place such funds on call in New York City. The surplus funds are frequently used also for the payment for raw sugar cargoes in advance of the "10 day after arrival" date specified in the contract with the planters. Such advance payments naturally earn discounts.

During periods of the year when the accumulations of refined sugar are great because of dullness in demand, the company finds it necessary to borrow money for short terms. The custom is to borrow such funds in San Francisco, if the time of the loan is to be 30 days or under, and in New York and Chicago when money is needed for longer periods. These borrowings are made on the basis of the annual and special financial statements of the company.

Forecasts of loans and borrowings are made bimonthly to provide the necessary minimum of time for the making of arrangements.

Accounting ratios.—The balance sheet and the income statement are the final measurements of business success. The facts given in these statements, however, mean little until their inter-relationship is established, for this relationship is the correct measurement of business efficiency. Actual amounts of inventories, plant investment, and current liabilities may be interesting, but the more important facts to know are the relations of these amounts to the turnover of inventories, the turnover of plant investment, and the amount of current assets, respectively.

In every branch of business or industry, certain accounting ratios are more or less normal or characteristic. Such ratios are computed by the majority of well-managed business institutions. Thus it is frequently possible to compare one firm's business ratios with those of others. Such comparisons represent an effective check on financial, operating, and distribution efficiency.

Ratios, though valuable, are not always absolutely reliable, because of constantly occurring new developments in business — changes in methods of production and distribution, improvements in operating processes, changes in character and quality of products, etc. Accounting or business ratios are dynamic in character and should be so considered.

Table 29 shows the accounting ratios for this company.

The real meaning of the ratios shown in the table cannot be had without taking into consideration the business conditions which brought about changes in them.

ACCOUNTING RATIOS

Item		Ratio	December 31, 1922	1923	1924	1925	1926	1927
1	*Current and Working Assets* To Current Liabilities (plus Liability to Producers)	Times	2.61	3.25	2.44	3.21	3.17	3.47
2	*Current and Working Assets* To Current Liabilities (excluding Liability to Producers)	Times	2.61	11.54	17.48	14.58	10.08	14.92
3	*Quick Assets* (Cash Accounts and Notes Receivable) To Quick Liabilities (Accounts and Notes Payable)	Times	1.11	4.78	7.21	8.87	3.87	4.48
4	Cash	Per cent	15.4	11.4	12.4	14.9	7.0	9.2
	Accounts, Notes, and Loans Receivable	Per cent	27.2	30.0	29.1	45.9	31.4	20.8
	Inventories—Raw	Per cent	15.2	9.5	3.2	0.2	0.3	0.3
	Inventories—Refined	Per cent	34.8	40.1	50.2	32.5	57.3	64.0
	Stores Other	Per cent	7.4	9.0	5.1	6.5	4.0	5.7
	To Current Assets	(Total)	100.0	100.0	100.0	100.0	100.0	100.0
5	*Capital Employed* (Stock, Surplus, and Bonds)	(Total)	100.0	100.0	100.0	100.0	100.0	100.0
	To Working Capital	Per cent	26.7	31.9	36.2	38.3	42.6	40.2
	To Fixed and Other Capital	Per cent	73.3	68.1	63.8	61.7	57.4	59.8
6	*Capital Employed*	(Total)	100.0	100.0	100.0	100.0	100.0	100.0
	To Borrowed—Bonds	Per cent	33.5	31.3	29.5	27.7	26.9	28.3
	To Stockholders—Preferred	Per cent	12.0	11.2	10.5	9.9	9.6	....
	To Stockholders—Common	Per cent	54.5	57.5	60.0	62.4	63.5	71.7
7	*Capital Turnover*—Sales of Refined Sugar (To Capital Employed)	Times	....	3.01	2.90	2.57	2.18	2.71
8	*Capital Employed*—per ton of sales	(Dollars)	....	$52.70	$49.80	$43.70	$49.50	$43.66

Because of the co-operative character of this organization, the acreage of cane sugar under cultivation, the actual crop, and weather and rainfall conditions affecting the grinding season and the yield, are factors reflected in inventories and manufacturing schedules. In the refined sugar market, many marketing factors are to be noted which affect the ratios of inventory; prices obtained must be considered in interpreting sales volume with capital employed, etc. Changes in methods of manufacture may effect changes in the fixed investment ratios.

The good financial standing of the company is shown in Item 1, which exhibits a ratio of current and working assets to current liabilities in excess of three-to-one for all years except 1922 and 1924. The year 1922 still showed the effects of the adjustment in the industry made necessary by the post-war deflation of sugar prices and the marketing of large stocks. The quick post-war recovery of this company is shown clearly in the ratio of 3.25 attained by the end of the fiscal year of 1923. A year later this ratio had dropped to 2.44. The reason for this was the unusually large liability to the producers. The year 1924 saw declining prices in the sugar market, calling for careful financing of inventories. Also the total deliveries of raw sugar for this year increased 31.5 per cent over the previous year. The result was a decrease in advance payments to the producers throughout the year. During 1923 the company advanced to the producers 87 per cent of the total value of raw sugar delivered, against only 77 per cent in 1924. These three factors account for the increase in the current liabilities. Reference to Item 2, which excludes the liability to the producers, substantiates the above generalization by showing a ratio of 17.48 in 1924.

As indicated in another section of this report, the liability to the producers is incurred under the co-operative agreement, whereby the company pays 75 per cent of the cost of the raw sugar upon receipt, the balance of 25 per cent being withheld until the results from the year's operating have been determined. This figure, in effect, is merely a book liability or a method of financing under a co-operative plan. The reason for the identity of the ratios under Items 1 and 2 on December 31, 1922, is that this liability to producers is fully discharged (in accordance with the agreement) as of December 15 of each year, and therefore does not appear in the balance sheet as of December 31.

Under Item 2 for 1926 is shown a ratio of 10.08. This is accounted for by dividends declared but not yet paid.

Under Item 3, the ratio of quick assets to quick liabilities ranges from 3.87 in 1926 to 8.87 in 1925. This variation is brought about by the elimination of raw and refined sugar inventory values and the liability to producers.

Reference to Item 4, which represents an analysis of the current assets, will show that while the proportion represented by cash plus accounts receivable was 38.4 per cent in 1926 and 60.8 per cent in 1925; a reverse condition for the same years is shown by the proportion represented by inventories; namely, 57.6 per cent in 1926 and 32.7 per cent in 1925.

Item 5 exhibits a healthy change in the capital employed—an increase in the percentage applied as working capital from 26.7 per cent in 1922 to 40.2 per cent in 1927, with a corresponding reduction in the ratio of the fixed investment.

The major change in Item 6, the analysis of capital employed, is due to the retirement in 1927 of the total preferred stock issue, a step made possible by the marked improvement in the available working capital. The effect of retiring this stock has been to reduce the percentage of working capital to total capital employed only 2.4 per cent, as shown in Item 5.

The price obtained for refined sugars in the different years has more of an effect than any other factor on capital turnover, Item 7. This is borne out by reference to Item 8, which gives the capital employed per ton of sugar sold, showing a decrease from $52.70 in 1923 to $43.66 in 1927. The only exception to this decrease occurred in 1926, the only year in the series that showed a decline in sales over the previous year. The year of 1926 showed a relatively low yield per hundred pounds of sugar sold.

The significance of the annual changes shown under Items 7 and 8 are discussed, in somewhat greater detail under the heading "Productivity of Capital," on page 232.

3. BUDGETING

Budgeting is a necessary function of modern management, and consists of systematic forecasting or planning applied to the conduct of a business, both from the point of view of fundamental financial policies and from that of current operating control. The time to plan control is in advance of actual operation. It is only when standards are carefully stated and definite relationships are established that a real basis for budget forecasting may be had.

Naturally enough, the budgeting done by this company originated largely in the finance-accounting division. This division also worked out the budgeting procedure, and methods to be used to correlate estimated budgets with actual expenditures. As stated elsewhere in this study, in connection with an analysis of the actual workings of the several budgets, this division furnishes all data necessary for the preparation of the budgets, and keeps the various executives who actually spend the allotted amounts, constantly informed of the relation between the budget and their actual expenditures.

The company first started to develop a system of budget forecasting during 1924, to be effective for the 1925 crop. The budgeting activities are still in the developmental stage, although much has already been accomplished. Budgeting was found of greatest worth as an aid in obtaining a careful appraisal of operations, and is of great assistance to the various department heads because of the extensive analyses of their own departments required in the preparation of the departmental budget.

Some of the principal advantages which budgetary control has achieved are:

1. There is co-ordination in all branches of the operating requirements. This co-ordination has reduced materially the investment in stores and supplies. The creation of a steady flow of materials to operating units has eliminated costly delays and disruptions in operating schedules.

2. Everyone "has a definite goal to shoot at." Labor requirements have been kept at a minimum, with an aim toward increased production and reduction in unit costs.

3. Product, operations, and equipment are being standardized.

4. Reduction of waste is encouraged by the maintenance of better balanced inventories of required stocks and containers (grades and packages) in close approximation to sales requirements.

5. Costs have been reduced through study and analysis incidental to the formulation of cost budgets, and through the follow-up necessitated by a comparison of actual expenditures with estimated budgets.

6. Budgets serve at all times as a reminder to compare actual performance with promise and standards, showing not only what may be done, but also what should be done.

The start was made in budgeting the costs of labor and of materials for the refinery. To prepare such budgets properly, a definite production program was necessary. It was imperative to plan and develop a more or less uniform rate of melt (production schedule) together with uniform rates of production of the several grades and packages. The budgeting idea was gradually extended until today there are in operation budgets for almost every field of activity in the company's business.

The detailed workings of the various budgets are shown in this study under the description of the operations of the divisions and departments to which each budget pertains.

4. GENERAL ACCOUNTING

This department compiles all accounts, records, and reports which are used by the general management in the conduct of the business. It keeps a general ledger comprising the controlling accounts of current assets, fixed assets, other assets, current liabilities, capital and surplus accounts, trading accounts, and operating expense accounts.

A subsidiary ledger is maintained to carry the detail accounts supporting and controlled by the general ledger. These subsidiary ledgers carry the controlling accounts for all subdivisions subsidiary to the general accounts, such as: cash or bank balances; accounts receivable; inventories of refined and raw sugar, stores and supplies; fixed assets (plant ledger); accounts payable and refinery clearing accounts.

Posting data, which come to this department in the form of summarized reports for a period, originate in the subdepartments from records of original entry controlling a detail function, as per the following examples:

1. Sales—expressed in pounds and dollars, from the tabulating department.
2. Distribution of audited invoices and record of cash disbursed, from "accounts payable."
3. Cash collections and their allocation to controls, from the cashier.
4. Detail of all expenditures at the refinery—costs, expenses, maintenance, betterments, additions, etc., from the refinery office.

This department is responsible for the preparation of all daily, weekly, monthly, and annual statements and reports. It has control and supervision over all subsidiary reports emanating from the subdepartments.

Complete files of all statements are kept in San Francisco; one working and reference set is kept in the vaults of the general office and one set in a local bank safety deposit vault, for protection against loss from fire or other sources. These statements are filed in binders with division tabs for each month.

5. ORDER DEPARTMENT

Copies of customer's orders reach this department from the sales department, in the form of telegrams, letters, and order blanks. Shipping orders for the most part merely contain shipping specifications for previously entered bookings or contracts.

Orders not covered by contract bookings are termed "new business." The work of this department requires close co-operation with the sales division and the traffic department. The personnel of the order department must have accurate knowledge of daily stocks of sugars available, terms of sale, and contract applications.

As the contract application of orders is an important function, it will be outlined before the order routine is described. With a change in price, customers book through their brokers their anticipated requirements on signed contracts. These contracts are forwarded to the sales division, which in turn dispatches them to the order department. Contract forms are placed in the contract ledgers, and the totals entered in the ledger controls. Shipping orders for these contracts, when received, are reduced to the 100-lb. bag equivalent, credited to the contract, and the remaining balance is extended. A daily statement is prepared showing, by brokers, the net obligations for future delivery on all contracts. This statement shows further the position of the sales division with reference to available sugars for sale, i. e., from the total sugars on hand is deducted the total of obligations, or the balance due on contracts. The remainder on hand is available for sale.

Orders when received are first checked for specifications, given an order number, and then passed to the contract clerk for entry, and thence to the traffic department for routing. Orders for shipment from the refinery at Crockett are relayed over the company's own leased wire to the refinery warehouse. Orders for delivery from local stocks are telephoned. Customer's orders are at this point transcribed on to the regular shipping-order form and placed in the tracing file, to await shipment and receipt of copies of order and shipping papers. This procedure may seem reversed, in that regular forms are not made out until after complete dispatch of the customers' order to the warehouses. The method, however, saves much valuable time.

Upon receipt from the warehouse copies of shipping orders and documents are checked with tracer copies, tracers are filed, and orders, with shipping documents attached, are forwarded to the billing department for invoicing.

6. CREDIT DEPARTMENT

This department has the responsibility of placing proper credit ratings and limits on purchases of customers, and the enforcement of collections in accordance with the terms of sale. Customers' orders and contracts are approved for credit before shipment of goods. A close follow-up of customers' accounts is kept to see that payments are made within the time of the terms of sale. This work calls for daily reviews of customers' accounts.

These reviews make it necessary for the credit department to work in close co-operation with the personnel of the accounts-receivable section in order to make the proper application of discounts adjustments, and to prepare customers' statements.

The department maintains close contacts with the sales department and the offices of the brokers. Advice is given regarding customers' financial ratings and information is exchanged on other matters affecting the relaship between the company and its customers.

The credit department maintains complete credit files of customers and prospective buyers. Three sets of credit files containing essential credit data are kept. One set is arranged geographically, another alphabetically, and a third by type of customer's business. The credit records contain rating reports (Dunn and Bradstreet), brokers' comment forms, financial statements and the analysis thereof, trade reports, collection letters, statements, etc. By constant follow-up these files are kept up to date on all data affecting the buyer's credit status.

The extent of losses on account of bad debts between 1922 and 1927 was 1/54 of 1 per cent.

7. BILLING

Copies of shipping orders, covering shipments from the refinery at Crockett and from stocks maintained in San Francisco, come to this department with shipping documents attached, after being checked for specifications in the order department. The orders are priced, and then passed to machine operators for invoicing. Direct automatic extensions of weights and amounts, together with additions, are made on the customer's invoices, the total weights and amount of all invoicing being carried by the machines. These totals are used as the pre-determined totals controlling the tabulating and accounts receivable departments.

After the machine operation, the shipping-order form itself is passed to a comptometer operator for the making of extensions. Before customers' invoices are mailed they are compared in detail with the completed shipping orders. This dual operation forms an effective check against errors in invoices.

The demands of the trade vary in respect to data desired on invoices and the number of copies required. There is therefore installed for quick reference a visible card index setting forth each customer's invoicing specifications.

Sixty-five per cent of all sugars sold in the Middle West and Southern territories are delivered from warehouse stocks. All such sugars are invoiced by the brokers' offices throughout the territory. It is the function of this department to audit this billing for terms, price, grade and package differentials, freight absorptions, extensions, and additions, before it is passed to the tabulating and accounts receivable departments. A predetermined total controlling the latter is made on an adding machine, both for weights and for amounts.

8. ACCOUNTS RECEIVABLE

This section keeps the ledgers containing detailed accounts with all customers, and is controlled by the general ledger. The work consists principally of posting invoices, credit memoranda, and cash, and of writing statements. The section co-operates closely with the credit department, which handles collections. Both this and the credit department are under the direction of the credit manager.

Invoices are received from the billing department, and segregated as to ledgers for posting to customers' accounts. While posting to the detail accounts is in process, a register or proof sheet of debits is compiled. The register must balance with predetermined totals compiled in the billing department.

Cash collections are checked by this department for correct applications and discounts and the ledgers are "stuffed" for posting. A novel machine application is installed in this section; when posting to customers' accounts, three forms, the customer's ledger sheet, the record of cash received, and the bank deposit slip, are made simultaneously. Three postings are thus made in one writing. The cash-received record and bank deposit slips, together with checks, are forwarded to the cashier for entry, endorsement, and deposit.

An important phase of the work of this department is the making of adjustments for contract applications and allowances for price declines, incidental to price guaranties. This necessitates the inspecting of credit memoranda, adjustment debits, and journal entries.

Customers' ledgers are arranged in geographic sequence, in accordance with the sales brokers' territories. Monthly trial balances of ledgers are made and forwarded to the auditing department for verification with controlling accounts.

9. ACCOUNTS PAYABLE

It is the function of this department to record all invoices received from vendors of materials, supplies, services, etc., and to make the proper distribution to accounts in the invoice distribution ledgers.

All invoices are checked in the purchasing department against purchase orders for quantities delivered, terms, prices, and extensions. The purchasing department in turn, forwards approved invoices to the auditing department, where they are audited and approved for entry and payment.

At the close of each month a journal voucher is prepared, summarizing the invoice distribution ledgers. The voucher is forwarded to the auditing department for its approval and then dispatched to the general accounting department for entry in the general books.

This department prepares voucher checks for the payment of invoices and maintains the detail check registers. The total of checks drawn daily is forwarded to the auditing department for entry in the daily bank statements. Voucher checks, with the original invoices attached, are forwarded to the auditing department for approval, and for cancellation of invoices, and thence to the proper officers for signatures. Signed vouchers, with all papers attached, are returned to the accounts payable section. The checks are then mailed to the vendors, and the original papers are filed.

At the close of each month a journal voucher is prepared summarizing the checks drawn for the month. The voucher is then passed on to the auditor for verification with total bank withdrawals. The auditor approves and passes the voucher to the general accounting section. By the use of the special bookeeping machine, combination records are made in one writing. For example, the posting of checks to vendors' accounts, and the making of voucher checks and the check record are all done in one operation.

10. CASHIER

This department's main function is that of recording and depositing all the cash receipts of the company. The principal source of cash income is, of course, from the sale of sugar and molasses. Minor revenues are received from the sale of real property to employees for homes, real estate rentals, and the sale of used materials. All cash receipts are deposited daily.

The work of this department differs from that usually found, because all disbursements other than petty expenditures are made in the accounts payable department.

Cash receipts from the sale of sugar and molasses are

THE FINANCE AND ACCOUNTING DIVISION 179

recorded by the accounts receivable department on detail "cash received" records. Through the application of machine accounting a bank deposit slip is made simultaneously with the "cash received" record. The latter, together with deposit slips and bank checks, is forwarded to the cashier, who checks the detail, endorses the checks on a check-endorsing machine, and deposits the proceeds daily in the bank.

The totals from the detailed "cash received" records are entered by the cashier in the summary of cash receipts. The detailed sheets are forwarded to the auditing department, where the figures thereon are used for compiling daily bank balances. At the close of each month the cashier prepares a summary of the month's receipts and forwards it to the general accounting department for entry in the general books.

The cashier's department prepares for the finance officer weekly and semi-monthly forecasts of receipts and disbursements, which are used in the preparation of financial budgets and the allocation of funds for operations and short-term investment. All notes, both receivable and payable, are handled by the cashier.

The official time of arrival of each sugar vessel is obtained from the Marine Department of the San Francisco Chamber of Commerce, for the purpose of calculating the base price upon which all sugars are settled. This price is based on an average of five market days prior to the arrival of a vessel, the arrival day, and four days thereafter, making ten in all.

Upon arrival of vessels in San Francisco, the planters' agents furnish the company with manifests showing marks, number of bags, and net weight. This information is used for the calculation of the approximate cost of the cargo and of the date on which the payment to the planter will fall due. The last is frequently needed for financial forecasting.

Upon completion of cargo discharge at Crockett a report of outturn is received in the San Francisco office, at which time the actual payment date is determined. One copy of the outturn is retained in the San Francisco office, and other copies are furnished to the planters' agents.

Entry of bags and pounds, as reported on outturn reports, is made in a raw-sugar book by this department. Polarization reports are received from the plant laboratory the following morning. By comparing these with the planters' figures, an average polarization is determined. The price paid is calculated on these averages, using a scale of "ups and downs" for sugars over and under 96 per cent.

Bills showing the original outturns with cost figures extended thereon by the agents are received and checked. The originals go to the auditing department to be approved for payment on the proper due date. A second copy is retained from which entries are made in the raw-sugar record.

11. CONSIGNMENT

This company has production far in excess of Pacific Coast requirements. It has therefore to seek distribution in the Middle West and in the South. In this territory the company is in direct competition with Southern, Atlantic seaboard, and Cuban cane producers, as well as with growers and manufacturers of beet sugar. To meet this competition and to have sugar available for immediate sale, the company is forced to maintain large stocks of sugar in some two hundred public warehouses throughout the territory.

It is the function of the consignment department to maintain complete records of the movement of sugars in these territories, in transit or in warehouses, and sugars sold from warehouse or from transit. All invoices for storage and handling of sugars in and out of warehouses are received in this department, checked with storage records and approved before going to the auditing department.

Reports and statistical statements are prepared on stocks and their distribution for the use of the sales, statistical, and general accounting departments. At the close of each month a trial balance is taken from the consignment ledgers and forwarded to the auditing department for verification with the general ledger controlling accounts.

12. TABULATING DEPARTMENT

This department uses electric tabulating machines for the compilation of statistical information from sales invoices. When sales invoices reach this department from the billing department, the indicating codes are applied, analyses and segregations are made, and cards are punched. All punch data, other than amounts, is checked with the invoices before tabulation. Verification of the card punching for amounts is made by tabulating the cards and by proving against predetermined totals compiled by the billing department.

Cards are then assembled or sorted preparatory to compiling the required statistical data. The major data covers: sales—both pounds and amounts by brokers; brokers' commission statements; sales segregation—by brokers and by states; grade and package segregation; prepaid freight analysis; sales expense analysis; and analysis of sales by business classification—manufacturers, jobbers, etc.

This department also prepares a monthly analysis of consignment sugar stocks, showing grades and packages stored at various points. A record is also prepared showing the monthly and yearly cumulative purchase record of each customer.

13. CENTRAL STENOGRAPHIC SERVICE

In October 1923 the company organized its central stenographic department to serve the several departments of the general office. This was done to facilitate the work of typing and correspondence and to provide for the flexibility necessary to take care of peak loads in the various departments. A further consideration was standardization of form and the quality of correspondence.

The department is in charge of a head stenographer, who makes the assignments to her five stenographers. The present estimated minimum requirement under the old system would be nine stenographers. This group handles the entire correspondence and the typing of all statements and reports. A correspondence manual has been prepared for the guidance of both the dictator and the stenographer. The company does not employ any phonographic appliances in connection with this work.

14. MAIL AND FILE SECTION

All incoming mail is opened, stamped, sorted, and distributed by this central department, and outgoing mail is collected, sealed, stamped, and mailed. Telegrams, radiograms, and cables are received, time-stamped, registered, and delivered. Regular schedules of collections and deliveries are maintained by messengers. These messengers are also available for special service, each department being connected with this section by means of an electric "buzzer" system.

For quick dispatch of information "key" departments are connected with the mail and file department by a pneumatic tube system. The department is equipped with all the latest appliances for opening and for sealing and stamping mail. Each desk throughout the office is equipped uniformly with three trays—incoming, outgoing, and file.

Mail to and from brokers is handled in distinctive envelopes to permit speedy preferential sorting. Incoming mail with remittances enclosed is dispatched to the accounts-receivable section for entry.

There are in operation here two duplicating machines for copying telegrams, orders, daily, monthly, and special reports, financial statements, trade letters, etc.

The Corporation does not have a centrally located file room. Each of the departments has its own files, readily accessible to its personnel. Papers withdrawn from files are placed in special baskets for re-filing.

All filing equipment is standardized for the ordinary routine files. Special equipment is used for handling such items as credit record cards, tariff files, etc. The filing system in the various departments is designed to meet specific requirements, either alphabetical or numerical. A geographic-alphabetic system is used in the credit department for filing customers' credit data cards.

Current files are periodically transferred to storage files in the general office and later transferred to the old-records room maintained at the refinery. Destruction of old records is in accordance with prescribed procedure.

15. TELEPHONE AND TELEGRAPH SERVICE

The company operates its own private exchange, comprising twenty trunk lines and fifty-four local station connections. Between the refinery at Crockett and the general offices the company operates its own leased telegraph wire, which is used for dispatching shipping orders to the warehouse and for the handling of interdepartmental messages.

16. PURCHASING DEPARTMENT

The purchasing department buys all materials and supplies. It is its responsibility to furnish materials and supplies of satisfactory quality at the most reasonable price consistent with delivery as needed. This department receives all invoices, checks prices and extensions, approves invoices, and passes them on to the auditors for final approval before payment. All credit memoranda are also checked in this department and passed to the auditors. This department takes care of all claims due to undershipment, poor quality, or to any other legitimate reasons. The purchasing agent is also in charge of disposing of old materials.

The purchasing agent, as head of the department, negotiates contracts for the purchase of materials and supplies, whenever necessary. He also supervises all contracts covering labor to be performed by outside firms, except contracts which have to be filed at the County Court House to cover bonds or liens. These special contracts are signed by the president and secretary of the company. The purchasing agent keeps in close touch with the different operating departments, and particularly with the stocks and stock-control sections, by visiting the refinery at Crockett at least once a week.

The assistant purchasing agent is in charge of the department in the absence of the purchasing agent. He is held responsible for all the detail clerical work performed by the other members of the staff. All incoming correspondence passes over his desk for inspection before distribution.

The invoice clerk receives all incoming invoices and credit memoranda and checks them against orders for verification of prices. The "trace" clerk follows up all orders placed with vendors. He is responsible for the proper delivery of the materials and supplies called for on the orders which have been placed. He is in daily touch with the firms from which materials are bought. In all instances of delay in delivery, he notifies the department concerned so that the necessary action may be taken.

He also keeps the different departments of the refinery notified as to deliveries on the outstanding orders. The order typist is responsible for the proper writing up of all orders, as placed, from the requisitions and specifications and with correct prices, and also for verifying them before passing them to the purchasing agent or his assistant for approval. The order typist sees that all orders are properly recorded in the register books and that copies are sent to all interested persons.

Purchasing procedure.—Requisitions for materials and supplies originate with the department requiring them, and are signed by the department head. One copy is retained by the department making the purchase request, and the other three are forwarded to the stock control section for checking. If the requisitions appear to be in order they are signed, and two of the three copies are sent to the purchasing department. One copy is kept for the stores department files, the original is placed in a binder to be kept on the order typist's desk, and the other copy is passed on to the assistant purchasing agent. The signature of the head of the department requesting the materials from the stock control section is sufficient authorization for purchase. All requisitions are numbered, in order to see that none go astray. After proper negotiations with the vendor have been completed and prices and delivery dates have been determined, the purchasing agent or his assistant records the date, vendors' name, requisition number, price, promised delivery date, shipping instructions, and any other information necessary.

The order typist proceeds to write out the purchase order, referring to the items specified on the original requistion, plus other data supplied by the purchasing agent. The order typist checks the items which have been placed on the requisition and types opposite each item the order number and name of vendor. All copies of the completed purchase order are turned over to the purchasing agent for signature. The original requisitions, after being completely checked, are then filed numerically by the order typist in a binder.

Claims.—The procedure covering the return of materials because of under-shipment, poor quality, defectiveness, or "ordered in error," is as follows:

The stores department is notified and issues a claim, on which are stated the reasons for return and a request for shipping instructions. Two copies of the claim are forwarded to the purchasing department. The vendor is then notified by the purchasing department of the contemplated return, and shipping instructions are requested. The stores department is then notified and shipment is made. The invoice clerk then bills the vendor, attaching to his file copy of the invoices copies of the claim and shipping instructions. For accounting purposes two copies are sent to the auditor. An entry is also recorded on the purchasing department copy of the order, and the claim is considered cleared. If replacement is wanted a new order is written, using the same order number but with the suffix "A."

Reference files.—An up-to-date file is kept of all the manufacturers of and dealers in goods used by the various divisions. Catalogs are filed alphabetically. Easy reference is provided for by a cross index to the material handled by each manufacturer or dealer. All purchasing-department correspondence is in reference to commodities, and is therefore filed according to commodities, with subdivisions numbered for quick reference. In files arranged by names of vendors are kept copies of purchase orders, invoices, etc.

17. STORES DEPARTMENT

The functions of this department may be classified into five major groupings: (1) to receive and store all incoming materials, supplies, and equipment awaiting use: (2) to disburse stores stocks on properly approved requisitions; (3) to maintain records of each item carried in stock; (4) to handle shipments and shipping papers on materials outbound, exclusive of sugar and molasses; and (5) to operate company trucks for local purchases and deliveries.

Primarily, the stores department is charged with the physical handling of materials. The control of inventories is vested in the stock control section of the refinery office. The storekeeper, however, keeps in touch with the control clerks and with the purchasing department, and assists in the planning of deliveries of materials and in maintaining proper stocks. The responsibility of the purchasing department for the movement of materials ceases upon delivery of materials in good order and in accordance with specifications.

The storekeeper keeps in close touch with other departments—particularly with the departments of operating and engineering—and maintains the necessary service of materials and supplies to the production, maintenance, and construction department.

All materials are classified into two principal groups: (1) stock items in stores, and (2) special orders covering materials purchased for special jobs. The latter group is made up mostly of non-standard items; however, stock items may be included where the job requirements are large and exceed the normal stores stock.

The purchasing department supplies this department with copies of all purchase orders for materials for the refinery. One copy, setting forth complete specifications, account number on which purchased, and order authorization, is given to the receiving clerk.

All materials purchased must comply with company specifications. Bone coal, starch, cotton sheeting, burlap, metals, castings, and fabricated equipment must pass the inspection of either the laboratory, the inspection department, or the engineering department before being released from the receiving room.

Materials for stock reach the stock rooms, are checked for quantities, and are placed in bins or racks for issue. Stores stocks are decentralized, because the plant is large, the departments consuming large quantities being widely spread and shops scattered. It is more convenient and economical to maintain a number of stores bases, each adjacent to or within close distance of the points of consumption. Withdrawals from stock rooms are made only upon requisition signed by authorized foremen. All requisitions are accounted for daily and forwarded to the stock control clerks. Bin tickets are placed on each bin showing date, requisition number on withdrawals, quantities received and withdrawn, and balance. Bin tickets show also brief descriptions of articles, code numbers, and maximum and minimum requirements.

When bin ticket balances reach the quantities shown under caption "Order When," entry is made on a "Request for Stock" form which is forwarded daily to the stock control clerks, who check and place requisitions with the purchasing department.

Complete stores records are kept in the refinery office stock-control section. The stores department keeps only arrival notices (receiving record), freight manifests (inbound and outbound), and inspection reports.

All merchandise being returned to vendors, and miscellaneous shipments from the refinery, whether by freight, express, or parcel post, are handled by this department.

The storekeeper is in charge of the company's fleet of trucks. This service covers pick-up and deliveries of supplies in the East Bay District, as well as service in the community of Crockett in connection with gardens, streets, and playgrounds.

18. TRAFFIC DEPARTMENT

This department handles all of the transportation matters of the company—the shipment of sugar from warehouses and the movement of materials and supplies inbound for use in manufacture, whether by rail or water. The bulk of the traffic department's work naturally deals with the movement of refined sugar, and the closest coordination exists between this department and that of the Sales Division and the order department. The company is a large consumer of materials and supplies, purchased in many markets; therefore a close relationship exists between the traffic department and the purchasing department, to obtain the best possible delivery and at the lowest cost.

With the wide distribution of its sugar, the company enters many markets. Sugar is shipped in several ways. Some shipments go all the way to their destinations by rail; others start out by rail and are trans-shipped by water; and still others move first by water and then by rail. This fact, coupled with the complicated rate structures which exist, makes the work of this department an important link in the distribution process. A constant study is made of the tariffs and rate schedules in a search for economical markets for the outlet of sugar, and in making rate adjustments in existing territories. This calls for the compilation and distribution of rate charts setting forth rates to the various points and the absorption to be taken by the company in competing against New Orleans and Atlantic Coast refineries.

This department represents the company in local traffic associations, and before the public service commission and legislative boards. It maintains complete files on commission rulings and orders and their interpretation as they affect the business.

The department prepares schedules of classifications

setting forth the proper description of all commodities, and the standardization of shipping papers. It cooperates with the operating departments and traffic bureaus in negotiating average weight agreements and demurrage agreements. Other important duties of this department are in connection with obtaining transportation privileges granted by carriers, diversion of cars in transit, reconsignment privileges, track storage, "free time," and switching.

Another important function is that of routing shipments and tracing them to their destination. In this respect the department is of service both to the Corporation and to its customers. Throughout the Eastern territory sugars are sold on terms that guarantee price upon arrival. The department must trace these cars and obtain from the delivering carrier the tracer record giving the date and time of arrival, as this information forms the basis for the estimate proving of invoices by the billing department.

The traffic department audits transportation company expense bills for rates, weights, and extensions, and certifies them to the auditor for payment. It also prepares and files all claims for loss, damage, and overcharge.

The files and records of this department comprise tariff files, bills of lading files, tracer files, car record books, and rate chart files.

19. INSURANCE AND TAX DEPARTMENT

In June 1921 the Corporation established a separate insurance department for the handling of all matters pertaining to insurance on company property and operations. Before 1921 this work was handled by the accounting department.

The established policy is to insure all property at full value. The many kinds of insurance incidental to the business, and forms under which such insurance is written involve constant, careful study and a great amount of detail. The following brief description gives an idea of the variety of insurance carried.

Fire Insurance

Sugar.—Fire insurance on sugar is carried in large sums on all sugar stored at Crockett and elsewhere. At certain periods of the year the amount of fire insurance on sugar reaches many millions. As sugar values fluctuate from day to day, the insurance department receives from Crockett a daily report showing the tonnage of raw and refined sugar stored in the warehouses. From the figures thus received the insurance department computes values based on daily market quotations of sugar. Sugar stored at points other than Crockett is insured up to the full value under a so-called "floater policy," which requires the company to report as of the last day of each month, the value of sugar at each location. The company has two types of policies, one of which affords protection up to $200,000 in any one warehouse, and the other up to $50,000 on any one dock, wharf, or pier. When actual values exceed these limits, the company places "specific insurance" to the extent of the excess.

Buildings and Equipment

Full fire insurance coverage is carried on all buildings and equipment except foundations, excavations, sidewalks, etc. The exclusion of the latter, which are items not wholly destructible by fire, results in a large saving in premium costs. Annually, the valuation department supplies the insurance department with appreciated and depreciated values on all buildings and equipment. From these the amount of insurance to be carried is determined. Fire insurance is also carried on various other risks, such as equipment in the San Francisco office, box brands, iron moulds, patterns, materials, and supplies.

All company buildings outside of the refinery are also fully covered. Houses being constructed for employees, under the plan described elsewhere in this study, are insured against fire while under construction. At the completion of each house, a separate policy is placed covering the amount of money loaned by the company.

Marine Insurance

All sugar and materials shipped by boat are fully covered by marine insurance. Upon request of customers, and for their account, the insurance department places marine insurance for all customer shipments destined for Pacific Coast ports.

Marine insurance is carried on hulls of tugs and barges to values given to the insurance companies by this department.

Molasses and Tanks Insurance

The company has four tanks for the storage of molasses, three at Crockett and one at San Pedro. These tanks and their contents are fully protected against fire, earthquake, tornado, collapse, explosion, and lightning.

Sprinkler Leakage Insurance

Sprinkler-leakage insurance is carried on materials and supplies at Crockett, and on sugar stored in warehouses at that location or in any warehouse throughout the country. This form of insurance is carried for protection against damage to sugar and stores which might result from breakage of sprinkler equipment.

Automobile and Truck Insurance

The present policies covering all cars and trucks owned by this company are known as "fleet policies"; that is, a certain number of cars are combined and insured under one or two policies in place of separate ones, with a corresponding saving in rate. The automobile insurance thus carried covers fire and theft, collision, property damage, and public liability. The same policies carry protection on cars which the company may hire with or without drivers, and also on cars owned by employees and used from time to time on company business.

Workmen's Compensation

For the past five years the Corporation has placed its compensation insurance with a participating stock company which returns a percentage of the total yearly premium over and above the actual cost. The premium returns, or dividends, have been large. As described elsewhere the company has achieved signal success in accident prevention and in the promotion of safety. These accomplishments have been registered in a constant reduction of its workmen's compensation rate. The present rate is $1.35 as against $2.24 in 1920.

Bonding Employees

Protection of this sort may be had two ways: first, by the bonding of individuals, and, second, by the bonding of positions.

The first type of bond insurance is being done away with and the second substituted in order to eliminate changes in policies due to transfers among the personnel. The cost of bonding positions is about the same as that for bonding individuals. The advantage lies largely in the elimination of much red tape.

To the above-outlined major coverages carried should be added the following types of insurance: check forgery, burglary and hold-up, elevator, public liability, and miscellaneous indemnity bonds.

A separate record, according to the various risks involved, is kept of all insurance placements, expirations, renewals, and cancellations. On the first of each month this department receives a statement from the insurance brokers listing the amounts of insurance in force as of that date. This list is checked, for correctness, against the company's records. All invoices for insurance premiums are sent to this department for checking and distribution. Complete policy files and records of premiums are kept in this department. At the close of each month journal vouchers distributing expired premiums are prepared for the general accounting department, together with a trial balance detail of unexpired premiums for verification with the general ledger control.

Losses sustained under the various policies are all handled by the department, in co-operation with the department involved in the loss.

The annual cost of the several types of insurance, as described above, is about one hundred and ten thousand dollars.

Taxes

All forms of taxes, excluding Federal income taxes, are handled by this department. The total tax bills covering corporate license, franchise, real property and personal property, represent an annual expenditure in excess of $200,000.00.

The department furnishes assessors with statements of values. In connection with real property taxes, the department obtains values from the plant ledger maintained by the engineering department of the refinery. The stock control section furnishes figures on stores investment; the refinery office, statements of sugar in storage. In addition to local taxes the company is obliged to pay taxes on sugars stored throughout its territories.

Accounting for taxes follows the same procedure as for insurance premiums, giving the accounting departments monthly the expired pro ratas and the trial balance of advanced taxes carried as a deferred cost to operations.

20. AUDITING DEPARTMENT

Prior to the organization of this department in 1922, all auditing was done by a firm of public accountants. Since then the large volume of detailed auditing, the verification of statements and account balances, and the control of interdepartmental balances are entrusted to this department. The scope of the public accountant's examination has ben reduced to the semi-annual verification of the balance sheet and operating results.

This department is concerned with examining, analyzing, reviewing, verifying, and approving (or disapproving) all accounting transactions before incorporation into the records. It also verifies the results of completed accounting transactions to show whether the conclusions drawn therefrom are proper and warranted. All accounting transactions and other matters of record pass through this department for audit, review of account distribution, and proper authorization and approval prior to entry in any subsidiary or general controlling records.

Briefly, the function of this department comprises the audit and approval of all invoices and disbursements, reconciliation of all cash receipts, and review and approval of all journal entries, as well as approval of claims and credit memoranda.

All detailed bank-account records are maintained in this department, and as cash receipts are reported and reconciled with bank deposits and accounts or other receivable credits, they are posted to their proper bank accounts. All check disbursements are reported to this department by the accounts payable department and likewise entered to their proper bank accounts. Bank statements and cancelled checks are sent direct to this department for monthly reconciliations and the balances are verified with the general ledger control account.

The departmental records and controls are so laid out

that the work of one department is complementary to that of another, making possible a continuous audit of all detailed transactions. Examples of this are shown in the shipments from the refinery and in the control over weights and values in the departments that handle contract records, billing, accounts receivable, and tabulating. All shipping orders after passing through the order and traffic departments are telegraphed to the refinery. Each morning the warehouse department wires to the audit department the figures for total tonnages shipped on the day before, and entry is made by the audit department to the inventory tonnage control account.

Copies of actual shipping bills are sent from the warehouse to the billing department, where actual billing is prepared. Before closing the day's billing, this department secures from the auditing department a release for the tonnage billed, to compare with the tonnage reported shipped by the refinery.

Office copies of the billings, if correct, are then sent to the customers' accounts section for entry to individual accounts. After the entry of a complete day's billing and before posting to the control accounts, the accounts-receivable department secures a release from the auditing department for values billed to customers' accounts. This must agree with values as billed by the billing department.

The tabulating department then punches cards covering tonnages shipped, distribution by territories, money values, tonnages by grades, freight charges involved, brokers' records for credit commissions, kinds of sugars shipped, and other data. Here again a daily summary is made, which clears through the auditing department and is verified with the figures of the other departments and then entered into the inventory- and sales-control records.

The auditing department likewise controls withdrawals from Eastern or other warehouses. Shipments made from warehouse stocks are first compared with wire reports from brokers' offices and are then entered into obligation-control records. The consignment department prepares a daily report which is sent to the audit department for verification with shipments, billings, etc., before entry into their consignment control records.

For the sake of brevity only the general routine of the accounting procedure and methods of control that affect shipments and inventories of sugars have been described. Many minor functions such as pricing, freight routing, brokers' obligations and contract records, freight applications, detail warehouse accounting, monthly trial balances, and closing journals are taken into account before the full accounting and auditing procedure is completed.

The auditing department makes regular monthly examinations and verifications of all detail trial balances, plant ledger accounts, budget accounts, payrolls, fixed assets and improvements, inventories of securities, cash funds, stores and supplies accounts, and outside operations. The staff of the department assists in the taking of periodic physical inventories, in examination of all outside or subsidiary operations, and in the analysis of customers' accounts, notes receivable, interest receivable, and loan or advance accounts, accounts payable and all deferred or accrued items, together with all revenue and expense accounts. This department is also responsible for the supervision, in the accounts payable department, of the preparation of franchise tax reports, special balance sheet or income statements, income tax reports, and other miscellaneous data and reports as requested by the Treasurer.

21. COMMERCIAL AND STATISTICAL RESEARCH

This department was organized to serve the three divisions of the business, Selling, Refining, and Finance and Accounting. The functions of the department can be segregated, therefore, into three parts: first, to accumulate and preserve the necessary statistical records; second, to interpret these figures into useful working data for the conduct of daily operations; and, third, to conduct commercial research deemed desirable and necessary. The department was started without definite organization and objectives, and has been built up as fast as its work could usefully be applied.

SALES DIVISION

The field of selling or distribution has so far claimed a large part of the attention of this department. A most thorough analysis of sales records was made. Records of sales to various classes of customers and to geographic areas were made available covering a long period of time. Accurate records of sales of each package and grade since 1922 were compiled. These have assisted greatly in sales planning. The sales Division is confronted with the problem of allotting to its various brokers the sugars which are available for sale. It must also control inventories which are carried on consignment at transit points.

Another type of statistical planning which has been done for the sales Division may be called "long term planning." This work consists in analyzing trends of population growth in the various sales areas, the trend of prices, and the trend of the consumption of sugar. Another factor considered in long-term planning is the varying growth of business among the various types of customers, such as jobbers, canners, chain stores, and candy manufacturers.

The results of various investigations and analyses which have been made for the Sales Division are used in the sales forecasts. Each broker is given a quota for the year and his actual performance is checked closely month by month. Seasonal variations of volume and the effect of price movements are taken into consideration in making these comparisons. By means of this constant check, sales plans may be revised whenever it seems necessary.

The analyses of distribution and the sales forecasts are used in the preparation of the sales budgets, which in turn form the basis for the preparation of refinery production schedules.

Refining Division

A considerable opportunity for statistical analysis is found in the refinery. The co-ordination of sales forecasts with stocks and production necessitates a constant study of plant facilities and station capacities. The operations of the refinery are checked monthly with unit costs in each of the departments and in the warehouse. Labor costs per ton of output at the different rates of melt are checked against standards set. The consumption of materials and supplies per unit of output, such as fuel oil, water, container materials, chemicals, and filter agents, are carefully analyzed monthly. Associated with consumption of materials and supplies is the study of turnover and investment in these materials, together with other operating and maintenance materials.

The constantly increasing ratio of packaged sugars, bales, boxes, barrels, and carton goods as compared with 100-lb. bag, called for studies of container and packaging costs and the compilation of cost-differential schedules.

In collaboration with production executives, studies have been made as to the most economical daily rate of melt and annual production.

Finance and Accounting Division

This division has a vital interest in, and makes use of all the data, studies and tabulations of a sales and production nature. It is also interested in statistics and research which concern the financial trends of the business. The balance sheet charges and financial ratios, the study of cash balances, and the application of funds, loans, and borrowings are most useful to the financial officer.

A problem which is receiving frequent attention is the turnover of inventories and of customers' accounts. The time elapsing between the purchase of the raw material and the receipt of the customer's payment for the refined sugar, determines the inventory period which must be financed.

The profitableness of the business is indicated by the margin between the cost of raws and the price received for the refined product. Current reports comparing these margins are prepared.

22. SALARY STANDARDIZATION

For purposes of salary administration a detailed study of all positions in the general offices was made in 1926, with subsequent follow-up. The survey involved the following:

1. Job analysis and specifications
2. Classification and grading of positions
3. Wage or salary setting
4. Methods for training and promotion

Job analysis.—An analysis of jobs was made and specifications were prepared to determine the essential requisites for each position, embracing the following:

1. Description of the work performed
2. Whether the work was of a strictly routine nature or varied
3. Whether position was to be filled by male or female employee
4. Salary limits
5. Personal qualities required for the position
6. Minimum educational requirements
7. Necessary training and experience
8. General understanding of business fundamentals

9. Purpose and use of business papers and documents
10. Use of office appliances
11. Other qualifications (specialized positions)
12. Line of promotion

The analysis of jobs brought out much detailed information as to the actual workings of the office—duplications, overlapping, and antiquated methods. As a result many economies were effected through modifications in method and procedure. The salary administration study also served as a means of assisting the office manager and the department heads in arriving at a more effective plan for the selection of help and for assignment to proper positions.

The above-described job analysis also served as a basis for determining: (1) the proper organization of the staff; (2) the need for the introduction of new mechanical devices; and (3) the correct distribution of the work.

The classification of positions was further divided into four groups, with corresponding salary increases. Advancement in grade is not dependent solely upon the length of service, but upon length of service together with demonstrated merit. The re-grading of employees is made annually on the anniversary of the induction of each individual into the position held. By thus distributing the grading, careful consideration can be given to the merits of individual cases for advancement. This degree of care was not possible under the old time "once a year for all" method.

Employees showing extraordinary ability and application may, at the discretion of the office manager, be recommended for advancement to a higher grade within less than a year.

Classification and grading.—A study of each department's organization and work showed typical positions in many. With typical positions classified, the next step was the classification of non-typical positions and the adoption of a standard classification for all employees. Positions and not persons were dealt with. The following position classifications were arrived at:

Department heads	Men
Assistants to department heads	Men
Chief accountants	Men
Senior clerks	Men
Junior clerks	Men
Statisticians	Men
Telegraphers	Men
Accounting machine operators	Women
Tabulating machine operators	Women
Telephone exchange operators	Women
Stenographers	Men–Women
Typists	Women
Clerks	Women

Salary setting.—The object here was to construct a schedule of remuneration which would be fair, more or less equalizing in relation to other positions, flexible in its application, one which would offer reward for individual merit, and yet would be within economic limits.

Consideration was first given to the methods of compensation, and the straight salary basis was chosen as the most applicable. The rate structure provides for certain starting salaries, to be paid during a probationary period of sixty days, followed by the minimum rate of Grade 1, which is gradually increased to the maximum of Grade 4. Employees advanced in position are paid the rate of their old position during the probationary period, and then gradually advanced as per schedule outlined.

Training and promotion.—To gain promotion the employee must be trained. Job analysis makes this sort of training for promotion possible. Training is visualized as follows: first, direct job training by the department head or under his supervision, giving exact and detailed instructions of the job and its relation to other jobs in the department or other departments; and, second, self-education. Self-education, it is hoped, will be furthered through lecture courses, correspondence courses, and extension courses. Vacation periods, necessitating temporary transfers, make it possible to train employees in work other than their own.

Employment.—The office manager is the employment officer in the San Francisco office. His activities regarding salaries and promotion are guided by the salary classification scheme described in this section. The office manager may dismiss employees.

Employee records.—The individual history of each employee is maintained on an "Employees' Personal Record" form, from the date of employment to the date of separation. A complete file of forms and reports in chronological order is maintained for each employee, including (1) "Application for Employment," (2) "Physical Examination," and (3) "On Roll" slip.

Vacations.—Annual vacations of fifteen consecutive days, inclusive of Sundays and holidays, are granted to all office employees who have given six months' continuous service prior to March 1 of each year. On or before March 1 bulletins are posted requesting that departmental vacation plans be submitted. Each employee then indicates to his department head the vacation period desired. The department head in turn submits the departmental vacation schedule to the office manager. The office manager, working with department heads, then lists the periods requested to determine the necessary program for relief help. Where schedules as requested interfere with the proper maintenance of office routine, the employee is notified and adjustment is made. About April 1 of each year the vacation schedule is approved and each employee is advised of the period granted him.

Sickness, accidents, and death benefits.—Employees of the San Francisco office, and those under the Finance and Accounting department at Crockett, are eligible to membership in the Disability and Mortality Divisions of the E. M. B. A., as described on pages 93-94 of this study. All the eligibles in the San Francisco office have actually joined the E. M. B. A.

23. CLASSIFICATION OF ACCOUNTS

A proper system of account classification is most essential to a correct analysis of the operations of any business institution. It is the means for locating facts and figures essential to an understanding of business results. This company has a comprehensive system of account classification. Because of the fact that this classification will be of utmost interest to the student of business organization and management it is presented in full as an Appendix to this study.

V. THE LEGAL DEPARTMENT

The legal department is not made subordinate to any of the three major divisions of the Corporation; instead, it functions much as an outside law firm might, in giving legal advice to all three of these divisions. For this reason the discussion of this department is here presented as a separate chapter.

The department was organized January 1, 1923. Prior thereto the Corporation secured its legal services through the retention of outside counsel. As the business increased and grew more diversified, it became increasingly difficult and inconvenient for department heads to consult with outside counsel about matters arising in their departments from day to day upon which legal advice might be desirable.

The principal advantage of maintaining a legal department, as against retaining an outside law firm, lies in the greater ability of the former to keep in touch with the daily affairs of the Corporation. The chief function of the legal department, therefore, is to serve as a preventive. Its efforts are directed toward keeping the company out of court by giving advice in business matters. To this end department heads and bureau chiefs have been encouraged to consult the legal department freely.

The personnel of the legal department must have a practical knowledge of the sugar business and a professional understanding of the law. The former is an attribute apt to be lacking in outside counsel.

The head of the legal department serves as assistant secretary of the Corporation, with particular reference to the duties imposed by law upon corporation secretaries.

An indication of the day-to-day service of this department is shown by the service it renders to the other departments in the form of advice, as follows:

1. The insurance department: With respect to insurance on

properties of the Corporation, workmen's compensation, public liability insurance, and insurance upon stocks of sugar in storage and in transit.

2. The tax department: With respect to matters of taxation arising in California and in the various other states in which the products of the company are distributed; also with respect to license taxes, franchise taxes, and Federal income taxes.

3. The purchasing department: With respect to the purchase of materials and supplies, including the viséing of purchase contracts.

4. The construction department: With respect to building contracts for new construction.

5. The credit department: With respect to the handling of credits of the customers upon the Corporation's books.

6. The auditor: With respect to legal angles incident to good accounting practice.

7. The industrial relations department: With respect to industrial relations between the management and its employees; also with respect to housing and real property activities in Crockett, including the preparation of building contracts, deeds, deeds of trust, promissory notes, and other documents.

8. The engineering and technical departments: With respect to patent matters arising in the plant.

9. The Sales Division: With respect to the legal angles incident to the sale of sugars and molasses; also with respect to the relations of the company with its competitors and with trade associations.

VI. PROGRESS AND RESULTS

1. PROGRESS IN EXTRACTION

From the economic as well as the technical standpoint it is of vital importance that the highest possible yield of refined sugar be obtained from the raw sugar handled. This is measured by what is termed the "extraction" of sugar.

The progress that has been made in increasing the extraction and in decreasing the losses of sugar since 1915 is shown in Tables 30 and 31 (pp. 208 and 209), in which the results obtained in 1915 are taken as 100 per cent and those obtained in subsequent years are shown as percentages of those for 1915. The results are expressed in two ways:

Table 30 shows actual extraction and losses in percentages of 1915 results (calculated as percentage on the sucrose in the raws).

Table 31 shows extraction results in terms of 1915, calculated on the assumption that raw sugars of identical composition had been used in all years.

A few words of explanation may be necessary to clarify the meaning of the figures shown in the tabulations referred to and to give a clear understanding of the terms used.

Polarization.—It should be explained that raw sugar, as received for refining, consists of about 96 per cent to 98 per cent cane sugar (technically termed sucrose) and 2 per cent to 4 per cent impurities and water. The term "polarization" expresses the percentage of sucrose present in the raw sugar.

Extraction.—In the process of refining the raws, some of the sugar (or sucrose) is lost, partly through mechanical or physical loss, partly through decomposition by heat and acidity in solution, and partly because the impurities prevent a portion of the sugar from crystallizing and thereby causing the formation of molasses which is practically a waste product. For these reasons it is impossible to recover all of the sugar in the raws. In ordinary refinery operation a recovery (or extraction) of 96 per cent to 99 per cent of the sucrose in the raws is obtained, depending on the composition of the raws and the efficiency of the work.

TABLE 30
Annual Extraction Results*—1915 to 1927

Year	Raws Melted Percentage of 1915	Polarization of Raws Percentage of 1915	Granulated Extraction	Total Losses
1915	100.00	100.00	100.00	100.00
1916	97.686	99.027	99.766	160.951
1917	103.757	100.061	100.647	80.454
1918	104.897	100.120	99.617	111.533
1919	124.840	99.983	101.053	68.235
1920	164.546	100.124	101.380	58.572
1921	113.151	100.560	101.758	46.945
1922	164.546	100.702	101.679	49.314
1923	156.060	100.59	101.667	49.688
1924	200.831	100.968	101.938	41.521
1925	221.112	101.013	102.016	39.152
1926	226.009	101.046	102.192	33.852
1927	235.921	101.197	102.247	32.169

* All results expressed as percentage of 1915 results.

It should further be explained that the soft sugar as sold contains a certain amount of molasses which would have been lost as a by-product if the soft sugar had not been produced. This, therefore, permits of a higher extraction than would otherwise be the case but it does not truly reflect the efficiency of the work at the refinery. In order to secure a measure of the improvement in results actually effected at the refinery, the sucrose in the molasses in the softs is deducted from the total extraction to give the granulated extraction. This represents the theoretical amount of granulated sugar that would have been produced had no softs been produced.

In order to measure the actual technical progress of the plant, the tabulations show only the comparative figures for "Granulated Extraction," exclusive of all benefits derived from the sale of molasses in softs.

TABLE 31
ANNUAL EXTRACTION RESULTS*—1915 TO 1927
Assuming All Raws of Same Composition as in 1927

Year	Raws Melted Percentage of 1915	Granulated Extraction	Total Losses
1915	100	100	100
1916	97.686	99.884	104.612
1917	103.757	100.241	90.367
1918	104.897	99.537	118.408
1919	124.840	100.967	61.469
1920	163.268	101.061	57.83
1921	113.151	101.180	52.979
1922	164.546	101.050	58.163
1923	156.061	101.097	56.285
1924	200.831	101.211	51.755
1925	221.112	101.255	49.999
1926	226.009	101.441	42.612
1927	235.922	101.453	42.16

* All results expressed as percentage of 1915 results.

Losses.—Losses include three general types:

1. Molasses Loss: This loss, as explained above, occurs because the impurities in the raw sugar prevent a portion of the sugar from crystallizing, causing the formation of molasses from which the sugar cannot be recovered. By improved methods it has been possible to remove more of the impurities in recent years and thereby reduce this loss.

(In the tabulations, molasses in softs, as well as actual molasses produced, is included in the losses, so as to eliminate the effect of sales conditions in the comparisons.)

2. Physical Losses: These losses include sugar that is

lost mechanically, as for example in waste products from cloth filters and char filters, entrainment in boiling of sugar and in escaping dust.

3. Decomposition Losses: These losses, which represent a considerable portion (20 per cent to 25 per cent) of the total losses, result from the fact that sugar in solution is very easily decomposed by heat and acidity.

In the tabulations, all three of these losses are included in the total.

2. INTERPRETATION OF RESULTS

In Table 31, it is shown that the granulated extraction by 1927 had increased 2.247 per cent as compared with 1915. In this same period the losses had been decreased 68 per cent.

These improved results have been due to four main causes:
  a) Increased polarization of raws
  b) Reduced molasses production
  c) Improved control of physical losses
  d) Improved control of decomposition losses

Increased polarization of raws.—Due to an increasing polarization of raws there has been a smaller introduction of impurities into the house and therefore a smaller production of molasses in recent years. As this has resulted from conditions beyond the control of the plant it does not reflect true technical progress in the refinery. For this reason the figures in Table 31 have been calculated in a manner which eliminates the effect of increased polarization, by showing the results which would have been attained had the raws for all years been of the same composition as in 1927.

It will be noted that, in Table 31, the year 1927 shows an increase in extraction of 1.45 per cent over 1915 and a decrease in losses of 58 per cent. These improved results may be attributed entirely to technical progress within the plant, the main items of which were:

Reduced molasses production.—This is due primarily to improved char filtration methods which were started in 1919 and 1920 and gradually developed in subsequent years.

Improved control of physical losses.—Between 1915 and 1920 a very strict control was developed to prevent ordinary physical losses through leaks or in waste products. This control has gradually been tightened up since that time.

Improved control of decomposition losses.—Since 1920 revised methods of alkalinity control and improved methods of temperature control have been developed, which have greatly reduced the decomposition of sugar in solution.

The combined effect of these improved technical methods, therefore, has been to reduce the losses of sugar by 58 per cent since 1915 and increase the extraction 1.45 per cent. The value of this increased yield, due to the technical progress of the plant, is equivalent to close to $1,000,000 per year.

3. REGULARIZATION OF PRODUCTION, 1923–1927

Two of the chief concerns of the management in recent years have been (1) regularization of production and (2) operation at maximum capacity for the greatest number of days consistent with supply of raws.

The sugar business is seasonal. More sugar, on the average, is consumed during the summer season of the year than during the winter. In many a refinery, production conforms to the seasonal demand. Not so here; the policy of this Corporation, during the last few years, has been to produce sugar as evenly as possible throughout the year, and store it pending demand from distributors and users.

Under proper conditions and with sufficient care, sugar can be stored for indefinite periods. The problem of regularization of operation therefore involved: (1) development of proper methods for storing and proper storage space and equipment, (2) regularization of delivery of raw cane sugar to the refinery, and (3) proper forecasts of demand, by grades and packages. Conferences were held with the planters for the purpose of bringing forcefully to their attention the economy of regular deliveries of raw sugar.

While the management is interested in the regularity of receipt of raws, it has to be on guard to avoid too large an accumulation of raws ahead of the refinery. The reasons for this are: (1) additional costs of unloading, piling, and delivery of raws to melt, (2) insurance costs on excess raws, (3) cost of moving supplies and preparing warehouse for excess raw storage, and (4) interest charges to be paid on account of excess raws not immediately usable.

The plant management considers a reserve of raws of about 25,000 tons, or ten days' supply, as the maximum desired. This balance, when backed up by regular arrivals of raws, has been found sufficient to operate the refinery without interruption.

The increased regularization of the operations of the refinery since 1923 is shown in Table 32 and Figure 10 (pp. 214-15), for each year between 1923 and 1927, and is based upon monthly rates of melt adjusted to the number of working days in each month, for the eleven operating months of each year.

The annual shut-down starts each year in November. To accomplish the orderly working out of sugars in process, a gradual reduction in melt takes place over the seven days prior to complete shut-down.

TABLE 32
REGULARITY OF REFINERY OPERATIONS (MELT) SHOWN IN TERMS OF
A PERCENTAGE OF AVERAGE MONTHLY MELT OF EACH YEAR

(Average monthly melt of each year = 100)

Month	1923	1924	1925	1926	1927
January	43.8	71.6	80.2	111.4	94.8
February	102.2	85.5	101.9	115.9	102.3
March	111.3	99.1	109.1	109.5	103.0
April	123.9	99.5	112.3	107.9	104.3
May	126.2	100.0	112.2	100.7	103.1
June	125.0	108.1	111.8	91.0	103.1
July	96.8	114.2	114.8	98.5	108.9
August	94.6	129.0	112.2	95.9	110.0
September	112.6	119.3	114.8	109.9	111.2
October	120.2	123.9	110.0	109.0	111.3
November	43.7	50.8	21.0	51.5	48.1

The chart of Figure 10 shows a definite improvement in regularity of operation from year to year. The most irregular operation of the period took place in 1923. During this year no correct information was readily available on the Hawaiian crop. The refinery ran as best it could on receipts of raws as they arrived. The next year, 1924, saw the beginning of experiments for correlating crop with refinery production. A considerable improvement in operation regularity was noticeable in 1924. The subsequent year, 1925, saw some definite results of the newly initiated program of regularization. Improvements in regularization during 1926 were made difficult by a retardation of crop due to unfavorable weather in the Islands. The year 1927 shows the most regular operations since 1923.

It is interesting in this connection to obtain, if possible, a mathematical measurement of relative regularity in terms of total general deviation from the mean from year to year. The following summary shows total annual percentage of deviations from the mean of each year:

214   THE C & H SUGAR REFINING CORPORATION

Year	Total of Percentage Deviation from Annual Mean
1923	242
1924	188
1925	180
1926	127
1927	114

The above composite summary shows by years, the total annual percentage of deviation from the average of each year. The total of deviations includes both deviations above the average and deviations below the average. The sum total of the two gives the extent of total deviation from the mean for each year. The table shows a steady and persistent lessening of irregularity from year to year. The irregularity of operations in 1923 was more than twice as great as in 1927; or, inversely, production was twice as regular in 1927 as in 1923.

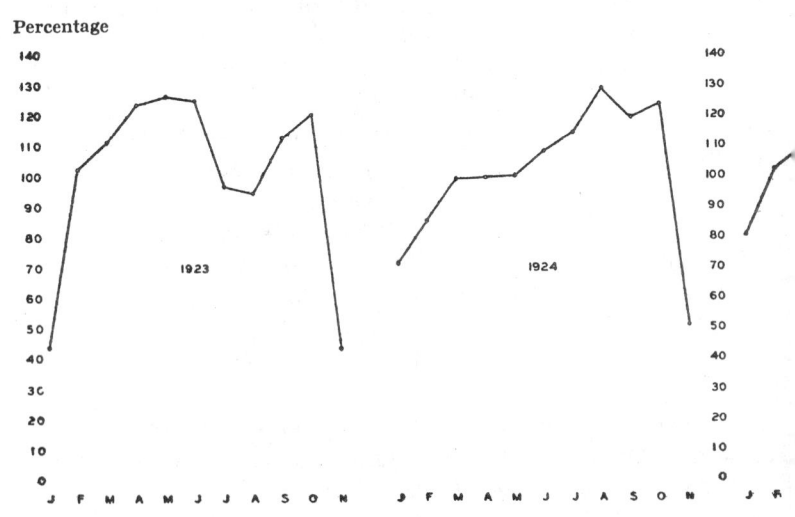

Fig. 10.—Graph showing relative regularity of refining operations number of operating days, 1923–27.

The saving in costs accruing from regularized capacity operation is shown in the next section of this study.

Comparison of seasonal trend of sugar production with seasonal demand for sugar.—The policy of production regularization really commenced in 1923. During that year, however, only the ground work was laid.

A graphic representation of the differences in the trend of production regularity, as compared with the average demand for sugar, is shown in Figure 11 (p. 216).

The production curve for 1924 strongly resembles the curve showing the average seasonal demand for sugar. For obvious reasons, the rise and fall in the production curve slightly precede the similar and corresponding changes in the demand curve. The two curves—the production curve of 1924 and the curve showing the demand —are otherwise almost alike. A totally different relationship is seen to exist between the demand curve and the 1927 production curve. The regularization of production

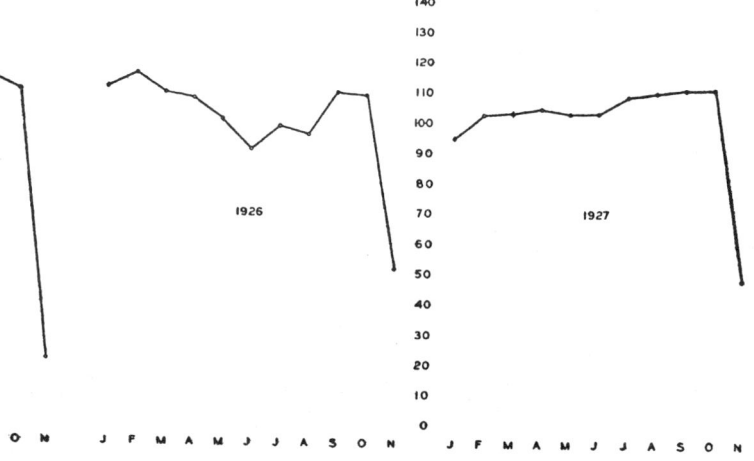

ms of a percentage of average monthly melt, adjusted to the monthly

has made the latter curve approach much more closely a straight line, and contains very few of the irregularities of the demand curve.

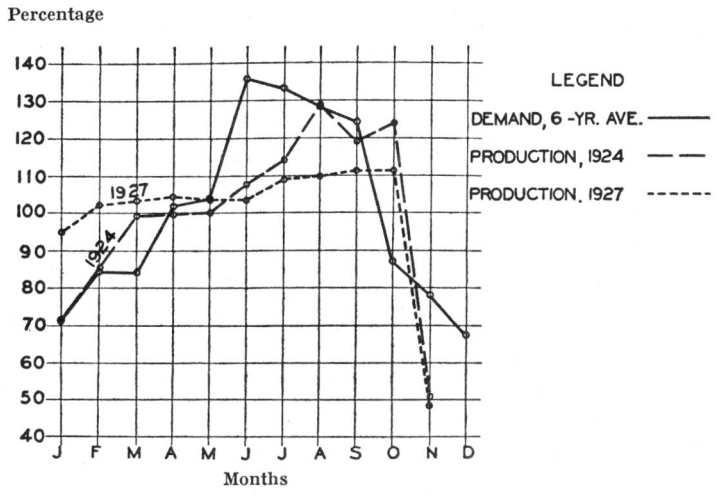

Fig. 11.—Comparison of seasonal trend of production in 1924 and 1927 with average seasonal demand for sugar

4. EFFECT OF RATE OF MELT UPON UNIT COST OF REFINING

The great savings in labor costs effected by running the refinery at maximum capacity may be seen from the figures of labor complements for each size of melt, and incidental costs of salaries and wages. The labor personnel required for the various sizes of melt is shown on pages 27 and 217 of this study, in connection with a discussion of labor budgets. The following table (Table 33) furnishes a comparison of relative increases in melt, men, and wages, in terms of a percentage of the requirements for an 1,800-ton daily melt.

The relative importance of the wage item may be appreciated through the fact that wages of labor constitute slightly more than 25 per cent of the total refining cost.

TABLE 33

COMPARISON OF RELATIVE INCREASE IN MELT, NUMBER OF MEN REQUIRED, AND WAGE COST

Melt (Tons)	Percentage increase over 1,800 Ton Melt		
	Melt	Men	Wages
1,800	100	100	100
2,000	111	104	104
2,200	122	107	107
2,400	133	109	108

The above table shows that by expending 8 per cent more in wages, the refinery can increase its output by 33 per cent. Output can be increased from 1,800 to 2,200 tons, or 22 per cent for a 7 per cent increase in expenditure on wages. Output can be increased from 2,200 to 2,400, or 11 per cent, for an increased expenditure on wages of only 1 per cent.

Figuring labor cost of one specific melt in terms of the cost of the preceding melt (as in the above table) shows the following results: Increasing the melt from 1,800 to 2,000 tons, or 11 per cent, would cost 4 per cent more in wages. An increase from 2,000 to 2,200 tons, or 10 per cent, would cost only 3 per cent additional in wages. An increase in melt from 2,200 to 2,400 tons, or 9 per cent, would increase labor costs only 1 per cent.

Some time ago a special study was made by the Finance and Accounting Division of the effect of the rate of melt and the regularity of operations upon the unit cost of refining. The results of this analysis are shown in the logarithmic chart, Figure 12 (p. 218).

Operating at maximum daily capacity for the greatest number of days per annum unquestionably tends to lower

218 THE C & H SUGAR REFINING CORPORATION

unit cost of refining. As this question was of importance in determining the relative economies of handling crops of various sizes, the study was given considerable thought. Careful analyses were made of all factors entering into cost calculations.

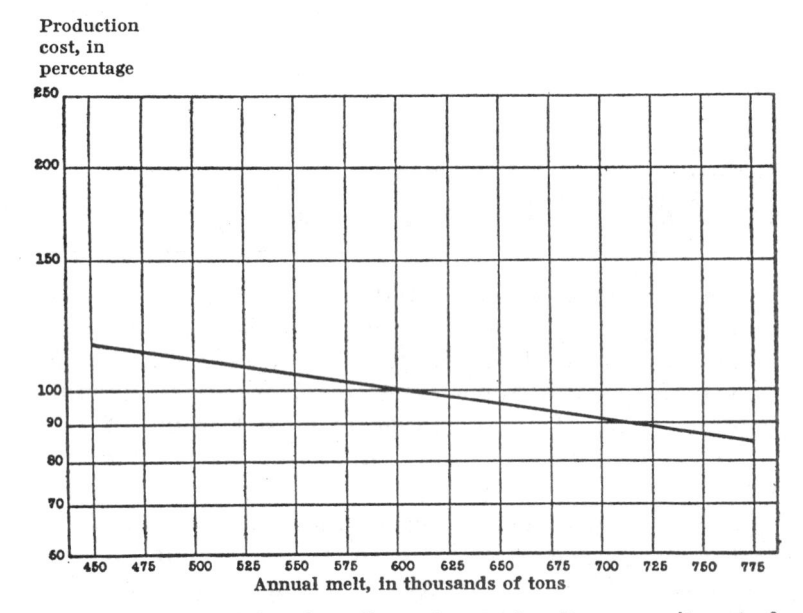

Production cost, in percentage

[Graph: x-axis "Annual melt, in thousands of tons" from 450 to 775; y-axis from 60 to 250; declining line from ~115 at 450 to ~85 at 775]

Fig. 12.—Graph showing effect of rate of melt upon unit cost of refining. Theoretical cost curve—450,000 to 775,000 tons

Costs, fixed and variable, were computed for various annual melts, as follows:

      450,000 tons
      500,000 tons
      550,000 tons
      575,000 tons
      600,000 tons
      625,000 tons
      675,000 tons

After plotting the above points, the curve of Figure 12 was extended for intermediate tonnages. Logarithmically plotted, the resultant curve approximates a straight line. The unit cost calculated for a melt of 600,000 tons was chosen as the base, or 100 per cent. Tonnages above or below this melt are expressed in percentage relationship to the base.

Many factors, large and small, technical and non-technical, enter into calculations of this kind, and to evaluate each correctly is difficult. However, all items of consequence were thoroughly analyzed, and those susceptible of mathematical computation were calculated. The best possible estimates were made for the remaining cost factors.

The ratios finally plotted may vary from time to time on account of price fluctuation in any one of the items bearing a relatively high percentage to the total cost—for example, wages, container materials, and fuel oil.

Expenditures were classified as variable and fixed. Variable items cover wages, raw materials and supplies, expenses, maintenance, and labor. Fixed expenditures cover insurance, taxes on plant and supplies, and depreciation on buildings and equipment.

The costs of some of the principal items were studied from the following points of view:

1. *Salaries and wages.*—The refinery labor costs were based upon the estimates prepared by the operating superintendent, for budget purposes, for melts ranging from 1,800 to 2,400 tons per day. While the wage cost in the operating department varies with the melt, the expenditures remain practically unchanged in the technical control, engineering, water and power, accounting, stores, personnel and general administration departments.

2. *Material and supplies.*—Under this heading the following analyses were made:

a) Containers: The total cost of containers varies

with the proportion of high-cost speciality packages to the total output. The records of actual sales performance, as shown elsewhere in this report, make it impossible to assume that the proportion of 100-lb. sacks to total sales remains constant. Accordingly, correction factors were used in estimating container costs at melts approximating maximum.

b) Fuel Oil: Actual consumption of fuel oil, per unit of output, is relatively higher at low melts because of excess exhaust steam to the atmosphere and other heat losses. Allowances were therefore made for these factors.

c) Kieselguhr, Bone Coal, Refining Chemicals, Lubricants, etc.: Past performance shows conclusively that the unit consumption of these items varies in proportion to the melt.

3. *Maintenance and repairs.*—For practical purposes the expenditure for labor and materials for maintenance may be considered as fixed, within certain ranges of melts. The analysis of these costs was therefore made in three groupings—450,000–500,000 tons, 500,000–575,000 tons, and 575,000–675,000 tons. Correction factors within each group were then applied.

4. *Fixed charges.*—The cost of insurance and taxes remains almost constant. Small variations do occur in some forms of personal property taxes and insurance premiums, because of increase or decrease in plant investment and stores. These variations, however, are negligible in their effect on final costs. Depreciation on plant investment was figured irrespective of melt; therefore the higher melts show a material decrease in the unit cost of depreciation.

5. LABOR STABILIZATION

Aside from reductions in costs and improvements in quality of product and service, the relative effectiveness of the industrial relations policy of the company is shown definitely in the progressive stabilization of its working force. As will be shown in detail in this section, the labor turnover among employees of the refinery has been cut down in 1927 to about one-third of what it was in 1923.

Gross labor turnover.—An analysis of labor turnover naturally begins with a statement of what is known as the gross labor turnover—that is, of the ratio of all separations, irrespective of cause, to the average working force. The following table (Table 34, p. 222) shows the gross labor turnover for each year since 1923.

The "lay-offs on account of annual shut-down" represent nominal separations from the payroll, during the annual shut-down, of employees who are automatically reinstated at the re-opening of the refinery after the shut-down. "Lay-offs at request of employees during shut-down" are vacations granted at employees' request during this annual shut-down. These employees, too, are reinstated at the expiration of the shut-down period.

The net or real labor turnover is therefore represented by separations due to: (*a*) discharges, (*b*) lay-offs for cause, and (*c*) quits (including died) or voluntary separations on the part of employees. The distinction between the terms "discharge" and "lay-off for cause," is described on pages 68 and 69 of this study under the heading of "Discipline and Discharge."

Before proceeding to an analysis of the net or real labor turnover, one more segregation of the gross turnover is of interest. By and large, there are two types of labor in the refinery: (1) common labor of the heavy lifting type, employed largely in the warehouse, for the handling of raw sugars upon arrival from the Islands and for the storing and shipment of the refined product; and (2) semi-skilled and skilled labor employed throughout the other parts of the refinery. The necessity for such a segregation arises from the fact that the mobility of labor is greater in the warehouse than in the refinery

TABLE 34
Gross Total Refinery Labor Turnover, 1923–1927

Year	Average Number of Employees	Accessions: Newly Hired	Accessions: Re-hired Within Six Months of Separation	Separations: Discharges and Lay-offs for Cause	Separations: Lay-offs Exclusive of Discharge and Lay-offs for Cause — Lack of Work During Operating Season	Separations: Lay-offs Exclusive — On Account of Annual Shut-down	Separations: Lay-offs Exclusive — At Request of Employees During Shut-down	Quit (Inclusive of Deceased)	Total	Gross Percentage of Labor Turn-over
1923	1,437	2,423	*	152	233	357	22	1,414	2,178	151.6
1924	1,464	799	238	111	101	170	31	610	1,023	69.9
1925	1,493	915	284	87	202	358	35	634	1,316	88.2
1926	1,451	541	379	82	142	87	49	481	841	58.0
1927	1,455	621	193	84	103	102	28	438	755	52.0

* Included under newly hired.

The following summary table (Table 35) shows the gross annual labor turnover for the entire plant, separately for the warehouse, and for the plant exclusive of the warehouse.

TABLE 35

PERCENTAGE GROSS LABOR TURNOVER, BY DEPARTMENTS

	1923	1924	1925	1926	1927
Entire plant	151.6	69.9	88.2	58.0	52.0
Warehouse	229.1	75.6	73.2	70.0	80.9
Plant exclusive of warehouse	140.4	69.0	89.8	55.5	47.4

The above table shows that the greatest turnover takes place in the warehouse. While for 1927, the gross turnover for the entire plant was 52.0 per cent, in the warehouse it was 80.9 per cent. The gross turnover for the plant exclusive of the warehouse was 47.4 per cent for 1927, as against 140.4 per cent in 1923. The gross turnover in the warehouse was cut from 229.1 per cent in 1923 to 80.9 per cent in 1927, a reduction of about two-thirds in the mobility of warehouse labor. The company realizes that its labor turnover problem is centered chiefly in the warehouse. The base wage in the warehouse is $4.96 per eight-hour day, as against $4.58½ for the rest of the plant. The management is trying to increase further the attractiveness of warehouse work and its efficiency through the payment of collective production bonuses above the base wage.

Net labor turnover.—Gross turnover has been reduced by almost two-thirds since 1923. The actual figures as shown in the last column of Table 35 are 151.6 per cent for 1923 and 52.0 per cent in 1927.

The gross figures of labor turnover do not indicate correctly the true mobility of labor in the refinery, inasmuch as they include lay-offs due to requested vacations, nominal or "bookeeping" lay-offs between the annual shutting down and reopening of the plant, and lay-offs of employees hired for special and distinctly temporary jobs. The last three categories of lay-off represent no turnover. Of a total of 103 laid off for lack of work during 1927, 79, or about three-fourths, were laid off because the nature of the position was temporary. Only 24, or about one-fourth, were laid off because of fluctuations in production budget or schedule.

By eliminating from calculation all separations not due to dissatisfaction on the part of the company or of the men, one may arrive at a percentage of actual or net labor turnover. This method of arriving at a statistical measurement of net turnover eliminates from consideration all separations due to lay-offs "for lack of work during operating season," "lay-offs on account of annual shut-down," and separations due to employee's request for temporary leave of absence. The first group represents terminations of temporary jobs. The last two constitute only "bookkeeping" turnover.

The following summary table (Table 36) presents the *net* labor turnover, for the entire plant, for the warehouse only, and for the plant exclusive of warehouse:

TABLE 36

PERCENTAGE NET LABOR TURNOVER BY DEPARTMENTS

	1923	1924	1925	1926	1927
Entire plant	109.0	49.3	48.3	38.5	35.7
Warehouse	176.6	47.1	55.2	69.4	76.7
Plant exclusive of warehouse	102.4	50.3	49.8	33.5	29.3

The above table shows, again, that the largest turnover takes place among warehouse employees. While the net turnover for the entire plant for 1927 was 35.7 per cent, the warehouse turnover was 76.7 per cent or almost twice as large. However, much progress has been made in reducing net warehouse turnover. The present figure—76.7 per cent—appears rather small compared with the figure for 1923—176.6 per cent. Exclusive of the warehouse, the net turnover for the refinery was 29.3 per cent in 1927, a reduction of more than two-thirds as compared with 1923.

Causes of all separations.—Table 37 gives the causes of separations for each year between 1923 and 1927.

TABLE 37

CAUSES OF SEPARATIONS

Year	Discharge and Permanent Lay-off for Cause No.	%	Lay-off Because of Lack of Work During Operating Season No.	%	Lay-off on Account of Annual Shut-down No.	%
1923	152	7.0	233	10.7	357	16.4
1924	111	10.8	101	9.9	170	16.7
1925	87	6.6	202	15.4	358	27.2
1926	82	9.8	142	16.8	87	10.3
1927	84	11.1	103	13.7	102	13.5
Average for five years	..	9.1	...	13.3	...	16.8

Year	Lay-off at Request of Employees During Annual Shut-down No.	%	Quit (Including Deceased) No.	%	Total No.	%
1923	22	1.0	1,414	64.9	2,178	100.0
1924	31	3.0	610	59.6	1,023	100.0
1925	35	2.7	634	48.1	1,316	100.0
1926	49	5.8	481	57.3	841	100.0
1927	28	3.7	438	58.0	755	100.0
Average for five years	..	3.2	...	57.6	...	.....

The five-year average in the foregoing table shows the greatest single cause of separation to have been "quits" or voluntary leaves. (In this item are also included employees who died—a rather small item in terms of numbers, as shown elsewhere.) The "quits" were responsible on the average for 57.6 per cent of all the turnover.

As previously pointed out, none of the lay-offs except those involved in discharges and "lay-offs for cause" represent real turnover. Hence no detailed discussion of these is necessary.

The fact that the employees are progressively more satisfied with their connection is shown in the slow but gradual reduction in the proportion of those who quit.

On the average, 9.1 per cent of all turnover was caused by discharges and lay-offs for cause. The proportion of turnover due to discharges, and lay-offs for cause has been increasing somewhat from year to year, except during 1925. This fact, however, cannot be attributed to carelessness and arbitrariness on the part of the management. As described elsewhere, final discharges or lay-offs (except for a few specific causes) are made only after an elaborate system of warnings, and after the infliction of lesser disciplinary penalties.

The generalization just made is borne out by a detailed analysis of the various causes of discharge and lay-offs for cause, presented in Table 39.

Reasons for voluntary separations.—Table 38 shows the detailed causes of voluntary separations, or quits, for 1926 and 1927.

The reason given for about 44 per cent of all voluntary separations is leaving "for other work." Almost 19 per cent of all "quits" in 1927 are ascribed to "work too hard, hot, etc." "Returning to the old country" was responsible for 10.6 per cent of the voluntary separations in 1926, and 9.4 per cent in 1927. Of such separations 1.9 per cent in 1926 and 2.1 per cent in 1927 were due to deaths.

Causes of discharges and "Lay-offs for Cause."—Table 39 shows causes for discharges and lay-offs for cause for 1925, 1926, and 1927.

TABLE 38
REASONS FOR VOLUNTARY SEPARATIONS OR "QUITS"

Reason Given	1926 No.	1926 %	1927 No.	1927 %
For other work	212	44.2	190	43.4
Because of shift work	23	4.8	5	1.1
Work too hard, hot, etc.	52	10.8	83	18.9
Because of reprimand	14	2.9	6	1.4
"Personal" reasons	11	2.3	27	6.2
Going into business	15	3.1	5	1.1
Returning to old country	51	10.6	41	9.4
Returning to school	17	3.5	28	6.4
To be married	3	0.6	5	1.1
Deported by authorities	2	0.4	...	...
Sickness	42	8.7	21	4.8
Deceased	9	1.9	9	2.1
"Family" reasons	30	6.2	18	4.1
Total	481	100.0	438	100.0

TABLE 39
CAUSES OF DISCHARGES AND "LAY-OFFS FOR CAUSE"

Cause	1925 No.	1925 %	1926 No.	1926 %	1927 No.	1927 %
"Services unsatisfactory"	6	6.9	24	29.3	20	23.9
Loafing	2	2.3	2	2.4	3	3.6
"Beating the whistle"	1	1.1	2	2.4	1	1.2
Smoking	..	....	2	2.4	1	1.2
Fighting	3	3.4	2	2.4	1	1.2
Drunkenness, disorderly conduct	5	5.7	1	1.2	3	3.6
Excessive absence	68	78.4	48	58.7	49	58.2
Excessive accidents	1	1.1	..	....	..	....
Miscellaneous	1	1.1	1	1.2	6	7.1
Total	87	100.0	82	100.0	84	100.0

The principal cause for discharges and "lay-offs for cause" is "excessive absence." This cause accounted for 58.2 per cent of all involuntary separations in 1927. This same cause was responsible for 78.4 per cent of all involuntary separations in 1925. In view of the fairness of the successive disciplinary steps leading to final lay-off for irregular attendance, this company's system of steadying attendance is clearly different, in practice, from the method usually found in industry for enforcing attendance—a lot of talk and no action.

The next greatest cause for discharge is the one noted as "service unsatisfactory." This cause was responsible for 23.9 per cent of the discharges in 1927 and 29.3 per cent in 1926. The proportion laid off for loafing increased from 2.3 per cent in 1925 to 3.6 per cent in 1927. This increase may be considered salutary; the great majority of the employees of this company work on "time," and the only way to get production is to discharge those who obviously loaf. "Beating the whistle" is a cause identical with loafing. The proportion of discharges in 1927 due to failure to produce was 3.6 per cent (for loafing) plus 1.2 per cent (for "beating the whistle") or 4.8 per cent. Drunkenness and disorderly conduct were responsible during 1927 for 3.6 per cent of all discharges.

Seasonality of labor turnover.—Since lay-offs for lack of work represent largely temporary jobs, and since lay-offs on account of annual shut-down and lay-offs at request of employees during shut-down represent no actual turnover (because of automatic reinstatement of employees upon annual reopening), the seasonality of the net labor turnover in this plant can be measured by the seasonality of discharges, lay-offs for cause, and "quits" or voluntary separations. Since voluntary separations are responsible for almost two-thirds of this total actual turnover, the figures of turnover seasonality shown herewith are influenced largely by the voluntary separations.

Table 40 shows the proportion of total annual labor turnover occurring each month, and the five-year average of turnover for each month of the year.

The chart, Figure 13 (p. 230), illustrates the seasonality of labor turnover shown in the table just presented.

TABLE 40

SEASONALITY OF LABOR TURNOVER

(Exclusive of lay-offs for lack of work)

Year	Jan.	Feb.	March	April	May	June	July
	%	%	%	%	%	%	%
1923	2.5	8.1	11.5	12.6	13.2	11.7	11.6
1924	5.9	5.9	9.7	11.2	13.4	9.9	8.9
1925	3.5	5.6	9.9	10.3	13.1	12.7	12.4
1926	6.8	5.2	10.6	10.1	12.1	11.7	9.1
1927	5.3	8.4	9.5	10.9	13.0	11.2	9.5
Average for five years ...	4.8	6.6	10.2	11.0	13.0	11.4	10.3

	Aug.	Sept.	Oct.	Nov.	Dec.	Total
	%	%	%	%	%	%
1923	8.0	8.6	7.3	4.2	0.7	100.0
1924	10.7	8.9	7.5	3.5	4.5	100.0
1925	8.9	8.1	9.3	3.1	3.1	100.0
1926	9.9	7.3	7.3	6.8	3.1	100.0
1927	9.8	6.2	5.6	6.7	3.9	100.0
Average for five years	9.4	7.8	7.4	4.7	3.6	.....

As already stated, the vital factor in determining seasonality is the voluntary separation or "quit." The number of such quits begins to increase with the passing of the winter. As spring approaches, and many openings for out-of-door positions occur, the extent of quits increases, the month of May seeing the largest number, after which it gradually diminishes. The tendency just mentioned is apparent in the turnover record of each year as well as in the average turnover for the five-year period.

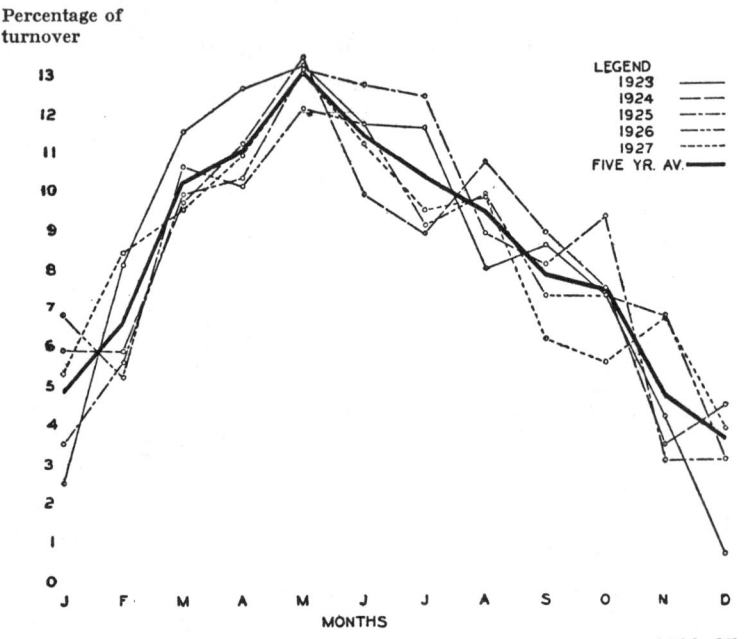

Fig. 13.—Graph showing seasonality of labor turnover, 1923–27

Estimated saving due to labor stabilization.—Aside from making the working personnel more effective, labor stabilization due to reduction in labor turnover represents considerable saving in money. Many estimates have been made from time to time as to the cost of breaking in new help in industry. Estimates vary from $200 to $300 per man, in occupations requiring much skill, to as low as ten dollars per man, in occupations where only common labor is employed. One may safely hazard the guess that this latter figure is altogether too low, and that the proper low figure would be much nearer $50.

In the tabulation presented in Table 41, showing reduction in the cost of maintaining the working personnel, the cost of breaking in a new employee was arbitrarily put at $35. This figure is considered conservative and its applicability reasonable only because of the fact that almost one-fourth of the newly hired employees in 1927 had been previously employed.

TABLE 41

REDUCTION IN COST OF MAINTAINING WORKING PERSONNEL OF REFINERY, 1923–1927

Year	Average Force	Accessions (No. Hired)	Total Cost of Breaking in New Help	Cost of Breaking in New Help per Man on Force	Index of Cost (1923=100)
1923.....	1,437	2,324	$81,340.00	$56.60	100.0
1924.....	1,464	1,037	36,295.00	24.80	43.9
1925.....	1,493	1,199	41,965.00	28.00	49.6
1926.....	1,451	920	32,200.00	22.20	39.3
1927.....	1,455	814	28,490.00	19.50	34.5

The above table shows the relative cost of breaking in help "per man on the force." This cost per man has gone down from $56.60 in 1923 to $19.50 in 1927, a reduction of 63.5 per cent. The last column shows that the cost of breaking in new help per man on the force was actually reduced from 100.0 per cent in 1923 to 34.5 per cent in 1927.

6. PRODUCTIVITY OF REFINERY LABOR

In 1927, the average annual labor productivity for the entire refinery, including the warehouse (as determined by dividing the total annual melt by the average number of employees) was 49 per cent above that of 1923.

The following table (Table 42, p. 232) shows a comparison of average daily labor productivity per man for the principal subdivisions of the refinery, for the years 1925, 1926, and 1927. Changes in average daily productivity are shown in percentages of the average daily productivity for the year 1925.

The table shows the following percentage increases in average productivity between 1925 and 1927: melting raws, 21.69 per cent; filtration, 16.76 per cent; refinery, 5.95 per cent; main packing station, 10.58 per cent; powdered sugar, 10.90 per cent.

TABLE 42

PERCENTAGE AVERAGE DAILY LABOR PRODUCTIVITY

	1925	1926	1927
Melting raws	100.0	100.77	121.69
Filtration	100.0	112.68	116.76
Refining	100.0	103.96	105.95
Main packing station	100.0	109.25	110.58
Powdered sugar station	100.0	99.19	110.90

7. PRODUCTIVITY OF CAPITAL

Capital productivity is shown herewith in two ways: (1) the ratio of the value of sales to total capital employed (annual business turnover), and (2) capital employed per ton of sugar sold. As shown on page 167 of this study in connection with an analysis of financial operations and accounting ratios, the increase in capital productivity has been as follows:

TABLE 43

CHANGES IN CAPITAL PRODUCTIVITY

Year	Ratio of Value of Sales to Capital Employed (Times)	Capital Employed per Ton of Sales
1923	3.01	$52.70
1924	2.90	49.80
1925	2.57	43.70
1926	2.18	49.50
1927	2.71	43.66

The figures shown in the column labeled "Ratio of Value of Sales to Capital Employed" show ratios of 3.01 and 2.71 for 1923 and 1927, respectively. This was due to declining sugar prices and not to business volume. The only year that did not show increased volume was 1926.

The amount of capital employed annually per ton of sales has declined from $52.70 in 1923 to $43.66 in 1927. This index of productivity shows continuous improvement in business results (that is, less capital was required per tons of sale) in each year except 1926.

The improvements in capital productivity shown here are very significant in view of the fact that the regularization of refinery operations (described on page 232) has caused appreciable increases in investment in refined sugar during certain periods of the year.

In this connection, however, it must be stated that the price obtained for refined sugar has more of an effect than any other item on capital turnover.

8. PRODUCTIVITY OF REFINERY MACHINERY AND EQUIPMENT

Good progress has been made in increasing the productivity of the investment in machinery and equipment. Table 44 (p. 234) shows the relative productivity of machinery and equipment by giving the average number of tons of sugar melted (refinery production) per $1,000 of investment in machinery and equipment, by years since 1922.

For each $1,000 invested in machinery and equipment concerned with direct refining, 89.3 tons of sugar were melted in 1927 as against 72.9 tons in 1922. For the investment in auxiliary equipment there were melted, in 1927, 1,448.0 tons per $1,000, as compared with 1,258.9 tons in 1922. The investment in "total refining" equipment (direct and auxiliary) produced 84.1 tons per $1,000 in 1927 as against 68.9 tons in 1922. The exception to the

TABLE 44

CHANGES IN PRODUCTIVITY OF MACHINERY AND EQUIPMENT

Classification of Machinery and Equipment	Number of Tons Melted per $1,000 of Machinery and Equipment					
	1922	1923	1924	1925	1926	1927
Direct Refining:						
Refining, packing, and control	101.0	94.9	114.6	123.0	123.6	123.2
Power equipment	531.0	490.6	599.1	679.8	664.4	691.4
Distribution of air, oil, water	1,085.7	814.2	993.7	1,086.3	1,105.4	1,127.7
Water delivery	958.1	941.1	1,154.8	1,255.0	1,281.8	1,338.8
Total direct refining	72.9	67.3	81.5	88.4	88.7	89.3
Auxiliary equipment (fire protection, stores, shops and tools, transportation, etc.)	1,258.9	1,252.4	1,481.8	1,620.4	1,510.5	1,448.0
Total refining (direct and auxiliary)	68.9	63.8	77.3	83.8	83.7	84.1
Warehousing	1,248.9	1,212.7	1,300.6	1,379.5	1,065.4	1,076.3
Grand Total, Machinery and Equipment	64.3	59.7	71.3	76.8	75.5	75.8

rule is found in warehousing, where the output per $1,000 of equipment declined from 1,248.9 tons in 1922 to 1,076.3 tons in 1927. This tendency toward increased warehouse costs is also shown on page 245. The reason there given for this tendency—namely, a very large increase in small-package production, and progressively larger refined sugar inventories—applies as well to the figures given in this section. Incidentally, warehousing accounts for only 3.72 per cent of the total business cost exclusive of the cost of raws.

The productivity per $1,000 for the grand total investment in machinery and equipment for the entire refinery, has increased from 64.3 tons in 1922 to 75.8 tons in 1927.

9. INSTANCES OF IMPROVEMENT IN MATERIAL AND EQUIPMENT

Of the hundreds of labor-saving devices installed during the past few years, only five will be mentioned, as illustrative of the co-ordination of work of the several departments. These are:

1. The Nelson Weighing and Conveying Installation
2. The Soft-Sugar Carton Packer and Weigher
3. The Melt Centrifugal Control
4. The Kieselguhr Regenerating Plant
5. The Oliver Filter Installation

Improvements originate in one or another of the departments. Some of the ideas are original, while others are adaptations of something an employee has seen in use elsewhere. The idea is worked over and written up in the department and copies are sent to the engineering department for study as to feasibility of plan and cost of installation. Changes are frequently made in the original plan by the engineering department. If the cost of installation compares favorably with the savings to be effected, the engineering department is authorized to proceed with the necessary construction (or purchase) and installation of the necessary equipment.

1. *Nelson Weighing and Conveying Installation.* — Prior to 1924 the raw-sugar bags were landed on the dock from the steamer and then trucked by hand, five bags to the truck, either to storage or to a belt leading into the refinery. The trucking method was found to be too slow to meet the demands for the quick discharge of steamers. At the suggestion of a member of the warehouse supervisory force, the present conveying and weighing installation was designed and manufactured by the engineering department, in collaboration with two outside companies engaged in the manufacture of conveying and weighing equipment.

The resultant saving in labor cost amounted to $0.149 per ton of sugar. The saving thus effected was in actual discharge of sugar, and does not take into consideration the saving in cost and trouble of taking care of the surplus men, under the old system, on days when no boats arrived. The Matson Navigation Company, too, gained much by this installation, through the quicker release of its vessels. The following gives a comparison of the direct labor cost under the old hand-trucking method and under the new:

```
       Hand-Trucking cost per ton.........$.168
       Nelson-Method cost per ton..........  .019
       Saving ............................  .149
```

The installation of this device enables nine men to do the work of sixty-six men with hand trucks.

2. *Soft-Sugar Carton Packer and Weigher.*—In 1926 an automatic carton packer was installed to pack brown sugar in one-pound cartons. Prior to this time, one-pound cartons were packed by hand. As this sugar is sticky, it was considered highly improbable that a machine could handle it. After much agitation on the part of the operating department for a mechanical means of packing the sugar, the engineering department, in collaboration with an outside Pneumatic Scale Company, designed and in-

stalled a machine which handles the sugar in a satisfactory manner.

Under the hand system of packing two girls made up a team, one to pack and one to weigh the cartons. A team of girls averaged about 75 cases of 24 one-pound packages per day of 8 hours. With this equipment production averages 500 cases per day of eight hours. Three operators are required, where under the hand method seven teams would be necessary to maintain the machine rate of production.

3. *Melt Centrifugal Control.* — The installation described herewith had the effect of increasing average labor productivity from 95.07 tons per man per day in 1925, to 193.80 tons in 1927. The actual reduction in cost per unit as a result of this installation was 46.28 per cent.

The melt centrifugal station consists of two mixers with eleven centrifugals to each mixer. Prior to 1926 the centrifugals were run by five men, so placed that four of the men ran four centrifugals each and one man only three centrifugals. This left three centrifugals on one of the mixers as spares, not needed to wash 2,400 tons of sugar per day of 24 hours.

During 1926 the operating department rearranged the duties of the operators and assigned two men to each mixer—one man whose duty it was to start and load all centrifugals which were running on that mixer and one man whose duty it was to shut off the power and apply the brake at the end of each centrifugal cycle. Besides these, there was one man whose duty it was to clean the centrifugal baskets for both mixers, making the total still five men per shift.

After the new method of operating was adopted, a study of the station showed that the two men whose duty it was to shut off the power and apply the brake could be dispensed with by substituting mechanical or electric devices, actuated by a timing arrangement to perform the necessary operations at the proper time. Recommendations were then made showing the saving which could be effected by such an installation, and the engineering department designed and built the present semi-automatic control for the melt centrifugals. This control system consists of the following major parts: a push button station located at each centrifugal, a supervising relay on a panel board, a magnetic switch, and contactors and solenoids. The operator presses a button at the push button station. This makes a contact which sets in motion the centrifugal and the supervising relay, which is really a timing device to synchronize each one of the various functions of the stations. As the centrifugal comes up to speed, the operator fills the basket with magma (sugar and syrup) by opening a gate from the mixer. When the basket is full, he closes the gate and goes on to the next centrifugal.

The supervising relay now starts to function, and after the centrifugal has been up to full speed for a predetermined time, the wash water is automatically turned on for a set time. Then, after another predetermined time, the power is turned off and the brake applied. This brings the centrifugal to a stop and automatically drops the washed sugar out of the basket into the melt tanks located below the centrifugals.

This station is now operated with three men per shift or nine men per day, a daily saving of the labor cost of six men.

4. *Kieselguhr Regenerating Plant.*—It is a recognized fact that the quality of refined sugar depends to a great extent upon the perfection with which its mechanical filtration system functions. The degree of perfection depends almost entirely upon the filter medium used. Kieselguhr, or diatomaceous earth, has long been recognized as a very good filter medium for sugar solutions. Therefore, everything else being equal, the plant using kieselguhr in its filters will, it is said, turn out a better

product than a plant using paper pulp or asbestos, or any of the other so-called "super" filter media. As superiority in the quality of the product has always been the aim of the Corporation, it has continued the use of kieselguhr. However, the problem of increased cost incidental to kieselguhr use had to be met.

After very exhaustive laboratory and plant tests conducted with regenerated kieselguhr, it was decided that the regeneration of spent, or once used, kieselguhr was a practical and paying proposition. The engineering department in collaboration with the technical and operating departments designed, built and operated the first kieselguhr regenerating plant to be run on a commercial scale.

The kieselguhr regenerating station has now been in operation since 1923 with much success, both from the point of view of cost and from that of operation.

5. *Oliver Filter Installation.*—The Oliver filter installation increased average labor productivity from 85.52 tons per man per day in 1925 to 171.86 tons in 1927. During 1919 and 1920 it became apparent that the capacity of the refinery would have to be increased to handle the increased output of raw sugar from the plantations. A survey of all stations was then made to find out which of the stations were capable of running at increased rates without any major changes, and which stations required rebuilding or remodeling to increase their capacity.

The sluice-water filtration station, or, as it was then called, the mud-press station, was one which required either more equipment or remodelling to increase its then maximum capacity of 1,950 tons per day. The mud-press station consisted of 14 Kilby plate and frame presses. The personnel requirement for these presses was 36 men and 3 foremen for the three shifts.

Because of the relatively large labor expense involved in the operation of the mud presses it was decided to investigate all mechanical filters then on the market. After a careful investigation and trial installation the Oliver continuous filter was adopted for filtering sluice water.

The installation of the Olivers made possible the application of many other minor changes which resulted in a more uniform operation, less sucrose loss, and other minor improvements.

The Oliver filter station is now run by three hand operators or nine men per day. The saving per 100 tons of melt over the old system was over 70 per cent.

10. INVENTIONS BY EMPLOYEES

It has been the policy to encourage employees to work out ideas which will contribute to a reduction of cost, an improvement in the quality of sugar, or the smoother running of the plant. As a result, the company was able to take advantage of many ingenious ideas contributed by employees. Ideas which were patentable, and possessed sufficient merit, were patented in the name of the employee at the company's expense. In all such cases, the company retained a shop license for the free use of the invention, the inventor retaining all other rights.

The following are some of recent inventions of employees for which patents have been either received or applied for:

1. ARMSTRONG-WOODFORD CONVEYOR:

   Joint development of chief draftsman and assistant master mechanic

   This conveyor is a novel departure from other portable conveyors and consists of twin screws on which the bags are propelled. It is made up of jointed sections, connected by universal joints, which eliminate the necessity of lining up and make it possible to quickly lengthen or shorten the conveyor. It has the further merit of easy portability and low cost and has been successfully applied.

2. ARMSTRONG CUBE-SPACING DEVICE:
    Invention of chief draftsman

   A simple attachment to the cube machine properly spaces trays under the drums, reducing spillage. This appliance greatly reduced the quantity of sugar to be reprocessed.

3. CARLSON SUGAR WASHER:
    Invention of assistant chief engineer

   Intensive tests between 1924 and 1925 proved conclusively the superiority of this washer over all others tried. In 1926 all white centrifugals were equipped with it.

5. CARLSON ELECTRIC COUNTER:
    Invention of assistant chief engineer

   This counting device is considered "fool proof" and the count secured very reliable.

6. TOOLS FOR APPLYING METAL FABRIC TO SWEETLAND FRAMES:
    Invention of chief engineer

   Invented and applied for patents on a number of such tools. Originated in 1924 and successfully used in manufacture of a large number of frames in 1924 and 1925. These special tools made possible use of metal fabric on Sweetland presses "with resultant large savings."

7. SUGAR GATES:
    Invention of chief engineer

   This gate is used in spouting, for the handling of all kinds of dry materials. It replaces the old slide or blast gates, which have been a constant source of trouble through sticking, and which it was impossible to keep tight.

8. PRESSURE-REGULATING APPARATUS:
    Invention of master mechanic

   This invention, which makes it possible to maintain a constant or a variable pressure in fluid systems, has found numerous applications throughout the refinery. At the present time it is used for automatic control of pressures on Sweetland presses, steam lines, and liquor lines. Additional use for this device will be found as automatic control is further developed at different stages in the process.

9. THREAD-CUTTING DEVICE:
   Invention of master mechanic and sewing machine mechanic

   All cotton-liner sewing machines in the bag room have been equipped with this device, which has materially increased the capacity of sewing machines and reduced unit cost by saving the time formerly required to cut the thread by hand.

10. MACHINE FOR WASHING SUGAR TRAYS:
    Invention of chief draftsman

    A machine of this type is now in service for washing and drying cube trays, replacing the laborious and costly hand washing and drying system formerly used. With this tray washer the services of only one operator are necessary, the operator feeding the used trays to the machine and seeing that the trays are stacking properly at the discharge end of the machine. The use of one cube-tray washing machine has effected an economy of labor on the cube station equivalent to the full time of three men.

11. PROGRESS IN COST REDUCTION

In evaluating progress made in cost reduction, one should bear in mind the fact that the volume of business of the Corporation, has, almost without interruption, been increasing. There was therefore a natural tendency for many fixed and other charges to automatically recede.

Before presenting some facts regarding progress made in cost reduction, it is necessary to show the relative importance of the various component parts of the total cost. The following table (Table 45) shows total business costs, exclusive of the cost of raw sugar. The expenditure on each specified item is shown as a percentage of the total business cost.

Taking the total business cost as 100, refining (that is, all processes involved at Crockett, inclusive of warehousing) accounts for 41.42 per cent, and selling accounts for 21.73 per cent of the total cost. It should be noted in this connection that the cost of selling includes all costs of freight absorption, storage, and consignment-point handling.

TABLE 45
DISTRIBUTION OF TOTAL BUSINESS COST, 1927
(per 100 lbs. of sugar)

Principal Items of Expense	Percentage of Total Cost
Refining	37.70
Warehousing	3.72
Selling	21.73
Administration	1.50
General office	1.16
Legal and "other" expense, federal tax, financial gains and losses	6.04
Commissions and cash discounts	16.83
Loss in refining	11.00
Outside operations	0.32
	100.00

Changes in relative importance of major cost items.—Table 46 shows annual changes, since 1923, in relative importance (to wholesale price) of some of the major items of expense, inclusive of the cost of the raw sugar.

TABLE 46
PERCENTAGE DISTRIBUTION OF TOTAL WHOLESALE PRICE TO MAJOR ITEMS OF EXPENSE

Item of Expense	1923	1924	1925	1926	1927
Cost of 100 lbs. of raws	80.1	80.0	77.5	75.7	79.4
Loss in refining	3.3	2.8	2.1	2.0	2.1
Cost of refining	7.7	7.8	8.8	9.7	7.9
Selling and overhead	4.1	4.5	6.8	7.5	7.1
Cash discounts	2.0	2.0	2.0	2.1	1.9
Commission	2.8	2.9	2.8	3.0	1.6
Total costs	100.0	100.0	100.0	100.0	100.0

Since 1923 there has been relatively little fluctuation in the proportion expended on raw sugar. The proportionate cost of "loss in refining" has been reduced from 3.3 per cent of the total in 1923, to 2.1 per cent in 1927. The slight decline in the proportion charged to "cash discounts," and the greater tendency in the same direction charged to "loss in refining," both emphasize the constantly decreasing margin between the price paid for raws and the selling price obtained for refined sugar. All refineries have been confronted with this problem since 1923, as a result of overproduction followed by greater competitive marketing. The proportion of total cost chargeable to "selling and overhead" has been increasing each year, from 4.1 per cent in 1923 to 7.1 per cent in 1927. However, statistical analyses presented elsewhere in this study reveal that the actual increase under this heading was due wholly to the inclusion of costs of freight absorption, handling, and consignment storage, because of extension of sales and changes in distribution methods. All other selling expenses and overhead sales costs have actually been declining.

In considering the figures presented in the table above, one should keep in mind that all items of expense (except that involved in selling) when considered in absolute figures per unit, have been going down.

As compared with 1923, costs in 1927 were: total—76.3 per cent; raws—71.4 per cent; refining—73.1 per cent; sales and overhead—126.0 per cent. The reason for the increased cost of these latter items has been shown in the comment of the preceding table. The cost of "loss in refining" in 1927 was only 46.2 per cent of what it was in 1923. In addition to the decreased cost of raws, the improvement in extraction (or recovery) and in operating efficiency is clearly shown in the column entitled "loss in refining." The slight increase in 1927 is occasioned by an average increase in the cost of raws over 1926.

The progress in cost reduction is shown more specifically in Tables 47 and 48 which deal with comparative unit costs and expenses (exclusive of cost of raw sugar) between 1921 and 1927.

TABLE 47
PERCENTAGE CHANGES IN RELATIVE COST OF PRINCIPAL ITEMS OF EXPENSE

Year	Total Cost	Cost of Raws	Refining	Sales and Overhead	Loss in Refining
1923	100.0	100.0	100.0	100.0	100.0
1924	95.0	89.4	90.1	98.5	75.3
1925	73.6	67.0	79.0	116.2	44.4
1926	66.8	59.3	79.1	116.0	37.8
1927	76.3	71.4	73.1	126.0	46.2

Table 48 gives an annual index of the major items of business costs, in terms of percentage of cost for 1921:

TABLE 48
ANNUAL INDEX OF COMPARATIVE UNIT COSTS

Department Cost or Classification	1921	1922	1923	1924
Cost of refining	100.00	87.86	102.57	88.60
Cost of warehousing, Crockett	100.00	81.18	105.21	77.57
Cost of selling	100.00	82.15	85.16	91.77
General administrative expense	100.00	74.27	71.07	67.71
General office expense	100.00	70.51	81.48	82.88
Total costs	100.00	79.15	89.90	85.34

	1925	1926	1927
Cost of refining	86.51	82.91	77.12
Cost of warehousing, Crockett	132.62	151.33	161.03
Cost of selling	102.31	95.40	102.15
General administrative expense	75.66	69.50	66.02
General office expense	73.08	76.66	75.77
Total costs	77.44	78.15	80.82

Cost of refining.—Relative costs are shown here in terms of the unit cost of 1921. The direct total refining costs have decreased 22.88 per cent since 1921, in spite of the fact that a 10 per cent wage increase was made in 1923, first in the form of a bonus (1923–1926) and since 1927 as an integral part of the wage. The underlying causes for the reduction in the refining cost are described elsewhere in this report. The cost of warehousing, however, has increased 61 per cent since 1921. This was due to: (1) progressively larger accumulations of raw and refined sugar inventories at certain seasons of the year, and (2) a great increase in the production and handling of small-package specialties.

Cost of selling.—With the exception of 1922 and 1925, selling costs have been getting higher every year. The selling cost in 1927 was 2.15 per cent greater than that of 1921. The increased cost of selling was due wholly to the increased cost of freight absorption, consignment storage, and handling, incidental to the expansion of sales territories. The actual unit cost of maintaining the central sales organization in San Francisco in 1927 was 12 per cent less than in 1924, largely because of the increase in the volume of business.

General administrative and office expense.—The unit cost of administration has declined by one-third since 1921. The grand total unit costs for the organization have been steadily declining since 1921, except during 1926 when they rose slightly, owing to a temporary decline in volume of sales brought about by competitive marketing. The general total unit cost in 1927 was one-fifth less than in 1921—80.82 per cent, to be precise.

Table 49 shows, in percentages of the total refining cost, the relative importance of the major items of expense in total cost of refining for 1927.

This table is to be used in connection with the analysis of progress of refining-cost reduction, shown in Table 50

(p. 248) so that the relative importance of cost reduction in each item of expense may be appreciated.

TABLE 49

DISTRIBUTION OF TOTAL REFINERY UNIT COST

Items of expenditure	Percentage of Total Refinery Cost
Manufacturing or operating	76.9
Technical control	1.8
Water and power	15.0
Engineering and maintenance	4.1
Purchasing and stores	1.4
Transportation	0.3
Industrial relations	2.6
Accounting and Statistical	0.7
General plant expense	7.0
Administration expense	2.7
Sub-total	112.5
Less—Refinery Income	–12.5
Total	100.0

With a very few exceptions, the unit costs of 1927 were lower than those of 1925. The exceptions are: transportation, industrial relations, and refinery administrative expense. The cost of industrial relations has gone up 8.23 per cent since 1925 on account of increased community activities, which are chargeable to the industrial relations account.

The radical increase in administrative expense (55.02 per cent in 1927) has been caused by a change in accounting methods. This increase, however, is insignificant in relation to total costs. The two items showing some real increases—transportation and industrial relations—account for only 2.9 per cent of the total refinery cost.

TABLE 50

COMPARISON OF UNIT COSTS OF MAJOR REFINING FUNCTIONS

Functions	Total	Functions	Total
Manufacturing or Operating (exclusive of warehousing)		Industrial Relations	
1925	100.00	1925	100.00
1926	95.93	1926	107.81
1927	90.21	1927	108.23
Technical Control		Accounting and Statistical	
1925	100.00	1925	100.00
1926	106.88	1926	91.80
1927	91.98	1927	79.38
Water and Power		General Plant Expense	
1925	100.00	1925	100.00
1926	90.08	1926	126.00
1927	79.11	1927	111.27
Engineering and Mechanical		Administrative Expense	
1925	100.00	1925	100.00
1926	73.49	1926	87.20
1927	66.20	1927	155.02
Purchasing and Stores		Total	
1925	100.00	1925	100.00
1926	110.74	1926	95.85
1927	93.94	1927	88.94
Transportation			
1925	100.00		
1926	120.97		
1927	101.61		

Much progress has been made in the reduction of unit costs in the major refining functions. The following table (Table 51) presents comparative unit costs for the major refining functions for 1925–1927. The unit costs for 1926 and 1927 are shown as a percentage of the unit cost for 1925:

TABLE 51

COMPARISON OF PERCENTAGE UNIT COSTS OF MAJOR REFINING FUNCTIONS

Major Refining Function	Cost Index (1925=100)		
	1925	1926	1927
Melting raws	100.00	99.48	89.67
Filtration	100.00	87.54	87.06
Refining	100.00	95.07	99.66
Packing	100.00	92.83	88.59
General Manufacturing Expense	100.00	90.16	65.80
Fixed and other charges	100.00	104.87	97.11
Total	100.00	95.94	92.98

The above table shows the following reductions in unit costs in 1927 as compared with 1925: Melting raws, 10.33 per cent; filtration, 12.94 per cent; refining, 0.34 per cent; packing, 11.41 per cent; general manufacturing expense, 34.20 per cent; fixed and other charges, 2.89 per cent. The total reduction for the entire group of functions shown above was 7.02 per cent.

GENERAL OFFICE UNIT COSTS

Frequent studies are being made for the purpose of revealing progress made in cost reduction and increased efficiency. The usefulness of such studies and the thoroughness with which they are made are shown in this section, which deals with the results of the last investigation into comparative general office costs, made early in 1928. The survey was made and data were prepared under the following heads:

A. Nature of increased costs
 1. Salary increases
 2. Increase in the number of employees
 3. Increased operating costs
  a) Rentals
  b) Supplies
  c) Telephone and telegraph
  d) Office expense
  e) Fixed charges
B. Causes of increase
 1. Increased volume of business
 2. Increased number of units handled
 3. Increased demand for statistical data and accounting records
C. Methods for control of office costs

Changes in costs. — The table presented herewith (Table 52) shows an appreciable increase in total expenditure. When reduced to a unit basis, however, the increased cost is relatively small. Sales have been used as a basis for calculating unit costs. The table shows the changes in general office costs, by years, from 1922.

TABLE 52

COMPARISON OF TOTAL EXPENDITURES, COST PER UNIT (100 LBS.), AND VOLUME OF SALES IN PERCENTAGE OF 1922

Year	Expenditure Index	Unit Cost Index	Volume Index
1922	100.0	100.0	100.0
1923	111.0	115.0	....
1924	128.0	117.7	....
1925	137.0	103.0	....
1926	134.0	109.0	....
1927	147.0	107.5	143.5

While total expenditures have increased 47 per cent since 1922, the unit cost has increased only 7.5 per cent. In the same time the volume of sales has increased 43.5

per cent. To locate further the specific point of increased costs, the total costs of the general office were analyzed by objects of expenditure, as follows.

Salaries and wages.—Salaries and wages paid represent 75 per cent of the total expenditure. The net increase in this item for the year 1927 as compared with 1922 amounted to 89 per cent of the total increased cost. The increase was distributed as follows:

1. Increases in salaries paid 53 employees—1922 to 1927—equivalent to 15 per cent over 6-year period .... 48.0 per cent
2. Increase in number of employees—7 employees, total annual compensation .... 27.5 per cent
3. Bonus—charged direct in 1927 only .... 24.5 per cent
  Total .... 100.0 per cent

Increases in the salaries of office personnel during the period under consideration accounted for 15 per cent of the excess cost. The general office has a relatively small number of employees, when the volume of sales and the extensive statistical and accounting activities are considered. Because of the great stability of the office force there has been a gradual advancement in grade, and today maximum salaries are paid in most positions.

In May, 1923, a salary bonus of 10 per cent was authorized. This added cost was charged to a general administrative account, not distributable to departments. The bonus was thought to be of a temporary nature and if charged to departmental activities, would have distorted comparative costs. The bonus was made permanent, however, in 1927, at which time the additional cost began to be allocated to departmental activities. This bonus accounts for nearly one-fourth of the excess of 1927 over 1922.

The increase in the number of employees is traceable to departments affected by sales volume, together with sales methods brought about by changes in marketing conditions. In 1927 sales were 77 per cent above those of 1921. The increase in total volume was accompanied by a reduction in tonnage per customer's invoice. The number of customers' invoices handled shows an exceedingly large gain and is one of the outstanding factors influencing the work in all departments incidental to the sales of sugar. Data on the number of invoices for the years 1921 and 1922 are not available. Increases in the number of customer invoices handled in 1927, in terms of 1923, were: Coast territory, 44 per cent increase; Eastern territory, 182 per cent increase. This increase was brought about by expansion of territory, by hand-to-mouth buying, and by competitive conditions which resulted in the replacement, in some of the large markets, of quantity buyers by smaller ones. The number of customers of the company in 1927 was 225 per cent of what it was in 1925.

Analysis shows an increasing sale through consignments, largely in the Eastern territories, from 31 per cent of total Eastern sales in 1922 to 60 per cent of total in 1927. The additional work incidental to increased consignment business is caused by the increased number of warehouses and the necessity for detail, grade, and package control in each. The checking of warehouse reports, storage rates, storage charges, and insurance involves time and much correspondence. All invoicing of sales by consignment is done in the brokers' offices. This invoicing must be audited at San Francisco for price, contract application, terms, freight absorptions, etc. The work in following up errors and adjustments has thrown a heavy burden upon the order, billing, tabulating, credit, and accounts-receivable departments.

Another important factor contributing to increased work and cost in the billing and tabulating departments has been the increase in specialty sales. Each of the specialties has its grade differential, while the freight expense varies with the container. The billing department must build up these prices for each item, for extension on the customer's invoice. When these invoices reach the tabulating department they must be broken down to determine: (1) the base price at which sugar was sold, (2) the grade and package differential, (3) the freight expense, and (4) the freight expense recovered.

Increases in the sales of grades and specialties were:

Solid pack sugars .... 100 per cent in 1927 over 1922
Boxes, all grades .... 44 per cent in 1927 over 1922
Bales Fine Standard and
  Berry .... 224 per cent in 1927 over 1922
Cartons .... 810 per cent in 1927 over 1923

Increased average productivity per office employee.—The reason why the increase in cost per unit was less than the absolute increase in cost is due to an increased productivity per office employee, due to improved methods, simplified practices, better control, the introduction of mechanical devices, and a greater extent of co-operation on the part of employees.

Table 53 shows the improvement in average productivity per office employee for 1927, in terms of the productivity of 1921:

TABLE 53
PERCENTAGE INCREASED PRODUCTIVITY PER OFFICE EMPLOYEE

Department	Percentage increase in 1927 over 1921
Order department	48
Billing	77
Tabulating	33
Accounts receivable	33
Consignment	18
Total office force	44

The above table shows an increase in productivity, between 1921 and 1927, ranging from 18 per cent in "consignment" to 77 per cent in the billing department. On the average, the productivity increased 44 per cent.

The changes in costs in several of the other departments, and the reasons for the increased costs, cannot be measured statistically. Comment will therefore be confined to a general statement of changes in amount of work in these departments between 1921 and 1927.

Insurance department.—Increased volume of sales and changing methods of distribution, have greatly increased the work of this department.

Credit department.—This work, formerly handled by one employee, now requires the full time of two. As already mentioned, the number of customers has more than doubled between 1925 and 1927. The competitive conditions which have brought about rapid changes in terms of sale, together with the increased volume of sales, has made the collection problem more difficult. The work of adjusting remittances where the customer has made the wrong application of allowances and discounts keeps the department busy. Customers frequently do not maintain complete files. In consequence, there is confusion between terms of future contracts and terms of contracts actually in force at time of purchase, and a large percentage of incorrect remittances.

The large increase in numbers of invoices, already referred to, was followed by an increased number of cash remittances, adding to complications and to the amount of work.

Traffic department.—The growing volume of sales and the increase in consignments and water shipments have added materially to the number of freight bills, the number of claims to be handled, and the work of car tracing. Expansion in territory necessitated a continuous compilation and application of added rate schedules.

Auditing department.—Prior to 1922 all auditing was done by an outside firm of public accountants. The outside accounting work is now confined solely to a periodic certification of balance sheets.

Accounting and statistical department.—In the period under review, one employee was added. The general office management, by proper allocation of work and the selection of efficient personnel, has enabled this department to keep abreast of all demands in spite of a great increase in requests for additional statements, new statistical data and a greater extent of research.

Expenses of general office.—The discussion so far has been confined to comparative costs of wages and salaries —the largest single item of general office cost. The wages-and-salaries item accounts for about three-quarters of the total cost of the general office. The remaining one-quarter is consumed by what is classified as expense. This classification covers supplies, telephone and telegraph, "other expenses, rentals, and fixed charges." The following table (Table 54) shows a comparison of the office expense cost for 1922 and 1927.

TABLE 54

CLASSIFIED ITEMS OF EXPENSE, 1922, 1927, IN PERCENTAGES

Item	1922 Percentage of Total	1927 Percentage of Total
Supplies	24.4	21.2
Telephone and telegraph	17.5	4.7
Other expenses	31.9	12.3
Rentals	20.5	50.5
Fixed charges	5.7	11.3
	100.0	100.0

The total net increase of this group was about 13 per cent. The cost of supplies actually increased only a few dollars in spite of the great increase in volume of business since 1922. Telephone and telegraph service costs have been cut in 1928 to about one-third of what they were in 1922. A similarly large reduction in the cost of "other expenses" has taken place. A net reduction has been effected in all items except rentals and fixed charges. The increased cost of rentals and fixed charges (insurance, taxes, and depreciation of equipment) was brought about by the enlargement of the offices when the present quarters were occupied in 1923.

APPENDIX

CLASSIFICATION OF ACCOUNTS

| Account Number ||| ASSETS |
Main	Sub	Sub	
110			CURRENT ASSETS
111			IMPREST FUNDS
	111	01	San Francisco
	111	02	Crockett
	111	03	Crockett Girls Club
	111	04	Seavey & Flarsheim, Kansas City, Missouri
112			CASH IN BANKS—SAN FRANCISCO OFFICE
	112	01	
	112	02	
	112	03	
	112	04	
	112	05	
	112	06	
	112	07	
	112	08	
	112	09	
	112	10	Bank of—Pay Roll Account
112			CASH IN BANKS—SAN FRANCISCO OFFICE
	112	11	Bank of—Special Account
	112	15	Transfer of Funds
113			CASH IN BANKS—CROCKETT
	113	01	Bank of—Payroll Account
	113	02	Bank of—Depositing Account
114			UNITED STATES GOVERNMENT SECURITIES
115			CUSTOMERS ACCOUNTS
116			ACCOUNTS RECEIVABLE
117			RENTS RECEIVABLE
118			NOTES AND LOANS RECEIVABLE
	118	01	Notes Receivable
	118	02	
	118	03	Loans Receivable—General
	118	04	Loans Receivable—Call
	118	05	Loans Receivable—Agents
	118	06	
119			NOTES RECEIVABLE DISCOUNTED
120			PROVISION FOR BAD AND DOUBTFUL ACCOUNTS AND NOTES
	120	01	Raw-Sugar Contract
	120	02	Hawaiian Plantation Feed Molasses Contract
121			PROVISION FOR CASH DISCOUNTS
122			
123			ACCRUED INTEREST RECEIVABLE

THE C & H SUGAR REFINING CORPORATION

Account Number			
Main	Sub	Sub	
124			
125			RAW SUGAR—BOOK VALUE
	125	01	Inventory
	125	02	Purchases—Delivered to Crockett
	125	03	Purchases—Delivered to Western Sugar Refinery
	125	04	
	125	05	Cost of Raw Sugar—To the Trade (Credit)
	125	06	Cost of Raw Sugar Sold—To W.S.R. (Credit)
126			REFINED SUGAR—BOOK VALUE
	126	01	Inventory—Cane
	126	02	Purchases—Cane
	126	03	Purchases—Beet
	126	04	Starch Used in Refining
	126	05	Cost of Cane Sugar Refined
	126	06	Cost of Cane Sugar Sold (Credit)
127			HAWAIIAN PLANTATION FEED MOLASSES—BOOK VALUE
	127	011	Inventory—Molasses
	127	012	Inventory—Freight
	127	02	Purchases
	127	03	Freight
	127	04	
	127	051	Cost of Molasses Sold—Molasses (Credit)
	127	052	Cost of Molasses Sold—Freight (Credit)
130			FIXED ASSETS
131			LANDS
	131	1	Plant Site
	131	11	Patented Lands
	131	12	Fee Simple Lands
	131	13	Franchise Lands
	131	14	
	131	2	Other Lands
	131	21	Town of Crockett
	131	22	Crolona
	131	23	Valona
	131	24	Colville Addition
	131	25	Crockett Heights No. 1
	131	26	Crockett Heights No. 2
	131	27	Edwards Ranch
	131	28	Tenney Terrace
	131	29	
	131	3	Lands at Point San Quentin
	131	31	McBryde Station
132			LAND IMPROVEMENTS
	132	1	Parks and Playgrounds
	132	2	Roads and Pathways
	132	3	
133			BUILDINGS AND STRUCTURES
	133	1	Buildings
	133	10	Plant Buildings
	133	101	Warehouses and Viaducts
	133	102	Refining group
	133	103	Power Plant
	133	104	Stores

APPENDIX 259

Account Number			
Main	Sub	Sub	
	133	105	Shops
	133	106	Office
	133	107	Miscellaneous
	133	108	
	133	12	Outside Buildings
	133	121	Transportation Bulidings
	133	122	Hotel Crockett
	133	123	Civic Welfare Buildings
	133	124	Rental Cottages and Buildings
	133	125	San Francisco Dock Office
	133	126	Buildings and Structures for Resale
	133	1261	Crockett Heights No. 1
	133	1262	Crockett Heights No. 2
	133	1263	Tenney Terrace
	133	1264	Crockett, Valona, Crolona
	133	127	
	133	2	Structures
	133	201	Bridges, Inclines and Approaches
	133	202	Wharves and Yards
	133	203	Fences Enclosing Plant
	133	204	Miscellaneous Civic Structures
	133	205	McBryde Pier
	133	206	San Pedro Tank and Barrel House
	133	207	
134			MACHINERY AND EQUIPMENT
	134	1	Plant
	134	101	Warehouse Equipment
	134	102	Refining, Packing, and Control Equipment
	134	103	Power Equipment
	134	1031	Steam
	134	1032	Electrical
	134	104	Distribution Equipment
	134	1041	Water
	134	1042	Air
	134	1043	Oil
	134	1044	Soda
	134	1045	Miscellaneous
	134	105	Water Delivery Equipment
	134	106	Fire Protection, Mains and Equipment
	134	107	Stores Equipment
	134	108	Shop and Yard Equipment
	134	109	Tools and Implements
	134	1091	General Plant
	134	1092	Construction
	134	110	Refinery Office Equipment
	134	111	Transportation Equipment
	134	112	General Miscellaneous
	134	113	
	134	114	San Pedro Molasses Equipment
	134	115	
	134	2	Outside
	134	201	Hotel Crockett Equipment
	134	202	Civic Welfare Equipment
	134	203	Rental Cottages and Building Equipment
	134	2041	San Francisco Office Furniture and Equipment
	134	2042	San Francisco Office Fixtures and Miscellaneous Equipment
	134	205	Miscellaneous Equipment

THE C & H SUGAR REFINING CORPORATION

Account Number			
Main	Sub	Sub	
135	134	206	BONE COAL
136			PLANS, SURVEYS AND APPRAISALS
	136	1	Plans and Specifications
	136	2	Surveys
	136	3	Appraisals
	136	4	Moving Picture Films
	136	5	San Francisco Office Library
	136	6	Refinery Library
	136	7	Patents and Trade Marks
	136	8	Brands, Electros, Cuts, etc.
	136	9	
	136	10	Miscellaneous
138			PROVISIONS FOR DEPRECIATION
	138	1	
	138	2	
			(Sub Accounts same as 132-133-134)
140			OTHER ASSETS
141			STORES AND SUPPLIES
	141	01	Stores
	141	02	Completed Containers
	141	03	Advertising and Educational Supplies
	141	04	Multi Color Press Department—Supplies
142			PREPAID SUGAR FREIGHT
143			DEFERRED CHARGES
	143	01	Unexpired Insurance
	143	02	Prepaid Taxes
	143	03	Prepaid Interest
	143	04	
	143	05	Refinery Clearing Account
	143	06	Accrued Water Expense—Water
	143	07	Accrued Water Expense
	143	08	Group Insurance—Prepaid Premiums
	143	09	Unamortized Bond Interest, Discount and Expense
	143	091	Interest
	143	092	Discount
	143	093	Expense
	143	10	Raw-Sugar Handling
	143	11	
	143	12	
	143	13	
144			SUNDRY ADVANCES
	144	01	Hotel Crockett
	144	02	
	144	03	Group Insurance Premiums
	144	04	
	144	05	Personal Accounts
	144	06	
	144	07	Publication Account
	144	08	

APPENDIX

Account Number			
Main	Sub	Sub	
	144	09	
	144	10	
	144	19	Miscellaneous
145			CONST. AND WORK IN PROCESS
	145	01	Shop Work in Process
	145	02	Plant Orders in Process
	145	03	Outside Improvement Budget
	145	04	Plant Improvement Budget
	145	05	Preliminary Surveys, Plans, and Estimates
146			
147			
148			
149			
150			INVESTMENTS
151			OUTSIDE INVESTMENTS
	151	01	
	151	02	
152			SPECIAL FUNDS
	152	01	
	152	02	
	152	03	
153			SINKING FUND
160			GOOD WILL

Account Number			LIABILITIES AND CAPITAL WORTH
Main	Sub	Sub	
210			CURRENT LIABILITIES
211			ACCOUNTS PAYABLE
212			
213			LOANS PAYABLE
214			NOTES PAYABLE
215			
216			ACCRUED PAYROLL
	216	01	Refinery Payroll
	216	02	Unclaimed Wages
	216	03	Premium Reserve
	216	04	
217			ACCRUED TAXES
	217	01	Contra Costa County
	217	02	Marin County
	217	03	State Franchise
	217	04	
	217	05	Federal Income Tax
	217	06	
	217	07	
218			ACCRUED INTEREST
	218	01	Notes Payable
	218	02	Loans Payable
	218	03	Bonds Payable
	218	04	
	218	05	

THE C & H SUGAR REFINING CORPORATION

Account Number			
Main	Sub	Sub	
219			DEFERRED CREDITS
	219	01	
	219	02	
	219	03	
220			DIVIDENDS PAYABLE
	220	01	Common Stock
	220	02	Preferred Stock
240			CONTINGENT LIABILITIES
241			RAW-SUGAR CONTRACT—SUPPLEMENTAL PAYMENT
242			HAWAIIAN PLANTATION FEED MOLASSES SUPPLEMENTAL PAYMENT
243			
250			FIXED LIABILITIES
251			BONDS PAYABLE
	251	01	First Mortgage 15 year, 7%, Gold Bonds, Due 1937
	251	02	
252			
253			
260			RESERVES
261			FIXED CHARGES
	261	01	Insurance
	261	02	Taxes
	261	03	
262			OTHER CHARGES
	262	01	Maintenance and Repairs
	262	02	Shut-Down
	262	03	Contingencies
	262	04	Bone Coal Renewals
	262	05	
	262	06	
290			CAPITAL STOCK
291			AUTHORIZED CAPITAL STOCK—COMMON
292			UNISSUED CAPITAL STOCK—COMMON
293			AUTHORIZED CAPITAL STOCK—PREFERRED
294			UNISSUED CAPITAL STOCK—PREFERRED
295			SURPLUS
	295	01	Surplus—Beginning of Period
	295	02	Surplus Adjustment—Credits
	295	03	Surplus Adjustment—Debits
	295	04	
	295	05	
	295	06	
	295	07	Surplus Appropriated—Sinking Fund Reserve
	295	08	Reserve for Sinking Fund
	295	09	
600			TRADING ACCOUNTS

Account Number			
Main	Sub	Sub	
610			SALES
	610	01	Cane Sugar—Carryover
	610	02	Cane Sugar—Contract
	610	03	Beet Sugar
	610	04	Raws to the Trade
	610	05	Raws to Others
	610	06	Refinery Molasses
620			RETURNS AND ALLOWANCES
	620	01	Cane Sugar—Carryover
	620	02	Cane Sugar—Contract
	620	03	Beet Sugar
630			CASH DISCOUNTS ALLOWED
	630	01	Cane Sugar—Carryover
	630	02	Cane Sugar—Contract
	630	03	Beet Sugar
640			COST OF SALES
	640	01	Cane Sugar—Carryover
	640	02	Cane Sugar—Contract
	640	03	Beet Sugar
	640	04	Raws to the Trade
	640	05	Raws to Others
	640	06	
700			CURRENT PROFIT AND LOSS ACCOUNT

Account Number			
Main	Sub	Sub	DISTRIBUTION BY OBJECTS OF EXPENDITURE
			To distribute the costs of the functions by objects, the first digit in the second sub-account will be used.
			The Objects of Expenditures are as follows:
		100	Salaries and Wages
		200	Materials
		300	Supplies
		400	Expense, other than Supplies
		500	Maintenance and Repairs
		600	Fixed Charges
		700	Other Charges
		800	Income

ITEMS CLASSIFIED AS MATERIALS

Acids
    Hydrofluoric
    Muriatic
    Phosphoric, Paste
    Phosphoric, Syrupy
Bone Coal
Blankets—Char Filter
Cloths—Sweetland Press Leaf

ITEMS CLASSIFIED AS MATERIALS (Continued)

*Container Material
Fuel Oil
Kieselguhr
**Lime (for Milk of Lime System)
**Soda Ash (for boiling out equipment)
Starch

> *All containers and container material, except material for making bags and liners, which is chargeable to SWO.
> **Charge Lime and Soda Ash used in the Boiler House (Booth Softeners) to "Supplies."
> All other items of Stores charged to Manufacturing are supplies.

| Account Number ||| MANUFACTURING |
Main	Sub	Sub	
330			MELTING RAWS
			DIRECT MANUFACTURING COSTS
	331	01	Cutting In—Cut in Station
	331	02	Cutting In—Hard and Sticky Sugar
	332	01	Conveying—Drag and Conveyor
	333	01	Washing—Minglers, Centrifugals
	334	01	Melting—Premelter, Melts
	335	01	
	336	01	
	337	01	
			INDIRECT MANUFACTURING COSTS
	338	01	
	338	02	
	338	03	
	339	01	Undistributed Charges—Supervision
	339	02	
	339	03	
	339	04	
	339	05	Undistributed Charges—Expense
340			FILTRATION
			DIRECT MANUFACTURING COSTS
	341	01	Defecation—Blow Ups
	341	02	Defecation—Milk of Lime System
	341	03	
	341	04	
	341	05	
	342	01	Cloth Filtration—Sweetlands
	342	02	Cloth Filtration—Oliver Filters and Mud Presses
	343	03	
	342	04	
	342	05	
	343	01	Char Filtration—Char Filters and Auxiliaries
	343	02	Char Filtration—Bone Coal Renewals
	343	03	
	343	04	

Account Number			
Main	Sub	Sub	
	343	05	
	344	01	Liquor Control—Receiving Tanks and Pumps
	344	02	Liquor Control—Liquor Gallery
	344	03	
	344	04	
	344	05	
	345	01	
	345	02	
	345	03	
			INDIRECT MANUFACTURING COSTS
	346	01	Char Revivification—Wet Conveying System
	346	02	Char Revivification—Kiln Driers, Coolers
	346	03	Char Revivification—Dry Conveying and Screening
	346	04	
	346	05	
	347	01	Kieselguhr Regeneration
	347	02	
	347	03	
	347	04	
	347	05	
	349	01	Undistributed Charges—Supervision
	349	02	
	349	03	
	349	04	
	349	05	Undistributed Charges—Expense
350			REFINING
			DIRECT MANUFACTURING COSTS
	351	01	Concentration—Evaporators
	351	02	
	351	03	
	352	01	Crystallization—Low Grade Pans and Auxiliaries
	352	02	Crystallization—Low Grade Crystallizers
	352	03	
	352	04	
	352	05	Crystallization—White Sugar Pans and Auxiliaries
	352	06	
	352	07	
	352	10	Crystallization—Soft Sugar Pans and Auxiliaries
	352	11	
	352	12	
	353	01	Washing—Low Grade Mixers, Centrifugals and Syrup Tanks
	353	02	
	353	03	
	353	05	Washing—White Sugar Mixers, Centrifugals and Syrup Tanks
	353	06	
	353	07	
	353	10	Washing—Soft Sugar Mixers, Centrifugals and Syrup Tanks
	353	11	
	353	12	
	354	01	Conveying—Wet White Sugars
	354	02	

266   THE C & H SUGAR REFINING CORPORATION

Account Number			
Main	Sub	Sub	
	354	03	
	355	01	Drying—White Sugars, Granulators, Driers, Magnetic Pulleys
	355	02	
	355	03	
	356	01	
	356	02	
	356	03	
	357	01	Screening—White Sugar Hummers and Newaygos
	357	02	
	357	03	
	358	01	Conveying—Dry White Sugar, Bins, Scrolls, Elevators
	358	02	
	358	03	
	359	01	
	359	02	
	359	03	
	360	01	Pressing—Cube and Cubelet Sugars
	360	02	Cleaning Cube Trays
	360	03	
	361	01	
	361	02	
	361	03	
	362	01	
	362	02	
	362	03	
			INDIRECT MANUFACTURING COSTS
	364	01	Molasses Handling
	364	02	
	364	03	
	365	01	Apparatus Cleaning System
	365	02	
	365	03	
	366	01	
	366	02	
	366	03	
	369	01	Undistributed Charges—Supervision
	369	02	
	369	03	
	369	04	
	369	05	Undistributed Charges—Expense
370			PACKING
			DIRECT PACKING COSTS
	371	01	Packing—Main Packing Station
	371	02	*Pack—Containers—Main Pack
	371	03	
	372	01	Packing—Small Package Station
	372	02	*Pack—Containers—Small Pack
	372	03	
	373	01	Packing—Solid Package Station
	373	02	*Pack—Containers—Solid Pack
			*Use these accounts for charges for made-up Containers and labor assembling.

Account Number		
Main	Sub	Sub
	373	03
	374	01
	374	02
	374	03
	375	01
	375	02
	375	03

INDIRECT PACKING COSTS

	376	01
	376	02
	376	03
	379	01

Undistributed Charges—Supervision—Packing House

	379	02
	379	03
	379	04
	379	05

Undistributed Charges—Expense

Account Number			
Main	Sub	Sub	MANUFACTURING

380			TRANSFERRING

POWDERED AND DESSERT

	381	01	Delivering Granulated from Warehouse
	381	02	
	381	03	Crushing and Conveying—Cut In—Mead Mills —Bolters
	381	04	
	381	05	Starch Introduction
	381	06	
	381	07	
	381	10	Packing—Bulk
	381	11	Packing—Cartons
	381	12	Containers—Packing—Bulk
	381	13	Containers—Packing—Cartons

BROWN

	383	01	Delivering Softs from Warehouse
	383	02	
	383	03	Crushing and Conveying
	383	04	
	383	10	Packing—Cartons
	383	11	Containers—Packing Cartons

INDIRECT COSTS

	389	01	Undistributed Charges—Supervision
	389	02	
	389	03	
	389	04	
	389	05	Undistributed Charges—Expense
	389	06	
	389	07	
	389	08	
	389	09	Building Expense

268 THE C & H SUGAR REFINING CORPORATION

Account Number			
Main	Sub	Sub	
390			GENERAL MANUFACTURING EXPENSE
			INDIRECT MANUFACTURING COSTS
	391	01	Supervision—Superintendent and Assistants
	391	02	Supervision—Shift Superintendents
	391	03	
	391	04	Supervision—Superintendent's Office
	391	05	
	391	06	
	391	07	
	392	01	Operating Systems—Dust System
	392	02	Operating Systems—Hot Water System
	392	03	Operating Systems—Drip System
	392	04	Operating Systems—Salt Water System
	392	05	Operating Systems—Signal Systems
	392	06	
	392	07	
	393	01	Reprocessing Damaged Refined
	393	02	
	393	03	
	394	01	
	395	01	
	395	05	Undistributed Charges—Expense
			SUGAR AND CONTAINER INSPECTOR
	396	01	Sugar and Container Inspector
	396	02	Supervision—Sugar and Container Inspector
	397	01	
	398	01	
	399	01	
	399	05	Undistributed Charges—Expense

Account Number			
Main	Sub	Sub	TECHNICAL CONTROL
400			TECHNICAL CONTROL
			DEPARTMENTAL EXPENSE
	401	01	Chemical Control
	401	02	
	402	01	
	402	02	
	403	01	Operating Control
	403	02	
	404	01	Instrument Control
	404	02	
	407	01	Special Investigations—Raw-Sugar Investigation
	407	02	Special Investigations—Other
	409	01	Undistributed Charges
	409	02	
	409	03	
	409	04	
	409	05	

APPENDIX

Account Number			WATER AND POWER
Main	Sub	Sub	
410			WATER
			DIRECT WATER AND HAULING COSTS
	411	01	Water Hauling—Tugs and Barges
	411	02	
	411	03	
	411	04	
	411	05	
	412	01	Water Hauling—McBryde Station Expense
	412	02	
	414	01	Water Purchased—Marin
	414	02	Water Purchased—Port Costa
	414	03	
			INDIRECT WATER COSTS
	416	01	Water Distribution—Barge Water System
	416	02	Water Distribution—Port Costa Water System
	416	03	Water Distribution—Drinking Water System
	416	04	
	416	05	
	419	01	Undistributed Charges—Supervision
	419	02	
	419	03	
	419	04	
	419	05	Undistributed Charges—Expense
	414	04	
420			STEAM POWER
			DIRECT OPERATING COSTS
	421	01	Steam Generation—Pumps, Boilers, Auxiliaries
	421	02	
	421	03	
	422	01	
	422	02	
	422	03	
			INDIRECT OPERATING COSTS
	425	01	Steam Distribution—Live Steam System
	425	02	Steam Distribution—Exhaust Steam System
	425	03	
	425	04	
	426	01	Building Expense
	426	02	
	426	03	
	429	01	Undistributed Charges—Supervision
	429	02	
	429	03	
	429	04	
	429	05	Undistributed Charges—Expense
430			ELECTRIC POWER
			DIRECT OPERATING COSTS
	431	01	Power Generation—Turbines and Auxiliaries
	431	02	
	431	03	
	432	01	Power Purchased

THE C & H SUGAR REFINING CORPORATION

Account Number		
Main	Sub	Sub

Main	Sub	Sub	
	432	02	
	432	03	INDIRECT OPERATING COSTS
	435	01	Power Distribution—Transformers
	435	02	Power Distribution—Power System
	435	03	Power Distribution—Light System
	435	04	Power Distribution—Direct Current System
	435	05	
	435	06	
	436	01	Building Expense
	436	02	
	436	03	
	439	01	Undistributed Charges—Supervision
	439	02	
	439	03	
	439	04	
	439	05	Undistributed Charges—Expense

Account Number			
Main	Sub	Sub	ENGINEERING AND MECHANICAL
450			ENGINEERING & MECHANICAL
			DEPARTMENT EXPENSE
	451	01	Engineering Expense
	451	02	
	452	01	Plant Valuation
	452	02	Consultants' Fees
	453	01	Mechanical Supervision—Master Mechanic and Assistants
	453	02	Mechanical Supervision—Shift Engineers
	453	03	
	454	01	
	455	01	Pump Room
	455	02	
	456	01	Plant Lubrication
	456	02	
	457	01	Fuel Oil Distribution
	457	02	
	458	01	
	458	02	
	459	01	
	459	02	
	460	01	
	460	02	
	461	01	
	461	02	
	462	01	Shop and Equipment Expense—Tool Room
	462	02	Shop and Equipment Expense—Shop and Mechanical Equipment
	462	03	Shop and Equipment Expense—Shop Buildings
	463	01	Locks and Keys
	464	01	Fire Prevention and Protection
	464	02	Fire Prevention and Protection—Fire-Fighting Equipment and Systems Expense
	466	01	Building and Equipment Adjustments—Abandonment—Wear and Tear

APPENDIX

Account Number			
Main	Sub	Sub	
	466	02	Building and Equipment Adjustments—Minor Alterations and Rearrangement Existing Facilities
	466	03	Adjustment Account
	469	05	Undistributed Charges—Expense

Account Number			PURCHASING—STORES—TRANS.—ACCOUNTING
Main	Sub	Sub	
	500		PURCHASING DEPARTMENT
	510		STORES DEPARTMENT
	510	01	Receiving and Storing
	510	02	Yard Gang
	519	02	Unallocated Freight and Express
	520		TRANSPORTATION
	520	01	Motor Trucks
	520	02	Gas Tractors and Equipment
	520	03	Electric Trucks
	530		ACCOUNTING AND STATISTICAL

Account Number			INDUSTRIAL RELATIONS
Main	Sub	Sub	
540			PERSONNEL DEPARTMENT
	541	01	Office Expense
	542	01	
	542	02	
	543	01	Safety—Accident Prevention
	543	02	Safety—Plant Protection
	543	03	
	543	04	
	544	01	Health and Sanitation—First Aid
	544	02	Health and Sanitation—Medical Examinations
	544	03	Health and Sanitation—Rest Rooms and Employees Lunches
	544	04	
	544	05	
	544	06	
	544	07	
	545	01	
	546	01	
	547	01	
	548	01	E. M. B. A. Claim Committee
	549	01	Undistributed Charges—Expense
550			COMMUNITY ACTIVITIES
	551	01	Civic Welfare—Community Center Club
	551	02	Civic Welfare—Girls' Club
	551	03	Civic Welfare—Community Auditorium

THE C & H SUGAR REFINING CORPORATION

Account Number			
Main	Sub	Sub	
	551	04	Civic Welfare—Back Ranch
	551	05	Civic Welfare—American Legion
	551	06	Civic Welfare—Public Library
	551	07	Civic Welfare—Boy Scouts
	551	08	Civic Welfare—Camp Fire Girls
	551	09	Civic Welfare—Sundry Civic Structures
	551	10	
	551	11	
	551	12	
	551	13	
	552	01	Health and Sanitation—Sewers, Roads and Streets
	553	01	Health and Sanitation—Garbage Disposal
	554	01	Parks and Playgrounds
	554	02	
	555	01	Gardens and Nursery
	555	02	
	556	01	Local Celebrations
	557	01	
	558	01	
	559	01	Undistributed Charges—Expense

Account Number			
Main	Sub	Sub	ENGINEERING
560			COMMUNITY ENGINEERING
	561	01	General
	561	02	Housing
	561	03	Sewers, Roads, Streets
	561	04	Maps
	561	05	Rights of Way

Account Number			
Main	Sub	Sub	GENERAL PLANT EXPENSE
570			GENERAL PLANT EXPENSE
	571	01	Refinery Grounds Expense
	571	02	
	571	03	Fences, Bridges, Viaducts
	571	04	Docks and Wharves
	571	05	Elevators and Manlifts
	571	06	Low-Pressure Air System
	571	07	High-Pressure Air System
	571	08	Pneumatic Tube System
	571	09	
	571	10	Photo Gallery
	571	11	Uniforms
	571	12	Inter-Department Messenger
	571	13	Sanitation and Cleaning—Regular
	571	14	Sanitation and Cleaning—Shut Down
	571	15	Undistributed Stationery and Supplies
	571	16	Plant Library
	571	17	Office Building Expense
	571	18	Auto Call System

Account Number			
Main	Sub	Sub	
	571	19	Undistributed Expense
	571	20	Ditto Work
	571	21	Claim Account
	571	22	Stores Inventory Adjustment
	571	23	Payroll Adjustment
	572	01	Lost and Overtime Adjustment
	572	1901	Regular Day Off
	572	2901	Overtime Allowance
	572	3901	Late or Tardy
	572	4901	Disciplinary Lay-Off
	572	5901	Unknown
	572	6901	Personal Time
	572	7901	Vacation
	572	8901	Sickness and Disability (Monthly men 1st 3 days)
	572	8902	Sickness and Disability (Monthly men after 3 days)
	572	8908	Sickness and Disability (Daily men 1st 3 days)
	572	8909	Sickness and Disability (Daily men after 3 days)
	572	9901	Short Shift
	572	9902	Shift Change

Account Number			
Main	Sub	Sub	ADMINISTRATIVE EXPENSE
580			ADMINISTRATIVE EXPENSE
	581	01	Plant Manager's Office
	581	02	Service Compensation
	581	03	Donations
	581	04	Consultants
	581	05	Special Experiments and Tests
	581	06	Suggestions and Awards
	581	07	Maps, Surveys and Appraisals
	581	08	Executive Salaries
	581	09	Undistributed Expense

Account Number			
Main	Sub	Sub	REFINERY INCOME
590			REFINERY INCOME
	591	800	Weighing Income
	592	800	Wharfage
	593	800	
	594	800	Sale of Old Bags
	595	800	
	596	800	Sales—Sundry Stores
	597	800	Sales—Miscellaneous
	598	800	
	599	800	Refinery Income—Undistributed

Account Number			
Main	Sub	Sub	WAREHOUSING
710			WAREHOUSING
711			RAW SUGAR WAREHOUSING

THE C & H SUGAR REFINING CORPORATION

Account Number			
Main	Sub	Sub	
	711	01	Raw Sugar Handling Charges
712			REFINED SUGAR WAREHOUSING
	712	01	Receiving and Storing
	712	02	Delivery for Shipment
	712	03	Warehouse Sanitation
	712	04	Reprocessing Refined
	712	05	Supervision
	712	06	Receiving and Storing: Belt Gang—1st Shift
	712	07	Receiving and Storing: Belt Gang—2nd Shift
	712	08	Receiving and Storing: Belt Gang—3rd Shift
715			GENERAL EXPENSE
	715	01	Equipment Expense—Conveying System
	715	02	Equipment Expense—Trucks, Scales, etc.
	715	03	Equipment Expense—Miscellaneous
	715	04	
	715	05	Building Expense
	715	06	
	715	07	
	715	08	
	715	09	
	715	10	
	715	11	
	715	19	Undistributed Expense

Account Number			
Main	Sub	Sub	EXPENSE
716			RAW SUGAR HANDLING
	716	01	Weighing
	716	02	Sampling
	716	03	Delivery to Storage
	716	04	Delivery to Refinery
	716	05	
	716	06	
	716	07	Supervision
	716	08	Undistributed Charges
	716	09	Raw Sugar Handling (Credit-Contra Account 711)

Account Number			
Main	Sub	Sub	OUTSIDE OPERATIONS
900			OUTSIDE OPERATIONS
910			REALTY
	910	01	Crockett Heights
	910	02	Crockett, Valona, Crolona
	910	03	Edwards Ranch
	910	04	Crockett Cottages
	910	05	Tenney Terrace
	910	06	
	910	07	

NOTE.—Account 711-01 Raw-Sugar Handling Charges is for office use only. In reporting to San Francisco report as 143 account.

APPENDIX

Account Number		
Main	Sub	Sub
920	910 910 920 922 923	08 09	OTHER OUTSIDE OPERATIONS Hotel Crockett

Account Number			SELLING EXPENSE
Main	Sub	Sub	
720			SELLING EXPENSE
721			DIRECT SELLING EXPENSE—CANE
	721	400	EXPENSE
	721	401	Brokers' Commissions
	721	402	Drayage
	721	403	Storage
	721	404	Loading Expense
	721	405	Switching
	721	406	Local Sugar—Freight and Toll
	721	407	Refined-Sugar Freight Expense
	721	408	Storage Allowance
	721	409	
	721	600	FIXED CHARGES
	721	601	Insurance
	721	6011	General A. Sugar in Storage B. Marine
	721	6012	Ocean
	721	602	Taxes
722			DIRECT SELLING EXPENSE—BEET
	722	400	EXPENSE
	722	401	Brokers' Commissions
	722	402	Drayage
	722	403	Storage
	722	404	Loading Expense
	722	405	Switching
	722	406	Local Sugar—Freight and Toll
	722	407	Refined-Sugar Freight Expense
	722	408	Handling Charges—Crockett
	722	409	Storage Allowance
	722	600	FIXED CHARGES
	722	601	Insurance
	722	6011	General A. Sugar in Storage B. Marine
	722	6012	Ocean
	722	602	Taxes
723			DIRECT SELLING EXPENSE—RAW
724			DIRECT SELLING EXPENSE—REFINERY MOLASSES
730			INDIRECT SELLING EXPENSE
	730	100	SALARIES
	730	101	Executives

THE C & H SUGAR REFINING CORPORATION

Account Number		
Main	Sub	Sub
	730	102	Clerks and Stenographers
	730	103	Salesmen
	730	104	Telegraphers
	730	105
	730	106	Telephones
	730	107
	730	300	SUPPLIES
	730	301	Stationery and Printing
	730	302	Office Supplies
	730	303	Miscellaneous Supplies
	730	400	EXPENSE
	730	401	Traveling Expenses
	730	402	Communications
	730	4021	Postage and Mailing
	730	4022	Telephone
	730	4023
	730	4024	Telegrams
	730	4025	Cablegrams
	730	403	Legal Expense—Other
	730	4031	Attorney's Fees
	730	4032	Collection Fees
	730	404	Dues and Subscriptions
	730	4041	Dues
	730	4042	Subscriptions
	730	405	Rentals
	730	4051	Office
	730	4052
	730	406	Entertainment
	730	407
	730	408
	730	409
	730	410	Sugar Samples
	730	411	Advertising
	730	4111	Entertainment
	730	4112	Subscriptions
	730	4113	Educational
	730	4114	Exhibits
	730	4115	Signs
	730	4116	Newspapers
	730	4117
	730	4119	Miscellaneous
	730	412	Reprocessing and Transferring Special Sugars
	730	419	Miscellaneous
	730	500	MAINTENANCE AND REPAIRS
	730	501	Furniture
	730	502	Equipment
	730	503
	730	600	FIXED CHARGES
	730	601	Insurance
	730	602	Taxes
	730	603	Depreciation
	730	6031	Furniture and Fixtures
	730	6032	Automobiles
740			ADMINISTRATIVE EXPENSE
	740	100	SALARIES
	740	101	Executives

APPENDIX

Account Number		
Main	Sub	Sub
740	102	Clerks and Stenographers
740	103	Chauffeur
740	104	Nurse
740	105	
740	300	SUPPLIES
740	301	Stationery and Printing
740	302	Office Supplies
740	303	Miscellaneous Supplies
740	400	EXPENSE
740	401	Traveling Expenses
740	402	Communications
740	4021	Postage and Mailing
740	4022	Telephones
740	4023	
740	4024	Telegrams
740	4025	Cablegrams
740	403	Legal Expense—Other
740	4031	Attorney's Fees
740	4032	
740	4033	Notary Fees
740	4034	
740	404	Dues and Subscriptions
740	4041	Dues
740	4042	Subscriptions
740	405	Rentals
740	4051	Office
740	4052	Garage
740	406	Entertainment
740	4061	Company Entertainment
740	4062	Outside Entertainment
740	4063	Honolulu Entertainment
740	4064	
740	4065	
740	407	
740	408	
740	409	Fees
740	4091	Directors
740	4092	Executive Committee
740	4093	
740	4094	Auditing (Outside)
740	4095	Medical
740	4096	Professional Services—Investigation
740	4097	
740	4098	
740	4099	Miscellaneous
740	410	
740	411	
740	414	
740	415	
740	419	Miscellaneous Expense
740	4191	Plant Valuation
740	4192	Maps and Surveys
740	4193	Service Compensation
740	4194	Patents and Copyright Expense
740	4195	Educational—Employes
740	4196	Special Services
740	4197	

278   THE C & H SUGAR REFINING CORPORATION

Account Number			
Main	Sub	Sub	
	740	4198	
	740	4199	Miscellaneous
	740	500	MAINTENANCE AND REPAIRS
	740	501	Furniture
	740	502	Equipment
	740	600	FIXED CHARGES
	740	601	Insurance
	740	602	Taxes
	740	603	Depreciation
	740	6031	Furniture and Fixtures
	740	6032	Automobiles
750			GENERAL OFFICE EXPENSE
	750	100	SALARIES
	750	101	Accounting
	750	102	Credit
	750	103	Cashier
	750	104	Accounts Payable
	750	105	Order
	750	106	Billing
	750	107	Accounts Receivable
	750	108	Consignment
	750	109	Statistical
	750	110	Insurance
	750	111	Traffic
	750	112	Information, Mail and File
	750	113	Telephone Exchange
	750	114	Janitor
	750	115	Messenger
	750	116	Auditing
	750	117	Tabulating
	750	118	Stenographic
	750	119	
	750	300	SUPPLIES
	750	301	Stationery and Printing
	750	302	Office Supplies
	750	303	Miscellaneous Supplies
	750	400	EXPENSE
	750	401	Traveling Expense
	750	402	Communications
	750	4021	Postage and Mailing
	750	4022	Telephones
	750	4023	
	750	4024	Telegrams
	750	4025	Cablegrams
	750	403	Legal Expense—Other
	750	4031	Attorney's Fees
	750	4032	Collection Fees
	750	4033	
	750	404	Dues and Subscriptions
	750	4041	Dues
	750	4042	Subscriptions
	750	405	Rentals
	750	4051	Office

APPENDIX

Account Number			
Main	Sub	Sub	
750	4052		Equipment
750	4053		Safe Deposit
750	4053		
750	4054		
750	406		Entertainment
750	407		
750	408		
750	409		Fees
750	410		
750	411		
750	419		Miscellaneous Expense
750	500		MAINTENANCE AND REPAIRS
750	501		Furniture
750	502		Equipment
750	600		FIXED CHARGES
750	601		Insurance
750	602		Taxes
750	603		Depreciation
750	6031		Furniture and Fixtures
750	6033		Automobiles

Account Number			EXPENSE
Main	Sub	Sub	
760			LEGAL EXPENSE
760	100		SALARIES
760	101		Executives
760	102		Clerks and Stenographers
760	103		
760	300		SUPPLIES
760	301		Stationery and Printing
760	302		Office Supplies
760	303		Miscellaneous Supplies
760	400		EXPENSE
760	401		Traveling Expense
760	402		Communications
760	4021		Postage and Mailing
760	4022		Telephones
760	4023		
760	4024		Telegrams
760	4025		Cablegrams
760	403		Legal Expense—Other
760	4031		Attorney's Fees
760	4032		
760	4033		Notary Fees
760	404		Dues and Subscriptions
760	4041		Dues
760	4042		Subscriptions
760	405		Rentals
760	4051		Office
760	4052		Garage
760	406		Entertainment
760	407		

THE C & H SUGAR REFINING CORPORATION

Account Number			
Main	Sub	Sub	
	760	408	
	760	409	Fees
	760	410	
	760	411	
	760	412	
	760	419	Miscellaneous
	760	500	MAINTENANCE AND REPAIRS
	760	501	Furniture
	760	502	Equipment
	760	600	FIXED CHARGES
	760	601	Insurance
	760	602	Taxes
	760	603	Depreciation
	760	6031	Furniture and Fixtures
	760	6032	Automobiles
770			TRAFFIC AND LAW ADMINISTRATION
	770	100	SALARIES
	770	101	Executives
	770	102	Clerks and Stenographers
	770	103	
	770	300	SUPPLIES
	770	301	Stationery and Printing
	770	302	Office Supplies
	770	303	Miscellaneous Supplies
	770	400	EXPENSE
	770	401	Traveling Expense
	770	402	Communications
	770	4021	Postage and Mailing
	770	4022	Telephones
	770	4023	
	770	4024	Telegrams
	770	4025	Cablegrams
	770	403	Legal Expense—Other
	770	4031	Attorney's Fees
	770	4032	
	770	4033	Notary Fees
	770	404	Dues and Subscriptions
	770	4041	Dues
	770	4042	Subscriptions
	770	405	Rentals
	770	4051	Office
	770	4052	Garage
	770	406	Entertainment
	770	407	
	770	408	
	770	409	Fees
	770	410	
	770	411	
	770	412	
	770	419	Miscellaneous
	770	500	MAINTENANCE AND REPAIRS
	770	501	Furniture

APPENDIX

Account Number			
Main	Sub	Sub	
	770	502	Equipment
	770	600	FIXED CHARGES
	770	601	Insurance
	770	602	Taxes
	770	603	Depreciation
	770	6031	Furniture and Fixtures
	770	6032	Automobiles
800			OTHER ACCOUNTS
801			CONTINGENCIES
820			INSURANCE, SICKNESS AND DISABILITY BENEFITS
	820	01	Insurance
	820	02	Sickness and Disability
	820	021	E. M. B. A.—Refinery Division
	820	022	Company—Refinery Division
	820	023	E. M. B. A.—S. F. Division
	820	024	Company—S. F. Division
830			PENSIONS—SALARIES
840			
850			ESTIMATED BAD AND DOUBTFUL ACCOUNTS
860			DONATIONS—CASH AND SUGAR
870			ESTIMATED FEDERAL INCOME TAXES
881			FINANCIAL GAINS
	881	01	Interest Earned
	881	011	General
	881	012	
	881	013	Calls Loans
	881	014	Agents Loans
	881	015	United States Government Securities
	881	016	Banks
	881	019	
	881	02	Discounts Received
	881	03	Exchange Earned
	881	04	
	881	05	
	881	09	Miscellaneous
882			FINANCIAL LOSSES
	882	01	Interest Paid
	882	011	Notes Payable
	882	012	Loans Payable
	882	013	Bonds Payable
	882	014	Bond Discount
	882	015	
	882	019	Miscellaneous
	882	02	
	882	03	Exchange Paid
	882	04	Bond Expense
	882	05	
	882	09	Miscellaneous

THE C & H SUGAR REFINING CORPORATION

Account Number			
Main	Sub	Sub	
890			COMMISSION EXPENSE—RAW-SUGAR CONTRACT

Account Number			WITHHOLDING PROVISION
Main	Sub	Sub	
1000			WITHHOLDING PROVISION
	1010		Raw-Sugar Contract Withholdings
	1020		Hawaiian Plantation Feed Molasses—Withholdings
	1020	01	Commission
	1020	02	Tankage
	1020	03	Expense
5000			CLEARING ACCOUNTS
	5001		PAYROLLS
	5001	101	Refinery
	5001	102	Selling
	5001	103	Administrative
	5001	104	General Office
	5001	105	Legal Department
	5001	106	
	5001	107	Hawaiian Plantation Feed Molasses
	5001	108	Traffic and Law Administration
	5001	109	Pensioners
	5001	110	
	5002		INSURANCE
	5003		TAXES
	5004		DEPRECIATION
	5005		
	5006		
	5009		ACCOUNTS RECEIVABLE AND PAYABLE—TRANSFER

Account Number			HAWAIIAN FEED MOLASSES
Main	Sub	Sub	
6000			REVENUES
6010			SALES
6020			COST OF SALES
6100			HANDLING EXPENSES
6110			RECEIVING, STORING, SHIPPING
	6110	01	Crockett
	6110	02	East San Pedro
	6110	03	Seattle
	6110	04	San Francisco Bay
6120			GENERAL PLANT EXPENSE
	6120	01	Crockett
	6120	02	East San Pedro
	6120	03	Seattle

APPENDIX

Account Number			
Main	Sub	Sub	
6200			SELLING EXPENSE
6210			DIRECT SELLING EXPENSE
	6210	400	EXPENSE
	6210	401	Brokers Commissions
	6210	402	Freight and Drayage
	6210	403	Containers
	6210	404	
	6210	409	Miscellaneous
6220			INDIRECT SELLING EXPENSE
	6220	100	SALARIES
	6220	101	General Office
	6220	300	SUPPLIES
	6220	301	Stationery and Printing
	6220	302	Office Supplies
	6220	303	Miscellaneous
	6220	400	EXPENSE
	6220	401	Traveling Expenses
	6220	402	Communications
	6220	4021	Postage and Mailing
	6220	4022	Telephone
	6220	4023	
	6220	4024	Telegrams
	6220	4025	Cablegrams
	6220	403	Legal Expenses—Other
	6220	4031	Attorney's Fees
	6220	4032	
	6220	404	Dues and Subscriptions
	6220	4041	Dues
	6220	4042	Subscriptions
	6220	405	Rentals
	6220	4051	Office
	6220	4052	
	6220	406	Entertainment
	6220	407	
	6220	408	
	6220	409	Estimated Bad, Doubtful Accounts
	6220	410	Samples
	6220	411	Advertising
	6220	4111	Entertainment
	6220	4112	Subscriptions
	6220	4113	
	6220	4114	
	6220	4115	Printed Matter
	6220	4116	Newspapers and Periodicals
	6220	4119	Miscellaneous
	6220	412	Contaminated Molasses Resale and Adjusts
	6220	413	
	6220	419	Miscellaneous Expense
	6220	500	MAINTENANCE AND REPAIRS
	6220	501	Furniture
	6220	502	Equipment
	6220	503	

THE C & H SUGAR REFINING CORPORATION

Account Number			
Main	Sub	Sub	
	6220	600	FIXED CHARGES
	6220	601	Insurance
	6220	602	Taxes
	6220	603	Depreciation
	6220	6031	Furniture and Fixtures
	6220	6032	
6250			COMMISSION EXPENSE
	6250	01	Commission
	6250	02	Tankage

INDEX

Absenteeism and tardiness, 68
Accident prevention, 71–73
Accounting, 105; accounting and forms of taxes, 194; assistance from Engineering and Maintenance Department, 106; cost accounting, 127–28; increase in work in, 159; stores accounting, 133–36; *see also* Classification of accounts, Finance and Accounting Division
Advancement in employment, 118–20, 201, 202–3
Advertising:
Brands, 153
Direct, 153, 154, 155
Motion picture, 153
"Personality" advertising, 153
Plant visitors, 153
"Something about Sugar," 153
Age distribution of employees, 87
Agreement, the co-operative, 3–8; chart of, 9
Aliens, percentage of, naturalized and declarants, 63
Allen, W. A., assistant editor of *Chemical and Metallurgical Engineering*, 29; quotation from an article by, 30–41
Americanization work, 63
Applications for employment, 63
Attitude toward suggestions and criticisms, 113–14
Auditing Department, 195–97

Billing, 175–76, 196
Blackstrap Molasses, 153; *see also* Molasses
Bonding of employees, 193–94
Bone char, 48; filtration methods, revised, 211
Brokers:
Classification of, 151
Commissions, Coast and East, 145
Delivery contracts, 139
Geographical distribution of offices, 144, 145–46
Quotas for the year, 198
Relations to jobbers, 139
Transactions of business through, 139
Budgets:
Of Finance and Accounting Division, 170–71
Of Refinery Division, 17–29, 113, 114–15, 116–20, 134
Sales forecasts and sales budgets, 150–51
Burlap bags, 51, 187

C. & H. Pure Cane Sugar, 153
California Beet Sugar and Refining Company, 2
Cane sugar:
Growing of, 4
History of, in the Hawaiian Islands, 1
Insurance on, 191
Monthly production of raw sugar in the Hawaiian Islands, 3
Shipment, from the Hawaiian Islands, 3
Uniform quality, 139, 154–55

Canning industry, consumption of sugar by, 147
Capital, employed by Corporation, total, 10; productivity of, 232–33; structure of, 8, 10
Chain stores, increase in sales to, 146–47
Classification of accounts, 257–84
Clubs:
 Blue Birds, 84
 Boy Scouts and Wolf, 85
 Camp Fire Girls, 84
 Community Center, 57, 82–83
 Girls' Club, 57
 Women's Club, 84
Colloids, 48
Community activities, sponsored by Company, 81–87
Concessions, avoidance of unethical competition, 141–42
"Consignment," 143, 145, 180–81, 197
Consumption of sugar, fluctuations in, 151
Contract with planters, 7–8
Conveniences for employees, 67
Co-ordination of functions, 12–14
Costs:
 Accounting, 127–28
 Administrative and office, 247–56
 Annual index of comparative unit costs, 245
 Changes in, 250
 Classified items of expense, 1922, 1927, in percentages, 255
 Comparisons, of direct selling expense, Coast and East, 145; of refining functions, 249; of relative increase in melt, number of men required, and wage cost, 217; of total expenditures, cost per unit (100 lbs.), and volume of sales in percentage of 1922, 250; of unit costs of major operating functions, 248; by years, 20, 23, 24, 25, 26, 27, 244, 245
Distribution, of cost of group insurance, 99; of total business cost, 1927, 243; of total refining unit cost, 247
Effect of rate of melt upon unit cost of refining, 216–20; graph of, 218
Fixed charges, 220
Industrial relations activities, 89
Insurance, 194; see also Employees' Mutual Benefit Association
Labor, 219; budget of, 25–29
Maintenance and repairs, 220
Materials and supplies, 219–20
Percentage distribution of total wholesale price to major items of expense, 243
Reductions, 242–56; in cost of maintaining working personnel of refinery, 1923–27, 231
Refining, 246; budget of, 21–25
Relative cost of principal items of expense, 245
Salaries and wages, 251; variations of, 219
See Sales, Taxes

INDEX 287

Credit Department, 174–75; increase in work of, 254
Crockett:
Christmas Festival, 86; see also Clubs
Corporation activities sponsored in, 82–87
Cost of living in, 55–56; see also Hotel Crockett
Living conditions, 81
A one-industry town, 81
Parks and playgrounds, 83–84
Sanitation, 85–86
Streets and roads, 86
Valona, west end of, 82
Crockett, Joseph B., 2
Customer classification, 146–48

Description of refining processes, 29–41
Development of understudies, 14
Discharges and lay-offs:
Causes for, 227–28
Causes for all separations, 225–26
Disciplinary lay-offs and permanent lay-offs, 68–70; lay-offs for cause, 227–28
Reasons for voluntary separations, 226–27
Lay-offs during shut-down, 66

East and South (River) sales territory, 139, 142–43; absorption to, taken by Company in competing against New Orleans and Atlantic Coast refineries, 189; auditing of billing to, 176; comparison of direct selling expense, 145–46; sales by consignment to, 143, 145
Educational activities, for the rank and file, 75–76; for furthering self-education, 203; for minor supervisory employees, 76–81
Employees, increase in number of, 252; see also Labor and Discharges and lay-offs
Employees' Mutual Benefit Association:
Average cost per member, 96–97
Benefits, cash, 91; medical and hospital, 91
Divisions, disability, 91; mortality, 92–93
Extended group insurance, 98–99; distribution of cost, 99
Financial status, 94–96
Membership, 93–94, 203–4
Revenue and expenses, 96; sources of, 91–92
Surplus, 97–98
Employment, 205; methods of, 63–64; see also Labor
Engineering and Maintenance Department:
Assistance in accounting of, 106
Development of personnel, 118–20
Engineering, 99–106
Line of responsibility, 114
Maintenance and repairs, 113–15
Mechanical operation supervision, 106–13
New construction, 115–20
Salvaging, 105

Engineering and Maintenance Department (continued):
Shift organization, 112–13
Standardization, specifications, 103–4
Extraction:
Interpretation of results, 210–11
Losses, 209–11
Progress in, 207–11
Summaries, annual, 207–11; in terms of composition of raw sugar, 207–11

Films, of community, refinery, and refinery processes, 90, 153
Finance and Accounting Division, 163–204; accounts payable, 177–78; accounts receivable, 176–77; auditing department, 195–97; cashier, 178–80; chart of, 164; classification of accounts, 204; current interest of, 199–200; financial operations and accounting, ratios, 165–70; general accounting, 172–73; main departments, 163; organization of, 163–65; records and accounts, 163–65; see also Billing, Budgets, "Consignment," Credit Department, Order Department, Purchasing Department, Research, Stores Department, Tabulating Department
Financial standing, 168
Fire Department, 112
First aid, 70–71

General office, 246, 247, 249–56
Grades and packages:
Errors in segregation, 130
Forecasts of sales, 151
Increasing ratio of packages, 199
No grading by quality, 53
Requirements, determined by sales forecasts, 18
Sales by grades, 148–50
Seasonal influence, 151
Standards of, 53, 54
Storage, 122
See Soft-sugar carton packers and weigher

Hawaiian Plantation Feed Molasses, 153
Hawaiian sugar plantations (owners of the California and Hawaiian Sugar Refining Corporation):
Advantages of co-operation, 5–6
Bargaining power, 4
Contract of, with California and Hawaiian Sugar Refining Corporation, 7–8
Co-operative agreement, 3–8, 9, 168–69
Correlation of crop production and refining, 214–15
Handling and selling of molasses, 129, 153
Value of, 3
History of the Corporation, 1–3
Hotel Crockett, 57, 85
Housing of employees, 73–75; Insurance on, 192

Industrial Relations Department:
Chart of Department, 58

INDEX

Cost of activities, 88-89
Disciplinary procedure, 68-70
Employment methods, 63-64
Normal force, 61
Organization, 57-60
Plant protection duties, 75
Policy of Department, 55-56
Public relations work, 89-90
See Accident prevention, Americanization work, Community activities, Educational activities, Employees Mutual Benefit Association, Racial distribution of employees
Inspection Department, 52-55
Insurance and Tax Department, 190-95; automobile and truck, 192-93; buildings and equipment, 191-92; fire, 191; marine, 192; molasses and tanks, 192; sprinkler leakage, 192; taxes, 195; see also Bonding of employees, Employees Mutual Benefit Association, Workmen's compensation
Interests of employees, in opinion of Company, 56
Inventions of employees, 240-42
Inventories, physical, 136-39
Invert sugar, 43

Job analyses, 200-201

Kieselguhr, 42; regenerating plant for, 235, 238-39

Labor:
Budget for first quarter, 1928, 27

Comparison of relative increase in melt, number of men required, and wage cost, 217
Distribution of, and payrolls, 131-32
Employment and personnel, 57-59, 203
Mobility of, in entire plant, in warehouse, 221-24
Normal force, 61
Productivity of, in refinery, 231-32; percentage increase in, per office employee, 253-54
Saving due to stabilization, 230-31
Seasonality of, 228-30
Stabilization of, 220-31
Turnover, gross, 221-23, 1923-27, 222, percentage, by departments, 223; net, 223-25, percentage, by departments, 224
See Discharges
Lay-offs, see Discharges and lay-offs
Legal Department, 205-6
Length of service of employees, 88
Living conditions, see Crockett

Mail and file section, 182-83
Manufacturing processes, description of, 29-40
Marketing, 139; see also East and South (River) sales territory, Molasses, Sales and Costs; Comparisons of direct selling expense
Material and equipment:
Equipment of special design, 116

290　THE C & H SUGAR REFINING CORPORATION

Material and Equipment (*continued*):
　Improvements, 235–40
　Oliver filters, 114; installation of, 235, 239–40
　Power generation and usage, 108–11
　Productivity, 233–35; changes in, 234
　Steam generation, 106–7
　Sweetland presses, 114
　See Stores Department
Matson Navigation Company, 3, 4, 236
Melts:
　Capacity of refinery, 3
　Centrifugal control, 235, 237–38
　Costs of principal items in relation to, 219–20
　Effect of rate of, upon unit cost of refining, 216–20
　Regularization of production in terms of average monthly melt, 213–15
Molasses:
　Blackstrap, 153
　Handling and selling of, 129, 153
　Hawaiian Plantation Feed, 153
　Insurance on tanks of, 192
　Kinds, 129, 153
　"Loss in Molasses," 207–11
　Marketing, 152–53
　Proceeds of sales, 153

Nelson Weighing and Conveying Installation, 235–36

Oliver filters, 114; installation of, 235, 239, 240
Operating Department, 48–51

Order Department, 173–74
Organization, character of, 10–14; chart of general organization, 11; of Refinery, 15–17
Origin of Company, 1–3
Output, 222
Ownership of Company, 3, 10

Patents, received and applied for, 240–42
Plant sanitation and cleanliness, 52
Polarization, 180, 201–11
Positions, classification and grading of, 201–2
Premium system of collective bonuses, 67
Price, base, 179; price paid calculations, 180
Productivity:
　Average labor, percentage increase, 253–54
　Of Capital, 232–33
　Comparison of budgeted with actual production, 1927, 20
　Of refinery labor, 231–32; of refinery machinery and equipment, 233, 235
　Regularization of, 1923–27, 211–16
　Schedule of, 19
　See Output, Stock production and stock records
Progress and results, 207–56
Purchasing Department, 183–86

Racial distribution of employees, 61–62
Rancho Canada del Hombre, 2
Raw sugar, 51, 121, 129, 180, 207–12; *see also* Polarization

INDEX

Refined sugar, 51, 122–24, 129, 148–50
Refining Division, 15–138; chart of, 16; departments, 15; description of refining processes, 29–41; general organization, 15–17; handling methods, 54–55; Inspection Department, 52–55; office, 127–32; operating control, 43–47; Operating Department, 48–51; operation at maximum capacity, 5, 15, 17; operation schedule for 1928, 17–18; physical inventories, 137–38; statistical analyses, 199; *see also* Budgets, Costs, Engineering and Maintenance Department, Industrial Relations Department, Labor, Stock Control Section, Technical or Chemical Control Department, Productivity, *and* Warehouses
Relationship between employees and Company, 55–57, 220–21
Research, commercial and statistical, 197–200; finance and accounting division, 199–200; refining division, 199; sales division, 198–99

Salaries and wages:
　Base wage, 55
　Comparison of relative increase in melt, number of men required, and wage cost, 217
　Cost, salaries and wages, 251; in relation to total refining, 219-20
　Method of payment, 66–67
　Net increase, 251
　Of new employees, 64
　Overtime, 65
　Payroll records, timekeeping, and actual payments, 131–32
　Premium system of collective bonuses, 67
　Salary setting, 202
　Salary standardization, 200–204
　Time-work and piece-work, methods of compensation, 51
　Of warehouse employees, 64
Sales:
　Central sales organization, 139–40
　Comparison of total expenditure cost per unit and total volume of sales in percentage of 1922, 250
　Cost of selling, 246; *see* Comparisons of direct selling expense, *under* Costs
　Customer classification, 147
　Division of Sales, 198–99
　Forecasts and budgets, 150–52; percentage of quota actually delivered in each territory, 152
　By grades and product, 148
　Increase of "specialty" sales, 150, 253
　Terms, Coast and East, conditions of, 142–45
　Volume, 140–42; average tonnage per customer's invoice, 141; increase of, 252

Sales (*continued*):
  See Advertising, Brokers, Budgets, Marketing, Molasses, Price, Research, Seasonality of demands for sugar, Varieties of product
Salvage, 105
San Francisco office, 129, 139
Seasonality of demand for sugar, 154, 211; compared with trend of production, 214–15; effect of, on amount of available funds, 165; method used to show, 154–62; seasonal influence on sales of grades and packages, 151
Shift, three 8-hour plan, 66; organization of, 112–13
Shipment of sugar:
  Facilities for car loading, 124
  From storage, 122–24, 189
  From the Hawaiian Islands, 3
  Marine insurance on, 192
  Routing and tracing, 190
  Time of arrival of sugar vessels, how obtained, 179
  Ways of, 189
Soft-sugar carton packers and weigher, 235, 236, 237
"Something about Sugar," 153, 154
"Specialty" sugars, 21; increase in sales of, 150, 253
Standardization:
  Of brands, 153
  Of filing equipment, 183
  Of parts, 103–5
  Of salary, 200–204
  Of stock piles, 138
  Of tier counts, 137
Starr flour mill, 2

Stenographic service, centralized, 182
Stock Control section, 133–36
Stock production and stock records, 128–30
Stores Department, 186–88; accounting, 133–36
Sugar Factors, Limited, 1, 2, 7
Sweetland presses, 114

Tabulating Department, 181, 196; tabulating work of Refinery Division, 130–31
Taxes, *see* Insurance and Tax Department
Technical or Chemical Control Department, 41–48; chemical control, 42–43; operating control, 43–47; special investigations, 47–48
Telephone and telegraph service, 183
Traffic Department, 189, 190; increase in work of, 254
Transfers, of employees, 65, 120; *see also* Discharges and lay-offs

Vacations, 65, 203
Valuation of properties, method of determining, 101–3
Varieties of product, 140
Visitors, reception of, 89–90, 153

Wage policy, *see* Salaries and wages
Warehouses:
  Automatic conveyor system in, 124–27
  Auxiliary, 120
  Mobility of labor in, 221
  Storage facilities, 120, 121

Warehousing in Eastern territory, 143, 180; withdrawals from, 196–97
See Salaries and wages, Racial distribution of employees
Water supply, 111–12
Wheatport, 1, 2
Women employees, 51, 64–65, 67
Work ratings, 69
Working hours, 66
Workmen's compensation, 73, 193